The Story of Yellowstone

Merrill D. Beal

Alpha Editions

This edition published in 2024

ISBN : 9789362927569

Design and Setting By
Alpha Editions
www.alphaedis.com
Email - info@alphaedis.com

As per information held with us this book is in Public Domain.
This book is a reproduction of an important historical work. Alpha Editions uses the best technology to reproduce historical work in the same manner it was first published to preserve its original nature. Any marks or number seen are left intentionally to preserve its true form.

Contents

PREFACE ....- 1 -

ACKNOWLEDGMENTS ....- 3 -

INTRODUCTION ....- 5 -

OUTDOORS ....- 6 -

Chapter I YELLOWSTONE —THE GEM
OF THE MOUNTAINS...- 8 -

Chapter II JOHN COLTER'S
DISCOVERY OF YELLOWSTONE..........................- 13 -

Chapter III INDIANS IN AND AROUND
YELLOWSTONE..- 32 -

Chapter IV PORTRAIT OF A TRAPPER
BRIGADE..- 42 -

Chapter V WERE INDIANS AFRAID OF
YELLOWSTONE?...- 53 -

Chapter VI SECONDARY VISITATIONS
BEFORE 1869 ....- 60 -

Chapter VII JIM BRIDGER—MAN AND
LEGEND...- 71 -

Chapter VIII FINAL DISCOVERY IN
1869 AND 1870...- 79 -

Chapter IX CREATION OF
YELLOWSTONE NATIONAL PARK ....- 94 -

Chapter X THE LAST ROUNDUP ....- 103 -

CHAPTER XI CHIEF JOSEPH'S TRAIL OF
BLOOD...- 119 -

Chapter XII TRAVEL AND
ACCOMMODATIONS—NEW
BUSINESSES ....- 140 -

Chapter XIII "THE YELLOWSTONE
IDEA" ....- 161 -

Chapter XIV GENERAL
ADMINISTRATION...- 176 -

Chapter XV THE NATIONAL PARK
SERVICE..- 197 -

Appendix I YOUNG MEN CAMPING IN
YELLOWSTONE WILDERNESS ....- 209 -

Appendix II THE PROBLEM OF
"COLTER'S ROUTE IN 1807" ....- 214 -

BIBLIOGRAPHICAL NOTE...- 227 -

BIBLIOGRAPHY ....- 229 -

FOOTNOTES ....- 240 -

PREFACE

Yellowstone National Park lives as a cherished memory in the minds of millions of people. Greater still is the number who anticipate a visit to this Wonderland. To nearly all, the Park stands as a symbol of the enrichment of the American way of life. And well it might, because it is a geological paradise, a pristine botanical garden, and an Elysium for wild game. But most important of all, it is a place of recreation for countless thousands who come to find a temporary escape from the pressure of a highly artificial life. Thoughtful people assent to the opinion of Wordsworth:

The world is too much with us; late and soon,

Getting and spending, we lay waste our powers;

Little we see in Nature that is ours;

We have given our hearts away, a sordid boon!

This Sea that bares her bosom to the moon;

The winds that will be howling at all hours,

And are up-gathered now like sleeping flowers;

For this, for everything, we are out of tune;

It moves us not. —Great God! I'd rather be

A Pagan suckled in a creed outworn;

So might I, standing on this pleasant lea,

Have glimpses that would make me less forlorn;

Have sight of Proteus rising from the sea;

Or hear old Triton blow his wreathed horn.

After many years of indifference to the claims of nature, the American people are coming into accord with the wise teachings advanced by John Muir more than fifty years ago. Today, legions of tired, nerve-shaken, over-civilized people realize that going to the mountains is like going home. They have found a brief sojourn in the wilderness a necessity of life. There is a balm in the sun, wind, and storm of mountain heights. There is healing in willow parks and gentian meadows. Cobweb cares of the world's spinning give way before the vibrant touch of Mother Earth when her children venture boldly into unbeaten paths. There they may attune their ears to strange sounds; their lungs respond to pine sap air. Jumping from rock to log, tracing rivers to their sources, brings men up from panting puffs to deep-drawn breath in whole-souled exercise unto a newness of life.

The story of Yellowstone has been told many times, but seldom does one catch that elusive something that so mightily impresses the sensitive visitor. The theme is at once so inspiring and grand, the details so varied and minute, as to challenge one's finest discrimination to seize upon the major features and bring them into relief. There is still much that is primitive in Wonderland, and in this setting it is appropriate to envision the salient traits of the Old West. Hereabouts was once enacted a colorful panorama of frontier life. There were Indians, trappers, miners, cowboys, rustlers, poachers, soldiers, and settlers. A description of these picturesque people and their ways might bring enjoyment to many. Perhaps the spirit of appreciation that characterizes this history is its chief claim upon the attention of Yellowstone visitors.

This monograph was written for them, and it represents a synthesis of many lectures that evolved in their presence, in the afterglow of Yellowstone campfire programs. Visitors whose enjoyment of life seems particularly enhanced by a visit to the Park may find the reason therefore in those lines:

One impulse from a vernal wood

May teach you more of man,

Of moral evil and of good,

Than all the sages can.

—WORDSWORTH

In the interest of economy of time in reading this history, it is suggested that chapters three, four, and ten might be skimmed. However, a knowledge of the Indians and trappers whose haunts and activities impinged upon the Park area is essential to a full appreciation of Yellowstone National Park in its western setting.

ACKNOWLEDGMENTS

Former Superintendent Edmund B. Rogers and Park Naturalist David de L. Condon gave me access to the records of the Park. Their interest in advancing the knowledge of Yellowstone has been keen and constant.

My Yellowstone Park ranger-colleagues also served as sources of information and occasional critics. It is probable that each of them will be able to identify an element of his own thought or expression in the narrative. As my campfire lectures evolved into a unified monograph, guidance was received from professional historians. They have been more critical than the rangers but not less kind.

At the State College of Washington, Dr. Herman J. Deutsch and Dr. Claudius O. Johnson made the college's Northwest Collection available. They also joined their colleagues, Dr. W. B. Thorson and Dr. C. M. Brewster, in making many fine and comprehensive criticisms, which combined to strengthen the narrative. Several of my colleagues at Idaho State College gave direction and increased purpose to the discussion of conservation and wild life principles. They are Dr. Ray J. Davis, Albert V. S. Pulling, and DuWayne Goodwin. Dr. Carl W. McIntosh, president of the college, has extended many courtesies. Professor Wallace E. Garets edited the manuscript.

Former Yellowstone National Park Naturalist, Dr. C. Max Bauer, gave encouragement from the inception of the study and reviewed the final draft. Other National Park officials from whom wise council and valuable suggestions were received include Dr. Carl P. Russell, former National Park Supervisor of Interpretation, and Dr. Alvin P. Stauffer, Chief of Research and Survey. The collaboration of J. Neilson Barry was invaluable in the exposition of the discovery phase in the chapter on John Colter. J. Fred Smith, Delbert G. Taylor, and Mr. and Mrs. George Marler have also given material support to this effort.

The illustrations are principally the work of William S. Chapman, North District Ranger.

The support of Yellowstone Park Superintendent Lemuel A. Garrison and Chief Park Naturalist Robert N. McIntyre in bringing forth this Third Edition under the auspices of The

Yellowstone Library and Museum Association is indeed appreciated.

Lastly, gratitude is due my wife, Bessy N. Beal, and our son, David, and his wife, Jean, for the typing of the manuscript and for the rendering of much additional service to this enterprise.
MERRILL D. BEAL

IDAHO STATE COLLEGE

POCATELLO, IDAHO

June 10, 1960

INTRODUCTION

It is interesting and significant that this book, telling the story of man in the area of our oldest National Park, should be available soon after a season of record-breaking public use of the area. During the travel year 1948, one million thirty-one thousand five hundred and thirty-one people visited Yellowstone National Park.

The discoverer of The Yellowstone Country early in the nineteenth century, and re-discoverers through the years prior to 1872, as well as all visitors to the Park before the advent of modern highways and automobiles probably gave no thought to the reality and problems of a million visitors a year.

Dr. Beal's well documented and carefully prepared book brings us through the history of man in a wilderness, through that period of history before annual visitation of a million visitors in that wilderness. Readers will find the story of the before-one-million-visitors-years most interesting. It is a period, especially since the establishment of the National Park in 1872, in which we as a nation were experimenting for the most part in wilderness preservation and, at the same time, encouraging its use. Dr. Beal's book covers a period in U.S. history when shameful exploitation of natural resources was common practice. The preservation of The Yellowstone Country as a National Park is an action during the period of exploitation, an action of which we can all be proud. The story of man in Yellowstone is a fascinating one. It can also be a challenge to everyone to assume responsibility in continued preservation of Yellowstone National Park so that future generations may benefit from all of the things that unimpaired natural areas can offer by way of recreation, education, and inspiration.

JOHN E. DOERR Former Chief Naturalist, National Park Service

OUTDOORS

O, give me a bit of the great outdoors
Is all that I ask of you,
Where I may do whatever I like
And like whatever I do.

Where the sky is the boundary up above
And the earth is the measure below,
And the trail starts on where the sun comes up
And ends where the sun sinks low.

Where the wind blows sweet as a baby's breath,
And the sun shines bright as its eyes,
And the showers come and the showers go
As the tears when the little one cries.

And the brook runs merrily through the glade,
Singing its gladdening song,
And the pine trees murmur their soothing sighs,
Still bearing that song along.

Yes, carry me back to the lake's white shores
With its deer and its lily pad.
Where the loon calls out into the moonbeams bright
Through the mist on the waters sad.

Let me hear the elk's far cry
As it sweeps through the forest deep,
Where the silence hangs as over the dead
At rest in eternal sleep.

I'll pitch my tent by some lonesome pine,
By the rippling water's edge,
With the great outdoors as my garden,
And the willows round as my hedge.

And surrounded by pretty flowers,
That perfume the gentle breeze,
I'll idle away the whole long day,
In the shade of my old pine trees.

And I'll watch on yonder mountain
The colors change with the day,
And I'll follow each shadow creeping
So silently on its way.

And then I'll give thanks to God above
And in gratitude I'll pause,
And I'll love, not hate, each care that comes
In that great big home—Outdoors.

—FRANK L. OASTLER

CHAPTER I
YELLOWSTONE—THE GEM OF THE MOUNTAINS

Yellowstone National Park was one of the last regions in the United States to come into the scope of man's knowledge. This fact is partly responsible for its development as a wild animal retreat. Grizzlies and people do not go well together under natural conditions. Yet nature has bequeathed a rare portion of her treasure upon this enchanting land that forms the crown of the Rockies. Within the confines of what the world calls Yellowstone the visitor may find great and wondrous manifestations of natural handiwork. Indeed, nature seems to have indulged in several grand orgies of creation. Here are lofty mountain majesties and shining rivers of silver and green wind athwart the heights and plateaus like living, breathing things. Everywhere the air is pierced by lodgepole pines. Erect they stand, bristling with fierce determination, while prone beneath their feet lie their uprooted brethren in tangled disorder and various degrees of decay.[1]

The whole plateau is dotted by myriad alpine lakes of surpassing beauty. Surely it is comparable to a vast sponge which receives a five-foot mantle of snow annually. From this precipitation sufficient water is derived to feed a legion of springs and streams. "The altitude renders it certain that winter comes early and tarries late; in fact, it is almost always in sight and liable to drop in any day."[2]

Deep and delicately etched canyons involuntarily shock the visitor as he views their kaleidoscopic grandeur. Massive mountains display their mighty ramparts in a silhouette that is unmistakable and unforgettable. Indeed, some of these serrated spires once served as pilots to the wayfarer; and Indians named them "Pee-ah," meaning large and permanent.[3] So are they still, mute testaments of the ages.

Surely such an impressive alternation of rivers, forests, lakes, canyons, and mountains is in itself complete. Someone has said, "Yellowstone has everything except a cave and a glacier." Actually, there are caves and glaciers in the Park's environs, but the most unique feature of all this Wonderland is its thermal activity. Thousands of hot springs and hundreds of geysers reveal strange secrets of the inner earth. Mammoth Hot Springs Terraces represents the actual process of a mountain turning inside out.

Yellowstone Park is roughly located between longitude 110° W. and 111° W. and latitude 44° N. and 45° N. In respect to Wyoming, the Park is located in the northwestern corner, encroaching slightly upon Montana and Idaho. The area comprehends three thousand, four hundred and seventy-two square miles, and the average elevation is eight thousand feet above sea level. Occupying a central portion of the Rockies' greatest girth, the Park's scenic position is most strategic. From the top of Mt. Washburn a majestic rock-ribbed panorama is disclosed. It is indeed a vast area, surrounded by lofty mountain ranges, some of whose towering peaks are reflected in Lake Yellowstone. This comprehensive view reminds one of a gigantic amphitheatre or, from another angle, a colossal orange juicer with the Yellowstone River as its spigot. At the river's outlet from the Park at North Gate the elevation is five thousand, three hundred and fourteen feet above sea level, whereas the maximum height of eleven thousand, three hundred and sixty feet is achieved on the summit of Eagle Peak on the southeastern boundary.[4] Cartographers have segregated the most conspicuous elevations into seven plateaus, three ranges, four ridges, and several minor units of mountains and hills.[5] Thirty-two mountain peaks loom above the ten-thousand-foot level, and another six exceed the eleven-thousand-foot scale.[6]

The Continental Divide winds among the Park's southern plateaus in the manner of a serpent. From these circumstances, Yellowstone Park has become truly the wondrous land of water and the source of that life-giving liquid to lands hundreds of miles away in all directions. Nowhere else does water so well display its varied charms. From the Divide's snowy, timber-rimmed pockets, icy rivulets flow into sylvan pools, thence to rushing rivers with thundering waterfalls. Other water issues from steaming vents and towering geysers connected with the earth's internal heat and weaves vaporous trails into streams called warm or fire rivers.[7]

Great rivers have their origins in its alpine parks, from whence they follow their devious courses to the several seas. Oh, the rivers of Wonderland, what strength and beauty they possess! There is the Yellowstone itself, arising upon Yount's Peak and its vicinity among the high Absarokas. It rolls northward through that vast lake of limpid blue referred to by the natives as "the smile of the Great Spirit." From the famous Fishing Bridge outlet it flows tranquilly again beyond Hayden Valley, but soon it flashes into milk-white cascades, a transitional phase of noisy preparation for its two great falls. These awe-inspiring plunges are one hundred and nine and a sheer three hundred and eight feet, for the Upper and Lower Falls respectively. At each point the river's mighty volume sets up an awful tumult of sound, earth tremor, and spray in the immediate environs. The river's pulsating reverberation seems to follow its imprisoned rush along a tortuous path for many miles toward the Missouri.

Another stream arises in the southeast corner of the Park that possesses equal might and great utility. By the natives it was known as "Pohogwa," or river of the sagebrush plains. The French called it La Maudite Riviere Enragee, meaning accursed, mad river, but American frontiersmen renamed it the Snake.[8] The latter name lacks something of the romance in the others but aptly describes this stream which everywhere exhibits some characteristic of reptilian behavior.

Two other interesting rivers arise in the Park and join a third a hundred miles beyond the northwest boundary of Yellowstone. The Madison's tributaries derive from meadowlands beyond Upper Geyser and Norris Geyser basins.[9] The Madison is a moss-bottomed stream with lusty aquatic life. The Gallatin, which heads in the range of the same name, has a dashing manner. It has carved its way among forests both living and petrified. Each river follows a parallel course until they merge with the Jefferson at Three Forks. As the triumvirate roll away together, one remembers the unity and friendship that characterized the three men for whom they were named.

Other sinuous streams are the tuneful Bechler, laughing Lamar, and sculpturing Shoshone. These streams possess attractions that appeal to fishermen, hikers, photographers, and artists. In Yellowstone, the two-ocean-drainage courses are almost as intricate and snug as a child's hands folded in prayer. At either Isa Lake, or Two Ocean Pass, a pebble tossed in one stream would start vibrations upon the "water-nerve endings" of Atlantic and Pacific river systems. In fact, the Yellowstone country is the apex of North America; it is essentially the Great Divide.

Yellowstone's summer climate is invigorating and delightful. Frequent, but fleeting, rainstorms tend to modify the prevailing atmospheric aridity. Evenings and nights are invariably cool. The highest temperature ever recorded at Mammoth was 92.4°, while the lowest on record was 66° below zero. This record low was taken at Riverside Station near West Gate on February 9, 1933.[10]

Such is the physical setting of this mountainous country. Its western slope was called the land of "Ee-dah-how." This was a Shoshone exclamation that means "Behold! the sun is streaming down from the mountain tops; it is sunup, time to get up!"[11]

It is expedient that a brief review of early American history should be given as a setting for the major interests in the drama of Yellowstone. The history of Wonderland falls logically into three periods: Archaeological characteristics and association; Modern discovery and exploration; Development as a pleasuring ground by the United States Government.

The greater part of the Yellowstone area was a part of the Louisiana Purchase, whereas that portion under the Snake River drainage appertained to the great Pacific Northwest. All of the territory involved once belonged to Spain. However, the Spanish claim was relinquished in a series of treaties beginning with San Ildefonso in 1800, wherein the province of Louisiana was retroceded to France under the dictation of Napoleon Bonaparte. The balance of Spanish interests above the forty-second parallel was extinguished in favor of the United States in 1819.

American acquisition of Louisiana from France grew out of several considerations. The frontiersmen of the Ohio Valley were chafing under foreign commercial restrictions at New Orleans. The officials of the government were distressed at the prospect of having the strong-willed Napoleon as a neighbor. President Jefferson cogently expressed the general concern by saying, "... from this moment we must marry the British fleet and nation."[12] However, the alarm was soon dispersed by an eminently successful negotiation. Jefferson had instructed Robert Livingston, the American Minister to Paris, to buy New Orleans and West Florida. The early part of the spring of 1803 found Napoleon hard pressed for money and disgusted with native resistance against his government in Haiti, led by the remarkable Negro, Toussaint L'Ouverture, whom Bonaparte called the "gilded African." By March, Napoleon realized that the Peace of Amiens was about to be ruptured and war with England resumed. In these circumstances he decided to dispose of his American holdings. This notable decision was effected while His Imperial Majesty was taking a bath. Consequently it was one of the cleanest decisions that he ever made! It was then that the "Little Corporal" directed J. M. Talleyrand to say, "What would you give for the whole of Louisiana?"[13] Livingston, who was a trifle deaf anyway, could hardly believe what he heard. After some parleying the deal was closed by Livingston and Monroe for $15,000,000; of this amount $3,750,000 was diverted to American citizens to meet private claims against the French government. Livingston showed prophetic insight when he said to Monroe, "We have lived long, but this is the noblest work of our whole lives...."[14] More than a dozen states have been carved out of the 827,987 square miles. It is probable that Old Faithful Geyser alone is worth far more than the original purchase price, should good taste allow an assignment of monetary value to such a natural wonder.

Notwithstanding the marvels of this alluring land, Yellowstone lay dormant, forbidding and inhospitable, until the last quarter of the nineteenth century. Why was its call to conquest so long unheeded? Seldom has an area so long ignored made such a phenomenal rise to fame. The answer to this question is fully explored in this narrative.

CHAPTER II
JOHN COLTER'S DISCOVERY OF YELLOWSTONE

It is a fairly well-attested fact that America was first discovered by Leif Ericsson about 1000 A.D.[15] However, as Mark Twain put it, "America did not stay discovered," and therefore Columbus is not to be denied. So it was with Yellowstone. The most significant feature of its early history lies in the inconclusive nature of the early reports concerning its position and character.

Yellowstone's isolation was not effectively invaded and broken until the decade of 1860. This narrative will explain how early, trapper observations drifted into oblivion, and later, miner excursions faded into indifference. Hence, the first conclusive visitations were those made by the Folsom-Cook party in 9 and the Washburn-Langford-Doane Expedition of 1870. Why did Wonderland remain unknown to the world so long? Surely the answer is found in its relative inaccessibility. Yellowstone is a sequestered region, mountain-locked by the Absaroka, Teton, Gallatin, Beartooth, and Snowy ranges. Here, then, is a plateau a mile and a half above sea level, encircled by a still loftier quadrangle of rocky barriers. Some of these culminate in peaks and ridges that rise 4,000 feet above the level of the enclosed table land.

Of course there were a few yawning, ever-difficult canyon approaches, cut by foaming mountain torrents and several high, snow-choked passes suitable for late summer use. However, they were far removed from the principal arteries of pioneer travel, and they still remain apart from the main avenues of trade. Even now, these same bulwarks of nature, and their concomitants of snow and wind, exclude traffic from the region for half the year. Consider, then, the situation when all travel was on foot or horseback, and bases of supply were far away from all approaches to this mountain crown. Adequate mountain exploration necessitated large parties and elaborate outfits in the middle nineteenth century.

From these circumstances it is easy to understand why Lewis and Clark missed Yellowstone. They adhered quite closely to the

Missouri River thoroughfare. However, as an incident of an extensive side trip on their return, Clark and a detail of ten took an alternate route that eventually brought them upon the Yellowstone River near the present site of Livingston, Montana.[16] Previously, while at Fort Mandan, they had learned that the Minnetaree Indian name for the river was "Mitsiadazi," which means Rock Yellow River. The French equivalent, Roche Juane, was also in common use among the Indians and trappers, although when or by whom the name was given is unknown. American trappers called the river "Yallerstone!" A segment of the stream was trapped in 1805 by Antoine Larocque's party of North West Company trappers. They struck the river at a point twenty trapping days above its mouth, which was reached on September 30.[17]

The fact of the name's currency is further attested by Patrick Gass' significant journal entry on July 1, 1806: "Perhaps Capt. Clarke [sic] who goes up the river here, may also take a party and go down the Riviere Juane, or Yellowstone River."[18] Beyond the Indian stream names, little information concerning the area was ascertained by Lewis and Clark at that time.

While Lewis and Clark did not add any knowledge of Yellowstone Park to their epic-making report, still it was a member of the party who first viewed its exotic beauty. However, before delineating Colter's discovery, the picture of the Park's isolation should be explored further.

The first thrust toward the Yellowstone country was made by the French explorer de Verendrye, who came near the northeastern border in 1743 when he crossed the lower Yellowstone River, leaving Wonderland still undiscovered.[19]

By 1810, the Missouri Fur Company established posts on the mouths of the Bighorn and at Three Forks of the Missouri. Notwithstanding these locations, there was little penetration of the "top of the world," as the Crow Indians called the Yellowstone country. Blackfoot Indian hostility forced the abandonment of the post at Three Forks and in the fall of 1810, Major Andrew Henry, one of the partners, led a small party into the Pacific Ocean drainage. They went up the Madison River, thereby skirting the Gallatin Range which bounds the Park on the west. They crossed a low pass and came upon a beautiful lake. Henry's name was given the lake (Henrys Lake) and also to its outlet (Henrys Fork of the Snake River), which they followed about forty miles below its debouchment into Snake River Valley. In a pleasant spot some four miles below the present St. Anthony Falls they erected Fort Henry, but they did not prosper there and, feeling discouraged and insecure, abandoned that post. In 1811, Henry released his trappers, and while they returned to the east by various routes all of them missed the Yellowstone region.[20]

W. S. Chapman
Sacajawea with Lewis and Clark.

As Henry's men circled eastward a much larger expedition was threading its course between the Wind River Mountains and the Tetons. In 1811, Wilson Price Hunt led the "Overland Astorians," a band of sixty trappers, toward the Pacific. They reached Henry's deserted post early in August. It is probable that a member of this party inscribed a rock "calling card" that reads: "Fort Henry 1811 by Capt. Hunt." This marker is now included in the historical collections of the Yellowstone Park museums. It was found at the fort site in 1933 and donated to the museum by Seasonal Park Ranger-Naturalist Merrill D. Beal.[21] Hunt's party unfortunately decided to switch from horses to hurriedly-made canoes, which were launched upon Snake River near the fort. The hardship, privation, and recurring peril experienced by this band are among the most severe ever encountered by civilized men. Although they were obliged to separate into three groups in order to subsist each part finally reached the mouth of the Columbia. In 1812, a smaller party called the "Returning Astorians," under Robert Stuart, probably discovered South Pass.[22]

Notwithstanding the extensive peregrinations of these splendid wayfarers, Lewis and Clark, Andrew Henry, and Wilson Price Hunt, Wonderland, large though it is, remained a place apart. Only one white man had been sufficiently venturesome to gain entrance into the enchanted land.

John Colter was the son of Joseph and Ellen Shields Colter. He was born in or near Staunton, Virginia, probably in 1775.[23] Little is known of Colter's youth except that the family moved from Virginia to the vicinity of Mayville, Kentucky, when he was about five years old. As John grew to manhood it is evident that he possessed a restless urge to be in the wilderness. An unparalleled opportunity to satisfy this desire came upon the arrival of Captain Meriwether Lewis on his voyage down the Ohio River. From this contact Colter joined the Lewis and Clark Expedition at Louisville, Kentucky, on October 15, 1803.[24] The following spring they were on their way up the Missouri. Doubtless he was already experienced in woodcraft and the use of firearms. Strong, active, and intelligent, he soon won the rank and privileges of a hunter.

Colter's fitness for the business of exploration was early recognized and universally accepted.[25] For two years he shared the expedition's many trials and triumphs, but they had obviously failed to satisfy his desire for adventure. Before the explorers returned, intrepid fur traders were moving westward along the great Missouri artery as was their custom. Two Illinoisans, John Dickson and Forest Hancock, were encountered west of the Mandan Indian Villages in what is now the state of North Dakota. They had high expectations of fortunes in fur, and from them Colter caught the trapping fever. This was early in August of 1806. They evidently recognized John Colter as a man after their own hearts and offered to furnish him an equal share of their supplies. Then, and there, they became boon companions, and Colter requested an honorable discharge from government service. This wish was granted with the understanding that no one else would request such consideration.[26]

The government party gave their comrade powder, lead, and other articles that would be useful to him. Is this not evidence that he was in the best possible standing with the company?

Indeed, he was an admirable embodiment of the American scout. He was a person of sturdy, athletic frame, above the average height. He was physically quick, alert, enduring, a fine shot, the ideal frontiersman. His greatest asset was an extraordinary coordination of thought and action. This balance, combined with an abundance of energy, made Colter particularly dynamic. Patient and loyal, he performed his duties faithfully. In tribute to him a creek tributary to the Clearwater River, near Lapwai, had already been named Colter Creek. In numerous references to him his associates did not once hint of any mean or selfish act. He was constantly possessed by good temper, and he was of the open-countenanced Daniel Boone type cast.[27] Surely Colter was fully qualified for high adventure because he was, indeed, a two-fisted man with the sinews of a bear and the surefootedness of a cougar. He was wholly unafraid of wild animals, savages, or elements.

From August until the spring of 1807, this trio of Dickson, Hancock, and Colter trapped and traded along the upper Missouri. Then Colter gathered his pelts and started for St. Louis in a canoe. At the mouth of the Platte River, toward the end of June, he met Manuel Lisa.[28] They also struck up a friendship and bargain. Colter was still set for adventure and his new friend had such an assignment. In this meeting the strongest and boldest of the early American trappers of the West met the greatest Missourian trader. Upon hearing Manuel Lisa's plans, the travel and weatherworn Colter turned westward for the second time, as a member of the Lisa party.

Manuel Lisa proposed the establishment of posts on both sides of the Continental Divide. His plan was to send men along the course of every stream and out among the wandering tribes of Indians, until the commerce of the entire country was in the control of the Missouri Company. He had with him some of the most intrepid Kentucky and Tennessee hunters, rawboned backwoodsmen with their long-barrelled flintlocks, which they usually carried across their knees while on the boat. It was a larger undertaking than any before, and he needed fighters who were experienced and daring from the start.

As they neared the mud-hutted village of the Arickaras the warriors swarmed forth but soon backed up before the leveled muskets of Lisa's hunters. The traders went ashore and smoked the pipe of peace with the chiefs. This heretofore warlike tribe thereupon became temporarily pacified and sought presents and traffic in scarlet cloth and trinkets. The trappers purchased ponies from these Indians and struck westward toward the Yellowstone Valley. In amazement they viewed the bad lands on the north of the Bighorn. The party arrived at the mouth of the Bighorn River on November 21 and began the building of Fort Raymond, usually called "Manuel's Fort," which was their first trading post.[29] They feared the Blackfeet Indians and considered it expedient to abide temporarily in the land of the friendly Crows.

According to the authoritative report of Henry M. Brackenridge, Colter was appointed to carry the news of this undertaking to all the Indian tribes in the south.[30] Since this is an original reference to Colter's assignment it should be quoted:

> He [Lisa] shortly after despatched Coulter [sic], the hunter ... to bring some Indian nations to trade. This man, with a pack of thirty pounds weight, his gun and some ammunition, went upwards of five hundred miles to the Crow nation; gave them information, and proceeded from thence to several other tribes....[31]

Thus, this rugged and dynamic man, now in his early thirties, entered the wilderness on foot and alone, into an area unknown to his race. The journey was a simple business enterprise. As he journeyed southward, he contacted the many Crow clans.

Although practically everyone assumes that John Colter discovered Yellowstone National Park in the early winter of 1807-08,[32] few realize that there is no conclusive evidence to support the claim. Therefore, a review of the proof is essential. The record is brief: Colter did leave Fort Manuel (Raymond) in the fall of 1807.[33] Yet the direction he took is not definitely mentioned, and no incident was specifically recorded of any unique visitation. Still, soon after this journey, Colter related strange tales of weird, natural phenomena.[34] Few of the stories he told were chronicled in detail. However, it is a matter of record that he claimed to have seen a large petrified fish nearly fifty feet long,[35] numerous hot springs and geysers,[36] and a great lake.

Manuel Lisa's Fort built in 1807.

Evidence that Colter saw a geyser basin is flimsy indeed. Notwithstanding the uncertainty of Colter's large travel experience, it is obvious that somewhere, sometime, he saw something that impressed him mightily. He must have waxed enthusiastic, because his recital evoked so much ridicule from the trapper fraternity. For a half a century, everywhere in the West, the mountain men argued and joked pro and con about the mythical marvels of "Colter's Hell." By 1837, the story had become common knowledge by reason of the following reference in Washington Irving's first edition of The Adventures of Captain Bonneville:

> A volcanic tract ... is found on ... one of the tributaries of the Bighorn.... This ... place was first discovered by Colter, a hunter belonging to Lewis and Clarke's [sic] exploring party, who came upon it in the course of his lonely wanderings, and gave such an account of its gloomy terrors, its hidden fires, smoking pits, noxious streams, and the all pervading "smell of brimstone," that it received, and has ever since retained among trappers the name of "Colter's Hell."[37]

Irving's description is significant because it is evidence of the "Colter's Hell" tradition current at that time. However, the location assigned is incorrect. No gloomy terrors or hidden fires exist on Stinking Water (now Shoshone River). As in other explorations of the Colter ones, Irving made guesses and assumptions.

Nothing has ever been found that states precisely when or where Colter saw the wonders of Yellowstone. Yet, the fact persisted that sometime between 1806 and 1810, somewhere between the Jefferson and Shoshone rivers he saw them! And strange enough, in the fullness of time, his spacious claims were wholly vindicated. This strange circumstance, therefore, presents the student of early Western exploration with one of the most difficult problems in regional history. Does the full discovery of Yellowstone Park in 1870, ipso facto, prove the tradition of John Colter's earlier visitation?[38]

In the Colter case there are only two elements of primary evidence. First, it is a matter of record that he made a journey from Fort Manuel in the fall of 1807 and subsequently returned with an astonishing story of natural wonders. Secondly, a famous map was published in 1814, based upon the compilations of Lewis and Clark. Upon this Map of 1814 appears a dotted line marked "Colter's Route in 1807."[39] It is generally assumed that the dotted line actually marks the route of Colter's journey from Fort Manuel. Although the route charted cannot be accepted literally, it is an important documentary link, worthy of the utmost study. There is little upon the map that would confirm the existence of Yellowstone's marvels beyond the phrases "Boiling Spring," and "Hot Spring Brimstone," but every trapper encountered boiling springs and waters impregnated with bubbling gases having sulphurous odors. These were not unusual. Hence, there is nothing indicated along that dotted line that would guarantee anything extraordinary.[40]

Still, the known facts of Colter's journey toward the headwaters of the Bighorn in the fall of 1807 and the representation of his extensive exploration to the west, a part of which is now Yellowstone National Park, upon the Map of 1814 is highly significant. For one thing, it proves that William Clark, who supplied the map sheets to Samuel Lewis,[41] the Philadelphia cartographer, was particularly impressed by Colter's journey, otherwise it would not have been incorporated upon this very important document.

According to this map, John Colter traveled in a southwesterly direction from the mouth of the Bighorn River.[42] He must have mapped the area because his route east of the Absaroka Range (Yellowstone's eastern boundary) conforms so accurately with existing geographic conditions that his journey to the Park's border may be followed like tracks in the snow. From Fort Manuel he ascended Pryors Fork some fifty miles to Pryors

Gap.[43] Passing through this opening, he crossed westward to Clarks Fork, which he ascended to Dead Indian Creek. From there he evidently quartered a divide to the south, which brought him upon a river called Mick-ka-appa, where he first smelled sulphur. So he renamed the stream Stinking Water River. It is known today as the North Fork of Shoshone River. In ascending this stream, Colter quickly gained elevation, and in a hanging valley about midway up the range he found a clan of Indians for whom he was obviously searching. On the Map of 1814 they are identified as "Yep-pe, Band of Snake Indians, 1000 Souls."

From these denizens of both prairie and mountain, Colter undoubtedly first learned of the Yellowstone marvels. The acquisition of this interesting information at a point in relatively close proximity to the features, together with other favorable conditions, impelled him to project an exploration of the "enchanted land." After listening to eloquent descriptions of the natural phenomena nothing could be more natural than for such an adventurous explorer to experience an intense desire to visit the country. Remember, his mission of informing the clans concerning the establishment of Fort Manuel at the mouth of the Bighorn River had been performed. Now he was on his own with leisure time on his hands. Although the season was advanced, late November often finds the Park open for travel. Tribal accounts describing a vast wilderness of multiform grandeur made the restless trapper burn with curiosity. One can easily envision him weighing the factors of distance, time, and the known hazards, until he struck a favorable balance. His sign talk in council with the chiefs could probably be sifted out and summarized in these terms: "Less than two hundred miles ... the trails are known by your scouts, and they are still open.... A matter of five or six suns ... your horses are fat and strong ... game is plentiful.... Well, what are we waiting for?"

Such an appraisal of the situation is in complete accord with the known realities. Colter was an experienced explorer; he knew how to conduct an expedition. This procedure eliminates the element of foolhardiness so conspicuous in the usual picture visualized of a solitary trapper on snowshoes, wending an uncertain course among river labyrinths running in various directions, mountain ranges of interminable lengths, and gargoylian lakes. Instead, the enterprise now conforms to a standard characteristic of Colter's levelheaded courage and judgment. Of course he may have gone alone and on foot, but if so why, after leaving the Yellowstone country, did he depart from the straight-of-way down Clarks Fork toward Fort Manuel and head back to the Yep-pe village as the map so clearly shows? Logic insists that Indian scouts were with him, or at least that he had borrowed a horse from them, which he was obliged to return. Thus, Colter's famous journey into the land of scenic mystery was efficiently accomplished late in November. With the aid of Yep-pe Indian leaders, if not under their guidance, he had gone where no white man had ever been before, and he still reached Manuel's Fort in good season, or else the Map of 1814 would not have been inscribed "Colter's Route in 1807."

But, where precisely in Yellowstone Park did Colter travel? This question poses an extremely difficult problem in research. (The serious student will find the many ramifications involved in the problem explored more fully in the Appendix.) Unfortunately the dotted line appearing on the Map of 1814, marked "Colter's Route in 1807," is of no help whatever in answering the question. In fact, the map complicates the problem because the geography depicted on the western loop, or so-called Yellowstone Park section of the map, is wholly fictitious. Unlike the valid section east of the Absarokas, the western section bears no similarity to anything in Yellowstone Park, Wyoming, Idaho, Montana, America, the world, or the moon! It is, in fact, a plat of bogus geography comparable only to the kind found in Jonathan Swift's Gulliver's Travels. In short, it is obvious that "Colter's Route in 1807," beyond the Yep-pe village, was not properly described because it depicts him as visiting the drainage of all the river systems within a radius of five hundred miles of that Indian encampment. The most obvious errors in that part of the map which impinges upon the western section of this so-called "Colter's Route" are:

(1) Three Forks are shown to the northeast instead of northwest.

(2) Lake Biddle, usually identified as Jackson Lake, could only be Brooks Lake and be on the Bighorn drainage. Jackson Lake lies due south about fifty miles, on the other side of the Continental Divide.

(3) The Rio Del Norte (Green River of the Colorado) is far and away to the south. It is grotesquely misplaced.

(4) The South Fork of Snake River is not depicted, neither is the Jackson Lake area.

(5) Upper Yellowstone River is not shown, and Lake Eustis (presumed to be Lake Yellowstone) is fantastic in all respects.

In view of these egregious errors it is a monumental mistake to insist, as so many authors in effect have done, that Colter was a human helicopter who hopped all over the Rocky Mountains in connection with his Yellowstone exploration. Actual geography and common sense prove that he could not possibly have made such an extensive journey, particularly so late in the season. Just as certainly, geography and common sense attest that in traveling a normal western loop essential to yield conformity with the map's figure eight[44] Colter would have seen precisely the type of country the Map of 1814 does not depict, but which, nevertheless, is actually there! A normal half circle would have brought him upon the Upper Yellowstone River, South Fork of Snake River, Yellowstone Lake, and the thermal areas at Thumb of Lake and Hayden Valley. These paint pots, hot springs, and geysers, particularly Dragon's Mouth and Mud Volcano, satisfy the descriptions he made and easily meet the requirement of the terms on the map, "Boiling Spring," "Hot Springs Brimstone," and also Washington Irving's reference "... of gloomy terrors, hidden fires, smoking pits, noxious streams...." In effect, these areas alone would qualify as "Colter's Hell."

                        J. N. Barry
               Eastern section of Colter's route.

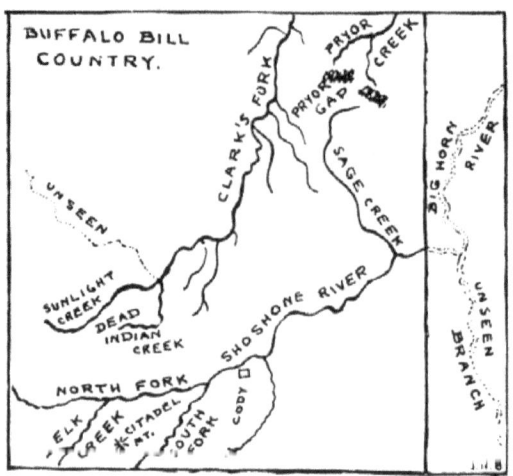

A true sketch of the Cody, Wyoming, area as it is mapped today.

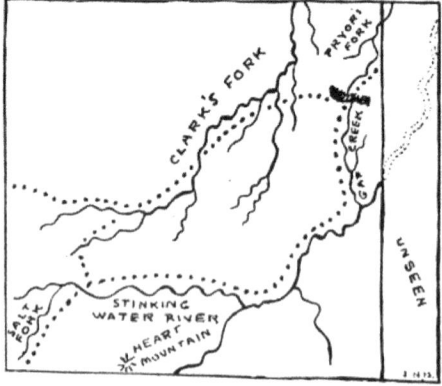

The east sector of Colter's route as depicted on the Map of 1814. Note the conformity with actual geography. The only material difference is in names.

It is now possible to accurately sketch both parts of Colter's famous journey. Firstly, from Fort Manuel he reached the Yeppe Indian camp and returned to the mouth of the Bighorn River where Fort Manuel was built, exactly as the map depicts. It is because of the accuracy of this section of the Map of 1814 that Colter's Yellowstone course may be now traced like tracks in the snow. Secondly, from the Yep-pe Indian camp, Colter ascended "Elk-Wapiti Creek" to its source; then crossing a range he came upon a mitten-shaped mountain, which he labeled "fossil."[45] From this landmark he probably descended Pass Creek to Thorofare Creek, which he followed to the Upper Yellowstone River. Then he ascended Atlantic Creek and crossed the Continental Divide at Two Ocean Pass. From here he descended Pacific Creek, skirted Big Game Ridge, and crossed the South Fork of Snake River, within the present confines of the Park. Thence, along Chicken Ridge, from whence he could frequently view South Arm, he headed toward Flat Mountain Arm, crossed Solution Creek, and struck West Thumb.[46] The validity of this itinerary is wholly sustained by the genuine features of this area as they appear upon the Map of 1814. Indeed, the route seems obvious and indisputable in view of the actual conditions existing. There are alternative routes within certain limitations. On a crude map where there are numerous similar streams various combinations are possible.[47]

Section from map of 1814 depicting Lewis and Clark route. Its legend reads: "A map of Lewis and Clark's Track, Across the Western Portion of North America, From the Mississippi to the Pacific Ocean; By Order of the Executive of the United States in 1804, 5, 6. Copied by Samuel Lewis from the Original Drawing of Wm. Clark."

Leaving West Thumb, Colter circled the Lake to its outlet and followed it to the Hayden Valley thermal area. Dragon's Mouth and the Mud Volcano were undoubtedly features contributing to the impression he carried away and transmitted to others. Even the "Hot Springs Brimstone" characterization on the Map of 1814 mildly suggests violent thermal activity. The phrase also suggests that Colter mapped a geyser basin.[48]

Colter's return route from Hayden Valley supplies the final link in the figure eight. To reach the Yep-pe Indian camp he might have veered to the northeast, crossed Yellowstone River at a ford below Dragon's Mouth, and ascended Pelican Creek or one of the tributaries of the Lamar River. After crossing the Absarokas, he evidently descended one of the creeks that empty into Clarks Fork. No one on earth can be certain about this part of his journey. There is no reference anywhere, and the Map of 1814 gives no clue. Still, he did reach a tributary of Clarks Fork, which he followed to its junction with Dead Indian Creek, thence to the Yep-pe band. As stated above, Colter left the Yep-pe village in returning to Fort Manuel by a different route than the one that brought him there. This fact, together with his return to the Yep-pe Indian camp, is of the first importance in assessing the validity of Colter's Yellowstone discovery.

While Colter's journey in Yellowstone proper was not comprehensive, still he was definitely oriented and reasonably precise. Truly, Colter crossed the eastern and central parts of Yellowstone's Wonderland, and he observed its features closely. Companions were duly apprised of these marvels. Members of the Lisa party thereafter referred to the region as "Colter's Hell." In May, 1810, when he reached St. Louis, William Clark was officially informed. It was then that Clark believed in Colter's story and passed it on to Nicholas Biddle and Samuel Lewis who were in Philadelphia. Notwithstanding considerable misapprehension as to facts, Colter's journey was nevertheless depicted after a fashion on the remarkable Map of 1814. Upon this evidence alone, John Colter became accredited as the first white man to enter the Yellowstone Park country, hence its first discoverer. Here, indeed, was a man worthy of making a great discovery. He was a dreadnaught, if there ever was one; completely self-reliant; unafraid of forests, deserts, rivers, or mountains, including all of their denizens; yet withal, a serious-minded person of integrity. He is entitled to everlasting credit in the field of western geographical exploration.

Eventually, Colter found himself back in Lisa's Fort. He had discovered the interesting Two Ocean Pass across the Rocky Mountains into the Snake River drainage. He was the first white man to touch upon the northeastern perimeter of majestic

Jackson Hole country. Then, as the climax of all, he was the first to climb still higher and gaze upon the marvels of a never-to-be-forgotten land. Has it ever been the fortune of any other man to explore such a vast domain of virgin territory? It is a strange paradox that, accustomed as mountain men were to impressive manifestations of nature, Colter's relation of Yellowstone's wonders only won him the distinction of a confirmed prevaricator.[49]

While Colter's experience after 1807 has little bearing upon the history of Yellowstone, it is a part of the heritage of the Old West and therefore essential for the unity of the narrative.[50] In the autumn of 1808, Colter and a companion named Potts invaded the hunting grounds of the Blackfeet Indians in the vicinity of Three Forks forming the Missouri. Early one morning they were setting a line of traps along either the Jefferson, Madison, or Gallatin rivers, about a day's travel from their point of junction.[51] As they were silently paddling the canoe, they heard a resounding noise that resembled the muffled pounding of feet. Colter was apprehensive about Indians, and since perpendicular banks obstructed their view he advised hiding. However, his impulsive companion accused him of cowardice; why run from buffalo? Almost within the moment a band of "Black Devils" burst through the thicket into full view. Colter kept cool and rowed for the bank. As they drew closer to the enemy, Potts dropped his paddle and picked up his rifle. This gesture was interpreted as an act of defiance by the Blackfeet braves. A stalwart savage leaped into the water and snatched Potts' rifle out of his hands. Whereupon, with an air of mastery that Indians respect, Colter stepped to the bank, wrested the weapon from the warrior's grasp, and returned it to Potts.

W. S. Chapman
Colter and Potts under attack.

The Blackfeet were now swarming through the brush, but Colter, calm and poised, raised his hand palm forward in the peace signal. Potts, now convinced that flight was the only hope, nosed the canoe toward mid-stream. Suddenly a bowstring twanged, and Potts cried out, "Colter, I'm wounded." Colter urged him to come ashore, but instead he leveled his rifle at an Indian and fired. Instantly a score of arrows entered his body or, in Colter's language, "he was made a riddle of," and he slumped lifeless in the canoe.[52] Calm and flintlike Colter stood his ground. As the chief sized up the situation, a dozen warriors identified the survivor as the white man who raised havoc among them in a battle with a band of Crow Indians.[53] This knowledge caused the braves to clamor for setting him up as a mark to shoot at, but their chief interfered. He stood in great dignity and said, "This is a brave warrior. We will see how bravely he can die."[54] Then, seizing the victim by the shoulders, he asked him if he could run fast. To this query Colter replied with a chop-fallen air that he was slow. Actually, he was an excellent sprinter. Several hundred Indians swarmed about, working up their emotions toward the victim. First they denuded him, then motioned him to move forward perhaps a hundred yards, from whence he was signalled to run toward a "v" shaped open prairie of some six miles expanse. Colter had drawn a chance to save himself if he could! He accepted the challenge and resolved to make the most of it. As the war whoops sounded, Colter was away with the dash of an antelope. He bounded and ran until his lungs burned within him, and he ruptured a blood vessel in his nose. On he sped, mile after mile, until the chorus of Indian yells grew fainter and fainter. All of Colter's muscles cried out for a moment's respite. He looked around and beheld a spear-armed warrior some twenty yards behind him, coming fast to split him in two. Upon impulse, Colter whirled in his tracks, and running obliquely, gave the signal for mercy. The reply was a thrust spear, but the brave made a false step, stumbled, and fell. He was obviously astonished at Colter's gory appearance. The badly launched spear struck in the ground and was broken off. In a surge of hope and strength, the powerful Colter lunged like a stag at bay, and overpowering the Indian, he seized the barbed half and impaled his fallen foe to the earth!

If the Blackfeet had possessed a spirit of chivalry they would have called quits to this ordeal by running and combat. Here was a man who had outrun the cream of the redskin sprinters and, unarmed, had slain an armed warrior. Surely such a performance should have won the captive's freedom. But the Blackfoot code made no allowance for heroic behavior in the enemy.

On came the braves, more ruddy than usual by reason of their exertions and more fleet than normal because of the caliber of the quarry. Colter needed no spear now; he fairly vaulted until he gained the river bank, and diving into the stream he concealed himself under a jam of driftwood or beaver dam that impinged upon an island. Here he secreted himself while they howled and thrashed about for hours, yelling, as Colter said, "like a legion of devils." When darkness came, like an angel of mercy, he dragged his aching body from its watery prison, silently swam across the river, and started the second excruciating lap in his race for life.[55] Manuel Lisa's Fort was two hundred miles away.

After seven days of hiding and nights of painful travel and exposure he found his way through Bozeman Pass and eventually reached the fort at the mouth of the Bighorn. During this "ordeal by travel" he had no sustenance other than roots known as psoralea esculenta, or sheep sorrel.[56] Again there was momentary disposition among the trappers to question Colter's veracity, but the evidence was unimpeachable, and it was written plainly where all might see. He seemed only a shadow of his former self.

According to James, even this terrible experience did not daunt the lion-hearted trapper, "Dangers seemed to have for him a kind of fascination."[57] Colter could not reconcile himself to the loss of the traps he had dropped in the river during the attack. Soon after his recovery, he ventured again into the forbidden Three Forks region. At his first night's camp he was attacked, but he contrived to escape. Whereupon, he vowed to his maker that he would never return.[58]

Acting upon this resolution Colter started his third voyage down the Missouri. While he was resting in one of the upper Minnetarre villages, probably in September of 1809, Manuel Lisa arrived. The Three Forks country was his destination and Colter must show him the way.

By midwinter a strong detachment was on its way, headed by Pierre Menard as bourgeois commander, Andrew Henry as field captain, and John Colter as guide. The party arrived at Three Forks on April 3, 1810 and built a post. Within a fortnight the Blackfeet attacked. Five trappers were killed, and most of the horses and equipment disappeared. It was a crushing blow to the enterprise, and for Colter, the final straw. James states that Colter came into the fort, spoke of his promise to God, repented of his foolhardy return, and said, "If God will only forgive me this time and let me off I will leave the country day after tomorrow and be d———d if I ever come into it again."[59] Several days later he and a companion slipped through the Indian lines and in due time reached Fort Manuel. From there the two men departed for St. Louis in a dugout and reached that frontier capital on the last day of May. They had negotiated the distance of 2,500 water miles in the incredible time of thirty days.[60] Is it any wonder that other trappers referred to "Colter's large experience"?

For over five years he had been among barbarian people, and of certain torments he had more than enough. His life had been one of hard toil and high adventure; now he would seek peace and quiet.

Captain Meriwether Lewis had passed away, but William Clark was a person of authority. He was Brigadier General of Militia and Superintendent of Indian Affairs. To Clark, Colter gave geographical data, a part of which appeared on the map published in 1814 in the Biddle-Allen edition of the journals. Colter was unable to collect the wages due him as a member of the famous expedition so he brought suit against the Lewis estate and secured partial compensation. His trapping claims for services to Thomas James were unavailing as the latter could not collect from the fur company. While in St. Louis attending to this vexatious business he undoubtedly related his experiences to General William Clark. The latter, in turn, passed the story along to John Bradbury, the English scientist, and James M. Brackenridge, an American author. Such men accepted his report at face value. Concerning him, James wrote, "His veracity was never questioned among us."[61] Lesser people were more incredulous, and Colter's reputation suffered accordingly.

Colter took up a tract of bounty land on the south bank of the Missouri in the vicinity of Dundee village, Franklin county. There the great wanderer, with his bride Sally, turned to the prosaic routine of farming. Wilson Price Hunt's expedition found him there and offered him a position as guide. Bradbury said he accompanied them for several miles, balancing in his mind the charms of his bride against those of the Rocky Mountains. However, the life of steady habits won, but not for long, as he died of jaundice in 1813.

During the subsequent half century Colter's reputation evolved by degrees through the following stages: bare-faced prevaricator, devil-take-care mountain roamer, accidental discoverer of Yellowstone National Park. From the present perspective he appears much more than a scout and explorer. He was something of an economist and prophet, because he is said to have told Henry M. Brackenridge that where he had been, "a loaded wagon would find no obstruction in passing over the Rocky Mountains."[62]

On Yellowstone maps a single conspicuous feature commemorates Colter's work. It is Colter's Peak near the southeastern point of Yellowstone Lake. May it ever stand aloof, towering and quite inaccessible; a fitting monument to a gallant scout. Such a man should never be forgotten because he was master of the untamed West.

CHAPTER III
INDIANS IN AND AROUND YELLOWSTONE

A description of the Indian background is an integral part of all early American history. An appreciation of the "Old West" is impossible without an understanding of the Indian problem.

Yellowstone was not the original homeland of any distinct Indian tribe. In comparatively recent time, probably about 1800, it became the refuge for a small and degenerate band of Tukuarika, or sheep-eating Indians. They had formerly lived in the Montana and Dakota country but had been driven into seclusion by the powerful Blackfoot nation. The several branches of Shoshones residing in Yellowstone environs were Bannocks, Snakes, Tukuarikas, and Flatheads. The Crows came from other Indian sources. All of these Indians possessed certain racial characteristics of the red race. In view of various conflicting ideas, a few observations about the people as a whole are expedient.

Indians are human beings possessing the sensibilities and emotions of white men. However, their manner of living and conception of life has been relatively low. Even so, it is difficult to generalize upon them as a people. As Chief Washakie once said, "Indians very much like white men—some good, some bad." It is generally conceded that they were proud, so haughty in fact that they lacked that quality of mind so essential to progress or adjustment, humility or teachability. They could not learn because they would not admit that they lacked anything. They were the "chosen people." Originally they looked upon the hard-working white people as slaves and referred to them by no other name.

As a rule Indian braves were arrogant lords, not to be degraded by menial toil. It was enough for them to expose themselves to the hardships of fighting and hunting. They would proudly bring home the trophies of war and the hunt. They were also diligent in caring for their weapons and horses in preparation for future exploits. Much leisure time was expended upon personal ornamentation and in talking about the news of the day and affairs of the tribe. The Indians' inordinate pride was revealed in every movement. The men in particular possessed a free and easy bearing. This natural grace of action was probably facilitated by their practice of living in a semi-nude condition.[63]

Indians were much more cunning and adroit than the wildest game. They were fleet and stealthy, deceitful and cruel. To gain an advantage over prey or an enemy by strategy was their greatest joy and constituted the primary requisite for leadership. To be mentioned by one's tribesmen as a great warrior or a cunning horse thief was the highest ambition of an Indian, and many were past masters at both these hazardous hobbies. The greatest among them was the one with the most "coups" to his credit, such as scalps, stolen horses, and captured enemies. Making coups entitled the brave to wear an eagle feather in his hair and emblazon it upon his robe; by this token he was distinguished for heroic action.[64]

On the whole they were revengeful and vindictive. If an injury, real or fancied, were done to them by a particular person, it was a solemn duty to retaliate either against him or someone else. Many cases can be adduced to sustain this principle. In 1809, a trapper named Carson accepted a banter from a band of Arickaras to shoot among their enemy Sioux, who were across the Missouri a half mile away. The reckless trapper shot and killed one of the Sioux warriors. The following year three white men were slain by the Sioux to expiate this crime. The Indian code demanded blood for blood, the more the better. They were seldom inclined toward chivalry; mercy had no part in their code. It was hard, relentless, and primitive. By the strong hand they lived, and by the strong arm only were they awed. Forays, feuds, battles, that was the life! They painted, dressed, danced, and prayed for war.

And yet, in a way, they had poetic souls. The beauty and grandeur of nature revealed itself in their dignified bearing. Many were majestic in appearance, poised of manner, and eloquent in speech. Some of them were gifted storytellers who entertained their hearers. Others were great speakers who instructed them in the legendary lore of the tribe. Still others were artists, musicians, skilled artisans in many lines; and there were medicine men.

Tribal organization was based upon the family unit, which was monogamous, except in the case of the chief men who usually had several wives. The chief's lodge occupied a central position in the village, with other leaders' abodes surrounding. The women, too, observed a style of dress in keeping with their respective stations. Heredity in leadership was unknown; men became chiefs by reason of their cunning and courage in war, wisdom in council, and generosity toward the tribesmen.[65]

In the matter of economics most mountain Indians were novices. It is undoubtedly true that early American settlers received important initial aid from the Indians in raising crops. They taught the whites how to raise the very products that still constitute the backbone of American production: maize, potatoes, tobacco, cotton, squash, and beans. But instead of improving along with the settlers, they generally preferred the ways of their fathers. They did not lack the means for the production and preservation of food so much as the energy and ability to anticipate future necessity.

In the Rocky Mountains, where nature was quite inhospitable (without irrigation), the natives were even less thrifty than elsewhere. When food was plentiful they would gormandize to the uttermost, living contentedly. When confronted by famine they would languish in starvation. Natural forces battered them roughly. There was fasting, but there were buffalo brains and tongues too—earth's supreme dish!

W. S. Chapman
Mountain Indian clan.

The women and girls were practically slaves to their husbands and brothers. They were inured in hardships and possessed much forbearance and self-denial. Their homemaking work was arduous. They dressed all game and gathered nuts, berries, fuel, and roots. They made bows, arrows, lodges, travois, and clothing. The packing and moving, striking lodges and general routine was women's work.[66] There was never the slightest disposition to complain among them; in fact, they were inclined to despise a brave who departed from the usual patterns. He would be called "old woman" and his squaw, if any, often received a castigation. Maidens were required to be modest, wear robes at all times, and look seriously upon life. Marriages were arranged by parents with the consent of near relations. The desires of the young people were given consideration, if reasonable, but the decision was made by the girl's father.

Meat was the mainstay of life among Indians, and a considerable supply was available before white men came. In spite of inadequate weapons, the natives had numerous effective methods of securing wild game. Most hunters were masters of what was called the cabalistical language of birds and beasts. By this means they were able to approach many animals closely and slay them. Bison were sometimes driven into natural arenas where a gory slaughter ensued. Occasionally these great beasts were maneuvered into runs, from which they were stampeded pellmell over a precipice.[67] Generally they were simply chased and shot down at full gallop. This procedure required great dexterity in loading and discharging weapons. Of course the hunter's full attention was given to the target because his hunting horse took care of himself. He anticipated every move of the prey. With eyes flashing, nostrils distended, and foam flowing from his mouth, the trained steed sprang after the deceptive buffalo in swift execution of his master's will.

The war horse was even more highly prized than a hunter. Animals of exotic appearance had double or treble value over ordinary steeds and were claimed by the chiefs. The proud warrior went to as much pains to adorn his horse as he did himself. Nothing could induce him to neglect or mistreat his favorite.

In their palmy days, the Indians largely confined their efforts to pursuit of big game. In later years they had reluctant recourse to smaller animals. Rabbits were encircled—sometimes by a chain of fire. Ground squirrels were drowned out, and all types of animal life were utilized for food. The products of the buffalo, deer, elk, antelope, goat, bear, beaver, and numerous small animals and fish gave them strength for the pursuit of more game and the enemy. Many different combinations of meat, roots, nuts, and berries were known to the Indians. Pemmican was a mixture of pounded dried meat, grease, and service berries. When properly prepared and packed in skins this food would keep indefinitely.[68]

The camas and yamp plants were the Indian's bread. These roots are about an inch in diameter, and they have a sweetish taste while fresh, but they are more palatable when baked in earthen ovens. Either of these roots contains nutriment sufficient to support life, and often mountain Indians were obliged to subsist on this slender fare.

From a white man's viewpoint the dominant element in Indian religion was superstition. A stark animism prevailed in every cult. They believed that the different animals had either good or evil spirits and that they should be revered or feared according to their nature. The sun in particular was an object of worship. Each young man diligently sought his own strong medicine. The ritual varied but usually involved solitude, exertion, fasting, and extreme exposure. During this vigil the youth received a new name and a symbol of power. In due time these signs of maturity were manifest among the tribe and a status therein was secured.

Illness and death were attributed to the influence of evil spirits. The chief remedy for sickness was the sweat house. This was a mystic shrine both for temporal and spiritual blessing. The health seekers would rub their bodies with the tips of fir boughs, and thus the steam would effectively penetrate their bodies in a few minutes. Several sweats, each followed by a dip in a stream, constituted a bath, except when the spiritual interest predominated. In that case the votary might remain in the sweat house for hours or even days.

In respect to amusement Indians had unusual interest. That they were stoical at all times is an erroneous idea. They laughed and joked and engaged in many games.[69] Their singing was largely extemporaneous, accompanied by instruments of the crudest type. A horse race had tremendous appeal for the "bucks," who sometimes gambled away everything they possessed, including their wives and children. In general, the social life of Indians was notable for its excesses. Certain seasonal festivals were held in which the element of worship was interwoven with hilarity. Before going upon a hunt the Indians were wont to clothe some of the hunters in hides of the game, buffalo, or elk. These "bucks" would then cavort around in the manner of the game desired. In all this there was an air of expectancy and supplication.

Smoking was another semi-sacred ceremony by which oaths and agreements were secured. A ritual was usually observed. They relied heavily upon innumerable supernatural symbols and routines.

Such were the general characteristics and customs possessed by all of the mountain Indians. A marked degree of differentiation among them would justify a brief description of each. Of course these differences are only apparent to the discerning eye. Factors of physiognomy, dress, and speech are recognizable upon close observation.[70] However, it is not an easy matter to express these different characteristics in words.

The Bannocks (also Bannacks)— This name is derived from the Shoshoni word "bamp," which means "hair," and "nack," which signifies "a backward motion." It is also said that these Indians made cakes from acorn flour, pulverized grasshoppers, and currant jelly which so resembled the Scotch bannock cake in shape and flavor that some Scotch trapper applied this name to the tribe. There were approximately two thousand Bannocks in 1810, and they claimed the country southwest of Yellowstone. It was this tribe which made a deep trail across Yellowstone in going to and returning from their buffalo hunts. Bannocks were tall, straight, athletic people, possessed of more physical courage than most Indians. In a defensive way they were the most warlike of all Indians.

The Shoshoni or Snake Indians— This tribe of natives lived in the upper Snake River Valley. According to Alexander Ross, the Snake Indians were so named because of their characteristic quick concealment of themselves when discovered. "They glide with the subtility of the serpent." However, Indians interpreted the word "Shoshoni" as meaning "inland."[71] Father DeSmet stated: "They are called Snakes because in their poverty they are reduced like reptiles to the condition of digging in the ground and seeking nourishment from roots."[72] They lived in peace with the Flatheads and Nez Percés in the north and were at war with the Blackfeet, Crows, Bannocks, and Utahs. The Snakes were dependable participants in the trappers' rendezvous so often held in the Green River Valley in the second quarter of the nineteenth century. TyGee was a leading chief during much of the nineteenth century. The Targhee Forest was named after this Snake chieftain. They were a short, very dark, heavy-set people, with small feet and hands but large chests and shoulders. Their disposition was quite peaceful and friendly toward other people, although they were very suspicious. They were excellent horsemen and good fighters when aroused. The whole nation consisted of about a thousand, but it was broken into bands, some of which were vital and murderous while others, such as the "Diggers," were degraded and impoverished. Their great and constant occupation was to obtain food, and they were disposed to eat almost anything.

Photo by W. H. Jackson
Family of Sheepeater Indians

Tukuarikas or Sheepeater Indians— "Tuku" means "mountain sheep" and "arika," "eat," or "Sheepeater." They were a slender, wiry people who possessed neither ponies nor firearms but used bows and arrows effectively. They wore furs and skins and lived among the rocks in the Gardner River canyon in Yellowstone and in the Salmon River Mountains of central Idaho. There were some two hundred Indians in the Yellowstone tribe. Their main support was from game and fish. These Indians did not possess any distinctive culture of their own, but, hermit-like, they seemed concerned only to carry on by themselves until further notice.

The Flatheads— This tribe lived in western Montana. The Flatheads roamed the prairie between Glacier National Park and the Bitter Root Range. Lake Flathead was their favorite rendezvous. These Indians supposedly derived their name from an ancient practice of shaping or deforming the head during infancy. However, in 1830, Ferris claimed that not one living proof of that practice could be found among them. They called themselves "Salish" and spoke a language remarkable for its melody and simplicity. They were noted for humanity, forbearance, and honesty. They were certainly one of the few tribes in the Rocky Mountains who could boast that they never killed or robbed a white man nor stole a single horse.

The Blackfeet— This was a branch of the great Algonquian Nation. They were the Ishmaelites of the west; indeed, they were the most "teutonic" of all American Indians. Their hands were against every man, and the hands of all men, both red and white, were against them.[73] Their habitat was the Marias River Valley in Montana, but they were known as the devils of the mountains and prairies. All who knew them agreed with trader Bird's observation made to Kenneth McKenzie: "When you know the Blackfeet as well as I do you will know that they do not need any inducements to commit depredations." They were always hostile and predatory, and their wanderings were most extensive. The tribal name, meaning "Siksi," "black," and "kah," "foot," alluded to feet made black by roving through the ashes of regions devastated by fires. The Blackfeet were great meat eaters and because of their energy they were generally well supplied. They had horses and guns from an early time, and they wore leather clothing, often highly decorated with beadwork.

The Absaroka or Crow Nation— Absaroka means sparrow hawk. The name was derived from a species found in Mexico. Does that imply a southern origin? Surely the name suggests their nefarious traffic in stolen horses. They would steal them on one side of the range and dispose of them on the other.[74] This was the strongest band of mountain Indians. That is to say, Crowland was a transitional area that skirted the east slope of the Rockies along the Yellowstone and Bighorn rivers. Therefore, these people were masters of both plain and defile. They were notorious travelers. They roved in several villages of six or seven hundred each. In fact, the phrase "all-pervading Crows" implies the character of their winging flight from mountain to prairie. Indeed, they prided themselves upon their superiority over all other nations. The men were tall, active, intelligent, and brave. They had a particular penchant for adornment. Rows of elk's teeth trimmed their garments. Men wore long hair; women, short. They referred to themselves as

"Absaroka" with great esteem. The tribal slogan was "Bac' dak Ko'm Ba wiky," meaning "While Crow live, Crow carry on."

They were a well-disciplined people. Women were given a voice in council but were most noted for their industry and skill. According to Warren A. Ferris, Crow women were notoriously unfaithful, which, if true, was measurably contrary to the general condition among Indians. Among the men lust for fame was the end and purpose of life. Crow war psychology was a blend of cruelty, vanity, greed, foolhardiness, and magnificent courage. Old Sapsucker was the most famous Crow Chieftain. He won this distinction by many years of fighting. Horses were at once their passion and glory. Even infants of two years could ride, while older youths rode horses that careened and dashed up and down among the most dangerous places. The nation of 3,500 people owned some 10,000 horses. Adult Crow horsemen were unexcelled. They combined agility and dignity to an unusual degree. Mounted on fine-mettled animals, without saddle or bridle, and bounding bare-bodied over the prairie in the panoply of speed and power, they were fine pictures to behold!

Crows made free booty of everything that chanced in their way. Horses in particular were the objects of their depredations. They developed astonishing skill and audacity in capturing them. As horse thieves they were world-beaters. "No legislative body on earth ever made an appropriation with half the tact, facility, and success." The following represents the mature judgment of James Stuart:

> One thing is certain: They can discount all the thieves I ever saw or heard of; in short, they have to be seen to realize their superiority over all thieves, either white, red, or black, in the world. They would steal the world-renowned Arabs poor in a single hour.[75]

Other mountain Indians whose activities had less bearing upon the Yellowstone area were the Herantsa or Gros Ventres. They referred to themselves by the former name; whereas the latter was a French designation. Of course, it was inappropriate because they did not have large paunches. Their homeland was the Wind River range.

East of Wind River lies the Laramie Plains, and there lived a band named Cheyennes. They were civil, well-behaved people, cleanly in their persons and decorous in their habits. The men were tall and vigorous, with aquiline noses and high cheek bones. Some were almost as naked as ancient statues and might well have stood as models for that purpose.

East of the Crow and Cheyenne homelands ranged various divisions of the great Siouan family. The Sioux of Dakota, Arapaho, Omaha, and Mandan were the most distinct clans on the near-eastern slope of the Rockies. These tribes were typical of the plains Indians and as mutually hostile as any of the others.[76]

Indian proper names were more appropriate than those given by the settlers. Some of the latter were commonplace, stupid, and, at times, ribald. The aboriginal tribes sensed the magnificence of nature. Therefore, their characterizations were both significant and euphonious. Montana was derived from "Tay-a-be-shock-up," "country of the mountains" or "land of the everlasting hills." Wyoming means "land of shining prairies." Utah means "the home of the high-ups," and Idaho, "sun descending upon the mountains."

All in all, the Indian regime of life was a curious blend of love and hate, of work and warfare. Indian life had as many facets as there were periods, places, and tribes involved.

CHAPTER IV
PORTRAIT OF A TRAPPER BRIGADE

The character of the barbarian elements that encircled the Yellowstone area has been given. Their position was sufficiently menacing to prevent penetration of the continental crown except by a chosen few. The relation of the trapper's activity to the Park can only be appreciated by an examination of the subject himself.

The Rocky Mountain fur trappers were a distinct group. They were just as singular in dress, interests, skills, and general characteristics as the cowboys and miners who succeeded them. When was their genesis and exodus? It falls entirely within the scope of nineteenth century history. Hence, the record is clear; it has few legendary figures. However, a generalized characterization would seem appropriate. Their predecessors were the earlier explorers of several nations, French, Spanish, English, with a sprinkling of other races. All of these elements pressed ever westward, chained by neither time nor distance. In their migrations from Kentucky to the River of the West (Missouri) excitement had become as necessary as life itself; adventure, as the breath of their nostrils. Until 1810 those woodsmen found hunting and trapping on the plains sufficiently challenging, but after the return of Lewis and Clark they donned buckskin suits and moved into the Rockies. From these shining mountains they were not to emerge until they learned by heart the geography upon the sundown side of the wide Missouri.

The French couriers of the woods were best endowed by nature for this roving life. Their easygoing temperament inclined them toward song and laughter. Their courage and gallantry adorned the barren path of life with the varied hues of their mercurial spirits. They never failed to adjust to the circumstances at hand, and the speculative character of enterprise could not wear them down. The Englishman had the necessary foresight and tenacity to effect such an organization and procedure as best calculated to bring adequate financial returns.

Beaver at Work.

However, the supreme mountain scouts were of American vintage. The best in the west were cool, longheaded, deadly-shooting backwoodsmen from Kentucky and Virginia. They had what it took to deal with Indian treachery, wild beasts, and constant danger in a thousand forms. The fur business demanded men of great force and energy. Hence, the successful trappers were hard-working, hard-fighting men inured to hardship and exposure. Their vanity was in fast riding, straight shooting, prowess in trapping and trailing, and enduring privation without wincing. However, most of them were capable of complete relaxation in the fashion of drinking and gambling. In fact, they were "white Injuns" and proud of the same class of achievements. The tides of trapper fortune were capricious. One year they rolled with promise; the next were empty as a beach. The competition was always keen, and they were ever on the move. "Old Roustabout," "Perpetual Motion," "Never Quit," and "Knock 'Em Stiff Hawkeye" were current nicknames in the Order. Some of them became veritable walking maps possessed of uncanny perception of distance, condition, and landmarks. All this knowledge was susceptible to sudden erasure by one deft blow of a tomahawk. Surely every trapper fully understood the meaning of the old Hudson Bay Company motto, "A skin for a skin."

The passing of time, together with kindly, indiscriminate sentimentality toward the lore of the Old West, has enveloped all of her buckskin-fringed denizens in an enchanting blanket of romance. Legend endows them with a uniform mantle of heroism and self-sacrifice. No great effort ought to be made to drag frontiersmen from these generous folds of fiction, because such a course might evoke the other extreme of shouting "Ichabod." However, a correct comprehension of reality should be the intelligent observer's constant aim.

Tramping this western wilderness was hardy-man's-pie, and one may search in vain for "cream puffs" in the trapper fraternity. Among this advance guard of the human flood were turbulent spirits. Surely persons of the wild and reckless type have their place in pioneering the way for the more conforming populace. Although they were generally of a kindred spirit, no company personnel ever conformed to a particular type. Indeed, a more heterogeneous assemblage could not be imagined. Some were cross-grained and lazy; some, young or superannuated; others, half-breed and faithless—a real challenge to the leadership of their employer. In time the ordinary men were weeded out, but those remaining were still as diverse as humans could be.

However, it was not as conscious agents of civilization that these rowdies entered the west. They reacted to the eternal impulse of personal curiosity and profit. For such ends they willingly perambulated the dreariest wastes, always at home, living from meal to meal, from day to day. Chance and danger were their daily lot and they gained the rare capacity to accept whatever came with good graces. Pleasant experiences produced rollicking good humor; hardships and trying scenes were soon forgotten. They became absolutely fearless, for destruction stalked them on every side in the form of famine, blizzard, wild beasts, and wilder savages. Death was a constant threat, but its grimaces only tended to develop men of nerve and hardihood who delighted in reckless feats. The trapper's universal insensibility to danger proves that the human mind, habituated to constant risk, becomes callous like the body subjected to exposure. There was the hazard of perishing from hunger and thirst, of being cut off by war parties of the Sioux who scoured the plains, of having their horses stolen by Absarokas who infested the skirts of the mountains, or of being butchered by the Blackfeet who lurked among the defiles.

Trapping did not require literacy, but skill was indispensable to success. The trapper had his A-B-C's to master. Any neglect of these lessons was at his peril. They were fur, meat, and danger. Signs of beaver, buffalo, and Indians must be read with the utmost accuracy. How did he perfect his craft?

Beginning with the objects about him, the trapper observed everything minutely. He learned to read the meaning of a turned leaf, a broken twig, and the behavior of domestic and wild animals. He achieved an intimate association with nature, and she talked to him. Not only did he form indelible impressions of topography by discerning senses, but he talked about them around the campfire. Each trapper learned from the others. One referred to this process as the Rocky Mountain college course.

W. S. Chapman
Part of a Trapper Brigade.

By reason of such apprenticeship frontiersmen were able to differentiate buffalo and grizzlies at astonishing distances. They read the clouds, understood bird flights, and sensed ambuscades. Practiced eyes, ears, and noses enabled them to classify Indians as to tribe, place, and even intent. They could converse with the representatives of many different nations and tribes. A smattering of French, Spanish, and several Indian languages—supplemented by signs—made conversation possible under all circumstances.

The trapper was not always at liberty. There were organization responsibilities. The fur brigade was under strict discipline. A junior partner in the company was usually in charge, and he was the law. There was a semi-military set of regulations regarding division of work; guard duty was rigorously enforced; efficient service and prompt obedience were required of every trapper.

Sometimes terrific exertion was involved in reaching a given trapping ground at the most opportune time. Upon one occasion Alexander Ross fairly forced his caravan to cleave a road through a snowbound pass. Said he:

> Making this road through the snow (seven feet deep) took the united labour of fifty men and 240 horses, with all the other available means within our power, for twenty-one days. It must be allowed to have been an arduous undertaking, with such a medley of people and so difficult to manage; and more so, when it takes into consideration that our supper at night depended on the good or bad luck of our hunters during the day. To their exertions and perseverance, indeed, no small merit was due.[77]

Such a time of travail was enough to elicit an occasional prayer from these sons of the wild. Men of few words, they could say what was needed in simple eloquence:

> Oh, God, may it please Thee, in Thy divine providence, to still guide and protect us through this wilderness of doubt and fear, as Thou hast done heretofore, and be with us in the hour of danger and difficulty as all praise is due to Thee and not to man. Oh, do not forsake us, Lord, but be with us and direct us through.[78]

One of the greatest among trappers was brigade leader Jedediah Smith, sometimes called "The Knight in Buckskin." Carrying a Bible and a rifle, he was equally proficient with each and had complete reliance upon both.

Mr. Ross has left a fine description of trapping routine:

> A safe and secure spot, near wood and water, is first selected for the camp. Here the chief of the party resides with the property. It is often exposed to danger, or sudden attack, in the absence of the trappers, and requires a vigilant eye to guard against the lurking savages. The camp is called headquarters. From hence all the trappers, some on foot, some on horseback, according to the distance they have to go, start every morning, in small parties, in all directions, ranging the distance of some twenty miles around. Six traps is the allowance for each trapper; but to guard against wear and tear, the complement is more frequently ten. These he sets every night, and visits again in the morning; sometimes oftener, according to distance, or other circumstances. The beaver taken in the traps are always conveyed to the camp, skinned, stretched, dried, folded up with the hair in the inside, laid by, and the flesh used for food. No sooner, therefore, has a hunter visited his traps, set them again and looked out for

some other place, than he returns to the camp to feast and enjoy the pleasures of an idle day....[79]

In this account there is an element of suppressed excitement and danger. Taking game is invariably a thrilling experience. Besides that, the covetous savages were frequently so menacing as to require almost constant vigil along the trap line. Trapper camps remained stationary only so long as two-thirds of the men were getting satisfactory results.

Setting beaver traps involved keen judgment, a deft touch, and precise arrangement. Indeed, it was a considerable art. Joe Meek left an accurate picture of his technique:

> He has an ordinary steel trap weighing five pounds, attached to a chain five feet long, with a swivel and ring at the end, which plays round what is called the float, a dry stick of wood about six feet long. The trapper wades out into the stream, which is shallow, and cuts with his knife a bed for his trap, five or six inches under water. He then takes the float out the whole length of the chain in the direction of the center of the stream, and drives it in, so fast that the beaver cannot draw it out; at the same time tying the other end by a thong to the bank. A small stick or twig, dipped in musk or castor (found in certain glands of the beaver) served for bait, and is placed so as to hang directly above the trap, which is now set. The trapper then throws water plentifully over the adjacent bank to conceal any footprints or scent by which the beaver would be alarmed, and, going to some distance, wades out of the stream. In setting a trap, certain things are to be observed with care; first, that the trap is firmly fixed, and at proper distance from the bank—for if the beaver can get on shore with the trap, he will cut off his foot to escape; second, that the float is of dry wood, for should it not be, the animal will cut it off at a stroke, and swimming with the trap to the middle of the dam, be drowned by its weight. In the latter case, when the hunter visits his trap in the morning, he is under the necessity of plunging into the water and swimming out, to dive for his game. Should the morning be frosty and chilly, as it very frequently is in the mountains, diving for traps is not a pleasant exercise. In placing the bait, care must be taken to fix it just where the beaver, in reaching it, will spring the trap. If the bait stick be placed high, the hind foot of the beaver will be caught, if low, the forefoot.[80]

Each trapper had two horses, one to ride and one to carry his trapping equipment and furs. Sometimes good fortune yielded a fur harvest that exceeded the trapper's carrying capacity. In that case he employed a device called a cache. A dry spot of earth on an incline was selected, well-camouflaged from Indian view. A hole large enough for a man to crawl into was then dug. As depth was attained it was widened to the desired proportions. Furs well wrapped would keep indefinitely in a properly constructed cache.

Essentials in the trapper's equipment were a bowie knife, ammunition, a hatchet, a revolver, and a rifle. The trapper's powder horn and bullet pouch, with flint and steel and other "fixins," were thrown over his left shoulder. These articles were his constant companions, ever ready for action.

W. S. Chapman
Gun and Powder horn.

Wearing apparel was pretty much standardized—a five-piece suit of buckskin, including smoked skin moccasins which would not shrink from the frequent wettings incident to the trapping season. The pants, shirt, long coat, and hat were made of the same material. Fringes at the seams gave a dash of ornamentation and hastened drying. Clothing was mostly "homemade" during the wintertime.

These accouterments were not only durable, but they were comfortable as well, and they were pleasant to the eye. That the latter item was a desideratum there can be no doubt. Indian maidens were fair to behold, and after all the trapper was human.

This phase of the trapper's life was cogently summarized by one observer:

> From all that I hear I conclude that in the palmy days of the fur trade, the bands of white trappers in the West were little

more than bands of white Indians, having their Indian wives, and all the paraphernalia of Indian life, moving from place to place, as the beaver became scarce, and subsisting like the Indians upon the products of the country.[81]

Squaw men were both numerous and respected. Lisa, Bridger, Provot, Ogden, Meek, Carson, Rose, McKenzie, and Beckwourth were wise and judicious men. They well knew the utility of the willing, efficient, and respectful Indian women for their own sakes. Then, too, there were political considerations which account for the fact that in some cases several squaws were taken at once, or in rapid succession. Marriage has always been employed as a means of ingratiation by the outsider. It may be said to their credit, with a few exceptions, genuine mountain men were faithful to their Indian wives.[82]

The Earl of Dunraven has left an excellent description of a squaw man's camp which he visited in Yellowstone Park during the summer of 1874:

> These men looked very happy and comfortable. Unquestionably the proper way for a man to travel with ease and luxury in these deserts is for him to take unto himself a helpmate chosen from the native population. No amount of art, industry, and study can rival the instinct displayed by savages in making themselves comfortable, and in utilizing for their own benefit all the accidents of Nature. Nobody can choose a camp as they can: nobody knows how to make a fire so quickly or so well: nobody can so wisely pick a shady, cool place in summer heat, or choose one sheltered from wind and storms in winter. With an Indian wife to look after his bodily comforts, a man may devote himself to hunting, fishing, or trapping without a thought or care. He may make his mind quite easy about all household matters. His camp will be well arranged, the tent-pegs driven securely home, the stock watered, picketed, and properly cared for, a good supper cooked, his bed spread out, and everything made comfortable; his clothes and hunting-gear looked after, the buttons sewn on his shirt—if he has got any shirt or any buttons; and all the little trivial incidents of life which, if neglected, wear out one's existence, he will find carefully attended to by a willing and affectionate slave.
>
> They had a lot to tell us also about their travels and adventures, about the wood and water supply, and the

abundance or deficiency of game. So we sat down on bales of beaver-skins and retailed all the civilized intelligence we could think of; and the women came and brought us ember for our pipes, spread out robes for us and made us at home; and the little fat, chubby children, wild and shy as young wolves, peered at us from behind the tent out of their round, black, beady eyes.[83]

The premier social event among mountain men was the annual rendezvous. This institution was inaugurated on Green River in July, 1824, by General William H. Ashley, owner of the interests that evolved into the Rocky Mountain Fur Company. The Ashley men traveled to the fur region in concert. Upon arrival, they were divided into "brigades" and dispersed into various districts with instructions to reassemble at an appointed time and place. In this manner the rendezvous became a sort of roving trading place; it served in lieu of a post. These shifting locations were occasioned by the need of forage for large numbers of horses. For sixteen years this combination of market, fiesta, and carousal held sway in such romantic spots as Green River, Ogden's Hole, Pierre's Hole—now Teton Basin in Idaho—and the Horse Creek-Green River country south of Jackson's Hole in Wyoming. In her book, The River of the West, Frances Fuller Victor tells of a rendezvous held by Jim Bridger and his trappers. The place was Hayden Valley; the season, 1838.[84]

Thither the company men, free trappers, and Indians foregathered. The business of exchange and supply was quickly transacted with beaver skins serving as money. Then came the celebration, and what a gala event it was. Trappers sought to indemnify themselves for the sufferings and privations of a year in the wilderness. Squaw men parted with their "hairy bank notes" in order to bedeck their spouses in bright cloth and gewgaws. Here were men with reputations to sustain, proud men with a streak of wild vanity: "Old Knock Him Stiff," "Old Straightener," "Dead-Eye Dick," "Broken Hand," Kit, Joe, and Jim. Most mountain men were openhanded, and they squandered a year's earnings in a few days of prodigal indulgence. Coffee and chocolate were prepared; the kegs were emptied; all pipes were kept aglow; free and generous spirits moved by day and night.[85] Truly this burnt and seamy-faced band was an all-American aggregation.

The veterans boasted "most enormous adventures" in mountain experience. Each represented himself as more than a match for any possible array of Indians or grizzlies. Narrations waxed romantic in the desire to astonish the new recruits. Extravagant and absurd as their yarns were, there was always a current of rude, good humor that allowed each listener to believe as little as he liked. There were rollicking, fiery, boisterous, swaggering southerners; quiet, steel-eyed northerners; mercurial French; loquacious Irish; calculating Scots; greedy middlemen; shrewd dealers; squaw men; Indian haters; Indians of many nations; pals; rivals; and enemies. Everyone was invited; no one was missing. It was a self-propelling circus, one show a year, the antecedent of roundup, rodeo, fair, and tournament.

Contests of skill were carried to a point of jeopardizing life. There were William Tell episodes and no mistakes, trials of speed and strength for both horse and man. There was plenty of flirting, feasting, carousing, and outright debauchery. All were on friendly terms today, but each was unconsciously aware that tomorrow their relationships would change, and woe unto him who was caught unaware!

The rendezvous was perhaps the most colorful, spontaneous, lusty, and romantic institution ever known among civilized men. It was conceived, nurtured, and abandoned within a score of years (1824-1840). A fleeting climax to a picturesque band—they came from everywhere, wrote a saga that reads like an epoch from a long-forgotten age, then vanished from the scene.

Actually they did not make a definite exit; they just faded away. Some, like Colter, turned into prosaic farmers; others became guides, only to lag superfluously upon the stage; some turned to trade; some, to government appointments as Indian agents. A few lingered on as trappers, sighing for the life that was gone forever. Trappers of the Great West—they had given their all and there were no regrets. Their levity and valor, their hardships and pleasure, what a medley it made. One of the French Canadians has left this testimonial:

> I have now been forty two years in this country. For twenty-four I was light canoe-man; I required but little sleep, but sometimes got less than I required. No portage was too long for me; all portages were alike. My end of the canoe never touched the ground till I saw the end of it. Fifty songs a day were nothing to me. I could carry, paddle, walk, and sing with

any man I ever saw. During that period, I saved the lives of ten Bourgeois, and was always the favourite, because when others stopped to tarry at a bad step, and lost time, I pushed on—over rapids, over cascades, over chutes; all were the same to me. No water, no weather, ever stopped the paddle or the song. I have had twelve wives in the country; and was once possessed of fifty horses, and six running dogs, trimmed in the first style. I was then like a Bourgeois, rich and happy; no Bourgeois had better-dressed wives than I; no Indian chief finer horses; no white man better harnessed or swifter dogs. I beat all Indians at the race, and no white man ever passed me in the chase. I wanted for nothing; and I spent all my earnings in the enjoyment of pleasure. Five hundred pounds, twice told, have passed through my hands; although now I have not a spare shirt to my back, nor a penny to buy one. Yet, were I young again, I should glory in commencing the same career again.[86]

The significance of the fur trade is graphically depicted by the National Park Service with charts, diagrams, illustrations, models, and dioramas in the Jefferson National Expansion Memorial, Scotts Bluff, Guernsey Lake, Fort Laramie, Grand Teton and Yellowstone National parks.

CHAPTER V
WERE INDIANS AFRAID OF YELLOWSTONE?

Beginning with the origin of Yellowstone as a National Park the idea became current that Indians were afraid of the area. The opinion is still widely held that they considered it a cursed domain, unfit for habitation. While it is true that superstition and taboo loomed large in primitive experience, there is no reason to suppose that Indians gave Wonderland a wide berth.[87] Rather, there is an abundance of material evidence that controverts this view. Furthermore, the proposition is at once illogical and untrue historically.

How, then, did this fiction originate? Probably the major reason is found in the fact that, with the exception of a small band of recluse-like Tukuarikas, or Sheepeaters, Indians did not live permanently in Yellowstone. This fact alone suggests that the region was not regarded as an appropriate abode. Only a pygmy tribe of about four hundred timid souls deemed it a suitable homeland.

These people were the weakest of all mountain clans. They did not possess horses. Their tools were of the crudest type; they lived in caves and nearly inaccessible niches in cliffs along the Gardner River, especially in wintertime. These more permanent camps were carefully chosen in the interest of security against other Indians. Superintendent Norris discovered one of them by accident:

> In trailing a wounded bighorn I descended a rocky dangerous pathway. In rapt astonishment I found I had thus unbidden entered an ancient but recently deserted, secluded, unknown haunt of the Sheepeater aborigines of the Park.[88]

This campground was a half mile in length and four hundred feet at its widest point, with a similar depth, "and hemmed in and hidden by rugged timber-fringed basaltic cliffs...."

In summer, the Sheepeater Indians ventured further into the interior, following the game upon the higher plateaus. There they erected:

skin-covered lodges, or circular upright brush-heaps called wickiups, decaying evidences of which are abundant near Mammoth Hot Springs, the various firehole basins, the shores of Yellowstone Lake, the newly explored Hoodoo regions, and in nearly all of the sheltered glens and valleys of the Park.[89]

In 1874, the Earl of Dunraven discovered such a camp just west of Mary Mountain on the head of Nez Percé Creek.

Superintendent Norris and his associates focused their eyes particularly upon evidences of Indian occupancy. In a dozen places they observed rude but extensive pole and brush fences used for wild animal driveways.[90] An especially strategic camp was discovered near the summit of a grassy pass between Hoodoo and Miller creeks. From this skyline perch, marked by forty decaying lodges, an entire tribe could command a view of all possible approaches for many miles. Fragments of white men's chinaware, blankets, bed clothing, and male and female wearing apparel bore mute but mournful witness of border raids and massacres. This was an Absaroka summer retreat.

However, there are few such evidences discernible today because snows are heavy and wind fallen trees profuse, while the character of Indian structures was flimsy. In fact, these Indians, on the whole, left fewer enduring signs of their dwelling places than beaver. Several log wickiups still stand in a pleasant fir grove in the triangle formed by Lava Creek and Gardner River above their point of union. These wickiups are readily accessible from the Tower Falls highway one half mile east of the Gardner River bridge.

What happened to the timid Tukuarikas? They simply vanished from the scene as the white men invaded their refuge. They left without a contest for ownership or treaty of cession. That is the way most Americans would have had all Indian tribes behave!

All mountain Indian tribes visited Yellowstone. We-Saw, Shoshoni guide for Captain W. A. Jones in 1873, said his people and also the Bannocks and Crows occasionally visited the Yellowstone River and Lake.

For one thing, Obsidian Cliff had the effect of a magnet upon them. It was their arsenal, a lance and arrowhead quarry. Arrowheads and spears originating here have been found in an area extending many miles in every direction. The obsidian chips, from which implements were assiduously shaped by the Indians, still litter the side hills and ravines in chosen areas all over the Park. Many fine specimens of arrowheads, knives, scrapers, and spears have been found at various places. The most notable finds have been around the base of Mt. Holmes, along Indian Creek, at Fishing Bridge, near West Thumb, in the Norris and Lower Geyser basins, and about the Lamar Valley. Actually, these artifacts have generally turned up wherever excavation for modern camps has been made.

Remnants of Sheepeaters' Wickiup

In P. W. Norris' Fifth Annual Report, 1881, there is a comprehensive analysis of the problem of Indian occupancy. Diagrams of four steatite vessels found in widely separated places are represented. Drawings of arrowheads and sinkers also occur, and figures 10 to 24, inclusive, depict the natural sizes of scrapers, knives, lance, spearheads, and perforators, mostly chipped from Park obsidian.[91] These artifacts were found in various places, such as caverns, driveways, at the foot of cliffs, and along creeks. Said Norris: "Over two hundred such specimens were collected this season."[92]

In his report of 1878, Mr. Norris states: "Chips, flakes, arrowheads and other Indian tools and weapons have been found by all recent tourists in burial cairns and also scattered broadcast in all these mountain valleys."[93]

Is it any wonder Indian artifacts are scarce in Yellowstone today? Still, they are frequently found when excavations are made. Winter snows, animal trampings, land slides, and floods have covered them. A few isolated items of discovery should be noted: arrowheads have recently been found on Stevenson Island, in lake gravel pits, about Buffalo Ranch, in the sewer line, near South Entrance, on the Game Ranch, around Norris, Lower, and Midway geyser basins, and at Fishing Bridge.[94]

Another evidence of Indian visitation was evinced by a network of trails. One of these followed the Yellowstone Valley across the Park from north to south. It divided at Yellowstone Lake, the principal branch adhering to the east shore and leading to Two Ocean Pass where it intersected the great Snake and Wind River trail. Since Indian trails multisected the Yellowstone area it is obvious that the region was a sort of no-man's land. Undesirable as a homeland, it was used as a summer retreat by many Rocky Mountain tribes. From this circumstance it may be assumed that an autumn seldom passed without a clash between the Bannocks and the Crows or the Shoshonis. Surely, the shrill notes of Blackfeet warwhoops have echoed in these vales. Campsites were well chosen both from the viewpoint of preserving secrecy and desirability as watchtower sites.

The most important trail, however, was that known as the Great Bannock Trail. The Bannocks of southeastern Idaho made an annual trek to the Bighorn Basin for buffalo. Their trail followed Henrys Fork of Snake River to Henrys Lake, an ancient Bannock rendezvous. From this notable camp the trail went up Howard Creek and crossed the Continental Divide at Targhee Pass. Upon reaching the Upper Madison Valley, the route passed Horse Butte and angled north of West Yellowstone townsite. A camp at Great Springs (now Cory Springs) was situated near the Park boundary.

In Yellowstone National Park, the Bannock Trail winds its devious way across the northern part. There are a half-dozen deviations from the main artery. Wayne Replogle suggests that weather conditions determined these alternations. High ground would be chosen enroute to the plains, but the return trip could be made along the streams. Other considerations might include security, grazing, and game. Entering the Park upon Duck Creek the Trail swung northward across Campanula Creek, paralleled Gneiss Creek to the point of crossing, then quartered southward, crossing Maple Creek and Duck Creek, on toward the head of Cougar Creek and its ample pasture lands.

From this area the Trail goes almost due north to White Peaks, which are skirted on the West. The Gallatin Range was crossed via a saddle north of White Peaks. The Trail then dropped upon the headwaters of Indian Creek and followed down to Gardner River. The route then looped to the left, across Swan Lake flats, on through Snow Pass, down the decline to Mammoth Hot Springs. From Mammoth the Indian thoroughfare struck right, recrossed Gardner River, and followed Lava Creek toward Tower Fall.

The Yellowstone River ford was located just above Tower Fall, near the mouth of Tower Creek. Vestiges of the trail may still be discerned along both banks of Yellowstone River. Other evidences, such as deep grass-sodded furrows, may be seen in the vicinity of junction of the Lamar River and Soda Butte Creek. One branch paralleled Soda Butte Creek to the divide and then descended Clarks Fork to the bison range. The alternate route continued along the Lamar to a secondary divide between Cache and Calfee creeks. This hog's back was then followed to the summit, and the descent was down Timber Creek to its confluence with Clarks Fork. The deep ruts worn by travois in these pilgrimages are still obvious in many places, although unused for three quarters of a century.

W. S. Chapman
Horse and Travois Transportation.

Can anyone doubt that the Bannocks made frequent and extensive excursions beyond this thoroughfare? Surely their young men ranged far and wide, prying into every nook and cranny of Wonderland. They undoubtedly fished in the great lake and river, hunted elk and bighorn, bathed in warm springs, and reveled in the beauties of the landscape. Any other view of the evidence would impute undue naïveté to human nature. After all, Indians were children of nature; the earth was their mother. In Yellowstone Mother Earth was especially intriguing. They might not understand her; they might entertain great respect for her strange manifestations, but cringing trepidation? Hardly! But weren't they afraid of the geysers? In 1935, White Hawk and Many Wounds visited the Park. They were members of Chief Joseph's band when it crossed the Park in 1877. When asked if the Nez Percé Indians were afraid of the geysers and hot springs they said no and implied that they used them in cooking.[95] Still the critic objects, saying the geyser and spring formations were all intact when the first white men came. Primitive people were seldom guilty of wanton spoliation. Hence, missing incrustations were not essential evidence of Indian visitation. They left nature's beauty as they found it, a proper example for all who might follow after.

Did Indians ever hear the legendary overhead sounds in the vicinity of Shoshone and Yellowstone lakes—those strange half-minute tunes like the humming of bees or echo of bells?[96] Perhaps they did. Any phenomenon audible to white men with the naked ear would be discernible to them because they were sensitive to nature and her communion was always welcomed. However, since Indians were without records and formal procedures for obtaining and preserving scientific knowledge they were tremendously limited in understanding. They operated upon a single dimension of experience. For instance, they could never realize that the fish they took from Lake Yellowstone was a Pacific Ocean species which could only have reached these inland lakes via the Snake River system, signifying that, in ages past, the great lake must have possessed an outlet in that direction. All such problems awaited the scientists, but red men still knew much in their own right.

Surely then, Indians were summertime visitors in Yellowstone. They literally swarmed around the lakes. The most unimpeachable testimony on this point comes from trapper accounts of actual encounters. This phase of the case is discussed in the following chapter. Their known presence in the wooded area was the greatest deterrent to the white man's interest. Few men voluntarily risk their lives for a view of nature's wonders. It is a historical fact that the Washburn-Langford-Doane party saw Crow Indians along the north environs of the Park and actually followed a fresh line of tracks into the Yellowstone area. Thus the scenic exploitation of Wonderland was not feasible until the Indians were rounded up and confined to the reservations. This program was accomplished in the states surrounding Yellowstone between 1860 and 1877.

This process of racial adjustment was not accomplished without minor repercussions upon Yellowstone. The exciting Nez Percé flight of 1877 is considered separately in Chapter XI. However, the very next year the Bannocks conducted an impressive horse-stealing foray against the property of laborers and tourists. These episodes resulted in unfavorable publicity from the standpoint of tourist interest in visiting Wonderland. In consequence two important steps were taken by the officials. In 1880 Superintendent Norris made a tour of all the Rocky Mountain Indian reservations. His mission was to secure solemn promises from the tribes to abide by the terms of their Washington treaties and in particular to stay away from the Park.[97]

These agreements were widely advertised, and in order to further neutralize any fear of Indian trouble a policy of minimizing past incidents was evolved. The recent invasions were represented as unprecedented, actually anomalous. Indians had never lived in Yellowstone, were infrequent visitors because they were afraid of the thermal activity! It was not a conspiracy against truth, just an adaptation of business psychology to a promising national resort.

CHAPTER VI
SECONDARY VISITATIONS BEFORE 1869

Parties in Search of Fur

The streams of the Rocky Mountains were thoroughly exploited by the trappers in the twenties and thirties. Notwithstanding the paucity of evidence concerning Yellowstone visitations, it is unreasonable to believe her great rivers were neglected. These phantomlike trapper men went everywhere, saw everything, tarried only long enough to strip furry coverings from the beaver, and vanished. On rare occasion a bit of artifact shows up: an initialed rock or tree, a broken trap or flintlock, a group of steel-cleaved trees, a trapper cabin, a rifle pit or cache.[98] These evidences bear mute testimony that hunters passed through Yellowstone. In 1880, Colonel P. W. Norris discovered an initialed tree one half mile above the Upper Falls. The significant legend, J.O.R. August 19, 1819, had every indication of authenticity.

In 1822, trappers engaged by Andrew Henry and General William H. Ashley entered the Rocky Mountains. Within that decade some of the men had unquestionably visited the Park area. Evidence of one such visit exists in a letter published in the Philadelphia Gazette, September 27, 1827, and reprinted in the Niles Weekly Register (Baltimore) the following week, October 6, 1827. Daniel T. Potts wrote this particular letter at Sweet Lake in the Rocky Mountains on July 8, 1827, and sent it to his brother Robert T. Potts of Philadelphia. This letter, which constitutes the first printed account of Yellowstone phenomena, is now on file in the Yellowstone Park Library at Mammoth. The section of the letter definitely descriptive of the Park area follows:

> ... the Yellow-stone has a large fresh water lake near its head on the verry [sic] top of the Mountain which is about one hundrid [sic] by fourty [sic] in diameter and as clear as crystal on the south borders of this lake is a number of hot and boiling springs some water and others of most beautiful fine clay and resembles that of a mush pot and throws its particles to the immense height of from twenty to thirty feet in height. The clay is white and pink and water appear fathomless as it

appears to be entirely hollow underneath. There is also a number of places where the pure sulphor [sic] is sent forth in abundance one of our men visited one of these whilst taking his recreation at an instan [sic] the earth began a tremendious [sic] trembling and he with dificulty [sic] made his escape when an explosion took place resembling that of thunder. During our stay in that quarter I heard it every day....[99]

Again, it is a matter of written record that Jedediah Smith and his associates "worked the country lying between the sources of the Missouri and Yellowstone rivers, finally going into winter quarters on the Wind River" in 1829. He was probably the man to whom Superintendent Norris referred:

I have always given much credence to a well-endorsed campfire legend of a mountaineer named Smith, having, prior to the days of Bonneville, written a narrative of his explorations of the Firehole regions, and being killed before its publication.[100]

It was in 1829 when Joseph Meek became separated from his associates of the Rocky Mountain Fur Company and wandered for five days in a southerly direction in the area that divides the drainage between the Madison and Gallatin rivers. The factors of time and place are entirely consistent with the report he gave:

Being desirous to learn something about the progress he had made, he ascended a low mountain in the neighborhood of his camp, and behold! the whole country beyond was smoking with vapor from boiling springs, and burning gases issuing from small craters, each of which was emitting a sharp whistling sound.[101]

Meek thought himself reminded of the city of Pittsburgh as he had once seen it on a winter morning. Meek also said that blue flames and molten brimstone issued from certain craters. Of course the brimstone was a slight exaggeration, but he undoubtedly believed it to be true.

There are still other references strongly indicative of the movements of those silent sons of the wilderness in Yellowstone. However, the journal of Warren A. Ferris, an employee of the American Fur Company, positively proves that he observed some of its mysteries. He first heard stories of astonishing marvels from a party of trappers at the rendezvous in 1833. These trappers confirmed other reports that were current, affirming that geysers really were as extensive and remarkable as generally represented. Backed by the united testimony of more than twenty men on the subject, Ferris decided to go there himself for the specific purpose of enjoying such an experience as would be afforded by water volcanoes.

In company with two Pend d'Oreille Indians he journeyed from Camas Creek through the "piny woods" to the Madison River, which he followed to the Upper Geyser Basin, where he camped. During the night of May 19, the thud and resounding of violent thermal action assailed him. Allow him to relate the story:

> When I arose in the morning, clouds of vapor seemed like a dense fog to overhang the springs from which frequent reports or explosions of different loudness, constantly assailed our ears. I immediately proceeded to inspect them, and might have exclaimed with the Queen of Sheba, when their full reality of dimensions and novelty burst upon my view, "The half was not told me."
>
> From the surface of a rocky plain or table, burst forth columns of water, of various dimensions, projected high in the air, accompanied by loud explosions, and sulphurous vapors, which were highly disagreeable to the smell. The rock from which these springs burst forth was calcarious [sic], and probably extends some distance from them beneath the soil. The largest of these wonderful fountains projects a column of boiling water several feet in diameter to the height of more than one hundred and fifty feet—in my opinion; but in declaring that it could not be less than four times that distance in height—accompanied with a tremendous noise. These explosions and discharges occur at intervals of about two hours. After having witnessed three of them, I ventured near enough to put my hand into the water of its basin, but withdrew it instantly, for the heat of the water in this immense cauldron was altogether too great for comfort, and the agitation of the water, the disagreeable effluvium continually exuding, and the hollow unearthly rumbling under the rock on which I stood, so ill accorded with my notions of personal safety, that I retreated back precipitately to a respectful distance. The Indians who were with me were quite appalled, and could not by any means be induced to approach them. They seemed astonished at my presumption in advancing up to the large one, and when I safely returned,

congratulated me on my "narrow escape."—They believed them to be supernatural, and supposed them to be the production of the Evil Spirit. One of them remarked that hell, of which he had heard from the whites, must be in that vicinity. The diameter of the basin into which the water of the largest jet principally falls, and from the centre of which, through a hole in the rock of about nine or ten feet in diameter, the water spouts up as above related, may be about thirty feet.—There are many other smaller fountains, that did not throw their waters up so high, but occurred at shorter intervals. In some instances, the volumes were projected obliquely upwards and fell into the neighboring fountains or on the rock or prairie. But their ascent was generally perpendicular, falling in and about their own basins or apertures. These wonderful productions of nature are situated near the centre of a small valley, surrounded by pine covered hills, through which a small fork of the Madison flows. Highly gratified with my visit to these formidable and magnificent fountains, jets, or springs, whichever the reader may please to call them, I set out after dinner to rejoin my companions. Again we crossed the Piny Woods and encamped on the plains of Henry's Fork.[102]

Ferris not only wrote the foregoing account in his journal, but his sense of its importance impelled him to expand it for publication. He submitted his "Life in the Rocky Mountains" to several papers. Subsequently the narrative appeared in the Literary Messenger of Buffalo, New York, in issues running during the early forties. The scholarly observations of Mr. Ferris were reprinted in The Wasp, a Mormon organ of Nauvoo, Illinois, on August 13, 1842. It was the best article prepared before 1870. Henceforth, the lack of knowledge about Yellowstone must be charged to common indifference and skepticism. The facts had all been well attested but slenderly disseminated.

Foremost among all trapper visitations in point of extent and accuracy were those of Osborne Russell. Between 1835 and 1839 he accompanied three specific Yellowstone expeditions. The first party, which numbered twenty-four, was organized at Fort Hall in June, 1835. Instructions directed them to proceed to Yellowstone Lake and return, hunting and trapping the intervening territory. Their route of travel was northeast to Jackson Hole, thence into the Absarokas. No one in the group had ever entered Yellowstone until July 28, when they descended the mountains into what they called "Secluded Valley."

The point of ingress was probably the upper Lamar drainage. There they encountered a small band of friendly Snake Indians, rich in pelts which they sold for a "song." Mr. Russell revealed an unerring instinct of appreciation for the area in his first and subsequent visits. Said he:

> We stopped at this place and for my own part I almost wished I could spend the remainder of my days in a place like this, where happiness and contentment seemed to reign in wild, romantic splendor, surrounded by majestic battlements which seemed to support the heavens and shut out all hostile intruders.[103]

W. S. Chapman
Trapper observing Riverside Geyser.

While his impression of security was to prove incorrect the reaction to grandeur was wholly sustained.

One trapper was lost, and after a futile search they reluctantly crossed the Yellowstone River. Their next camp was in Gardner Hole, named for trapper Johnson Gardner, formerly an Ashley employee, who had worked the area several years before. Russell's party then crossed the Gallatins and joined Jim Bridger's company in making a stand against the marauding Blackfeet.

The next season found Russell attached to Bridger's party and again on his way to Wonderland. They entered from the southeast along Yellowstone River. By mid-August they reached the lake. Two weeks were spent in trapping the lake and Gardner Hole streams. Russell again expressed his unqualified partiality for this region.

Mr. Russell's final and most significant visit occurred during July and August of 1839. Upon this occasion there were only four in the party. They entered the Park by way of Snake River, passed the lakes now called Lewis and Shoshone, and visited the geyser basins. The white formations reminded the trappers of some ancient cities' ruins. Mr. Russell's description of Grand Prismatic Spring is satisfactory as of today. From the Firehole Basin they circled the Park clockwise and came to rest on Pelican Creek, near Yellowstone Lake's outlet. The date was August 28, 1839; the time of day, 4.00 P.M. Russell had taken a swim in the lake; White was sleeping; the Canadian and Elbridge were hunting elk. In these circumstances a large band of Blackfeet made a surprise attack. Russell and White were both wounded but managed to escape. The next day they were joined by the Canadian. Together, and on foot, the three trappers wound a tortuous course to the Thumb of Lake, and thence south to Jackson Lake. After many harrowing experiences and much discomfort they reached Fort Hall on September 6. A week later Elbridge also reached the fort, and in a short time they were all ready for new adventure.

Another party of forty men went through almost the identical experience in 1839. They entered the area via the Snake River, crossed the Divide, and trapped the upper Yellowstone to the lake. Near its outlet they fought Piegan Indians and lost five men, with the same number wounded.[104] Yellowstone was not a choice trapping ground and the risks involved by reason of remoteness and Indian menace offset the margin of profit.

Upon interrogation relative to Yellowstone, Captain Bonneville said, "You ask me if I know of the thermal springs and geysers. Not personally, but my men knew about them, and called their location the 'Fire Hole.'"

From these sources it is apparent that many trappers traversed the "crest of the world," and its secrets were common knowledge among the whole fraternity. The evaluation placed upon these singular experiences would naturally depend upon the judgment of the several hunters. Father DeSmet took the liberty of placing their reactions upon a superstitious basis. He said the region was considered an abode of evil spirits. The eruptions were supposed to result from combat between infernal spirits. This was probably the view of some, but all hunters were not such tyros in natural science. Indeed, it is quite reasonable to suppose that at least a few were first-rate naturalists. However, some of them were killed in the wilderness; others withdrew to other fields of interest; and none of them envisioned any lively public concern over scenery. A few had gone to the trouble of recording and relating their experiences only to be laughed to scorn or made the butt of jokesters. Why should honest men like Colter, Meek, and Ferris go out of their way simply to be dubbed outlandish prevaricators? Of course, the answer is found in the fact that as a class they deliberately brought such a reputation upon themselves. Take the case of Joe Meek. Upon one occasion his party was floundering about in the Gallatin Valley. Meek suggested that their bewilderment might be lessened by climbing a high peak and getting their bearings. No one would accompany him so he went alone. When he returned there was considerable interest in his experience. Naturally his ego expanded; he took on a knowing air. He erroneously contended that he could see the Yellowstone, Missouri, and Snake rivers from the lofty height. Later, the brigade leader sent Moses "Black" Harris to another high point to reconnoiter. When he returned the men pressed him for information, and, not to be outdone, he declared that he saw "the city of St. Louis, and one fellow drinking a beer."[105]

Therefore, two conditions combined to withhold the knowledge of Yellowstone wonders from the world. The men who knew of her marvels were seldom equipped to describe or interpret them, and the public was in no better state to accept them. Hence, this trapper lore was barren of result, locked up as it was in the minds of generally illiterate men. It all but perished with them and had no definite bearing upon the final and conclusive discovery. For more than a generation the tales of trappers were bandied around on the lips of indifferent mountaineers. In this rough dress the wonders of Yellowstone were either received with uncivil incredulity or as a joke to be indulgently humored.

Conclusive evidence of the trappers' discovery and exploration of Yellowstone has been adduced. The fur traders were well acquainted with every portion of it, but their knowledge passed with them. Only a tradition persisted. In 1860 the elements of this tradition came within a rifle shot of conversion to truth. During the latter fifties the United States government had a corps of Topographical Engineers in the upper Missouri country. Only a double assignment to Captain W. F. Raynolds saved the Park from official discovery in June, 1860. He was directed to explore the country from which the headwaters of the Yellowstone, Gallatin, and Madison rivers originated. He was also told to be on hand north of the Canadian border on July 18 to observe the eclipse of the sun.

The expedition traversed the Wind River Valley, crossed Union Pass, and turned north. From a position nearly opposite Two Ocean Pass the party attempted to knife its way through the Absaroka Mountains, but it was June, and the defiles were choked with snow. Guide Jim Bridger pleaded with them to swing south and enter the plateau from Snake River. He told them they couldn't get through, that even a "bird wouldn't fly over there without takin' a supply of grub along." But the time was short, and Captain Raynolds reluctantly turned away from the prospect of verifying "marvelous tales of burning plains, immense lakes and boiling springs," to witness the certain obliteration of Old Sol. It was a lucky choice for the future of Yellowstone because discovery in 1860 could hardly have been so propitious as it was a decade later.

PARTIES IN SEARCH OF GOLD

Another series of partial exploration was inaugurated in the early sixties by the Argonauts. Nature's distribution of precious metals is rather far-flung in western America. Therefore, miners were not inclined toward geographic discrimination. Spirit brothers to the trappers, they searched the Rockies with wonderful energy and daring. Deep snow, arctic cold, yawning precipices, and fierce Indians were all defied in their eager quest for a new Eldorado. It would have been strange indeed if they had missed the Yellowstone country.

Gold seekers were hardy, optimistic, and foot-loose. Ever impatient of restraint, they responded like mercury to the fever of a "gold excitement." To them every range, mountain, and gulch offered a challenge that required acceptance. Actuated by a single thought, these colorful adventurers literally swarmed to the Pacific coast in '49. Subsequently, a backwash rolled over into Nevada and Idaho. In the sixties Montana received a portion of the overflow. The Bitter Root Range was prospected with a "fine tooth comb." In feverish haste these prospectors encompassed the whole of Yellowstone. However, this vast volcanic plateau provided little inducement to tarry, while other regions in close proximity yielded one of the greatest treasure troves on earth. In the decade of 1860, Alder Gulch, Bannock, Virginia, Leesburg, Butte, Helena, and Anaconda were magic names. What chance for attention had Yellowstone's mountain-locked mysteries in such a maelstrom of lusty life and immediate material reward?

The DeLacy party represents the most notable gold-inspired visitation. This party, consisting of twenty-seven men, left Virginia City on August 3, 1863. They crossed southeastern Idaho, thence to Jackson Hole. They followed the Snake River into the Park and discovered the fact that Lewis and Shoshone lakes were a branch of the Snake River drainage. In fact, the larger lake was named DeLacy, but unfortunately it was later renamed Shoshone by the Hayden Survey. DeLacy's party crossed the Divide, and on September 9 they entered the Firehole Basin where they "nooned." They were actually in the midst of the Lower Geyser Basin, picking their way cautiously because "the ground sounded hollow beneath our feet." Allow Mr. DeLacy to describe their reactions:

> The water of these springs was intensely hot, of a beautiful ultramarine blue, some boiling up in the middle, and many of them of very large size, being at least twenty feet in diameter and as deep. There were hundreds of these springs, and in the distance we could see and hear others, which would eject a column of steam and with a loud noise. These were probably geysers, and the boys called them "steamboat springs." No one in the company had ever seen or heard of anything like this region, and we were all delighted with what we saw.[106]

Had Walter W. DeLacy been more of a naturalist and less the prospector he might have achieved the distinction of being the real and effective discoverer of Yellowstone. However, he and his associates were looking for gold, and while they saw many wondrous things they failed to appreciate them. They were in a hurry. Even so, the time was not ripe for any special interest in Wonderland. Montana was only a name signifying rowdy mining camps. There were no newspapers to herald the discovery, no telegraph to transmit the news. Indeed, general attention was focused upon the Civil War.

However, DeLacy drew a more accurate map of the area than had been drafted before. Actually, he alone correctly represented the drainage of the Shoshone basin as tributary to the Snake River, a point which even later explorers such as Folsom, Washburn, and Hayden failed to observe. He also kept a daily journal, but it was not published until 1876. Walter W. DeLacy was, therefore, just another explorer who failed to take "time by the forelock" and, hence, lost an opportunity to win considerable fame.

While the DeLacy party prospected the southwestern section of the Park, a similar group, led by a man named Austin, explored the eastern periphery for the same purpose and with better success.

James Stuart might logically have been Yellowstone's honor man, but the breaks were against him. He and his brother Granville were outstanding leaders in Montana's pioneering. In the spring of 1863 James Stuart led an exploratory party into the lower Yellowstone. They were searching for gold, but fate so arranged that six miners who intended to join them (the Fairweather party) had the great good fortune of finding the famous Alder Gulch, whereas the main expedition under Stuart experienced a serious battle with the Crows, in which two men were killed and three wounded.[107] After their unpleasant encounter this party encircled the entire "crest of the world," traveling sixteen hundred miles.

James Stuart was a natural leader of men and a superb Indian fighter. In 1864 he organized and directed a frontier militia to punish Indians for the outrages before mentioned and others perpetrated in the vicinity of Deer Lodge. This party crossed the lower Yellowstone River, skirted the Absarokas to Shoshone River, thence proceeded westward. At least a part of the expedition returned by way of Yellowstone Lake and Canyon, but Stuart was not in that particular division. Because of his sterling worth and vast experience he was the unanimous choice for leader in the final discovery effort of 1870, but misfortune dogged him to the last. He was summoned for jury service, and the court refused to excuse him for a pleasure trip!

In 1864 H. W. Wayant and William Hamilton led a party of approximately forty miners, with horses and pack train, into the

Lamar Valley. Their horses were stolen by Indians near Soda Butte, but the mules would not stampede. Wayant, Harrison, and ten others with their mules ascended Cache Creek to Index Peak. Later they circled back by way of Amethyst Mountain to Tower Falls.

Later in the same year, 1864, a small company of miners, including George Huston, Rube Libby, George Hubbard, Soos, Lewis, and a Mexican, made a cursory trip in the Park area. They entered the region from the west and ascended the main Firehole River. They were startled by the eruption of the Giantess and other geysers, but they passed by with a glance and dismissed them as of slight importance.[108] An account of this journey was discussed with L. M. Freeman, a newspaper reporter, at Emigrant Gulch. He arranged to have it published in the Omaha Herald.[109] Other prominent miners whose explorations in Yellowstone are well known were C. J. Baronett, Bart Henderson, H. Sprague, Frederick Bottler, Adam Miller, and Adams and Crandall. The latter two were killed by Indians in the Hoodoo region in 1870, while Adam Miller and two companions narrowly escaped.[110] It would appear that probably a dozen nondescript mining groups had some contact with the region during the sixties. Yet these miner meanderings did not definitely confirm the actual existence of Wonderland, even though they added another chapter to an increasingly impressive legend. However, the persistence of this marvelous legend between 1820 and 1870 was largely due to the influence of Jim Bridger.

CHAPTER VII
JIM BRIDGER—MAN AND LEGEND

It is customary to assign an extraordinary disregard for truth to Jim Bridger. At times he appears as a rantipole hero, and undoubtedly he drew the long bow to unparalleled tension in matters of adventure. Still, he achieved excellent recommendations for reliability and trustworthiness from all the government officials who had business in the West. Surely Bridger was such a contradictory personage as to warrant investigation. Jim was the son of James and Chloe Bridger. He was born in Richmond, Virginia, on March 17, 1804. The Bridgers moved to St. Louis about 1812. The father died in 1816, and Jim became a flatboat operator; then, an apprentice in Phil Creamer's blacksmith shop. There his interest was first pointed to the West. In 1822 he became a member of Andrew Henry's party and departed for the Indian country. There is some evidence that he was the young man in the detail which deserted Hugh Glass in the time of his great need in 1823.

Bridger was a large man, fully six feet high, all rawhide and mountain-wise. He was wiry in action, with a quick, dangerous movement in handling weapons. His hair was auburn; his eyes were light blue. They were keen, friendly eyes in conversation but veritable hawk eyes for the game trail which he followed at maximum speed. Jim was shrewdly intelligent, although he could neither read nor write. He learned to speak French and Spanish from other trappers. In addition, he spoke several Indian languages, and he was able to communicate with all tribesmen by means of sign language. Indeed, he had a reputation as an entertainer among the natives. However, it is said that he exercised reserve and caution because he was suspiciously alert against deception of any kind. His very life depended upon accurately seeing and interpreting the signs of the wilderness. When serving as a guide for the army Jim once reported a thin column of smoke many miles away. Several officers trained field glasses upon the designated point without seeing any. They expressed their doubt of its existence. Jim was indignant: "Dam paper-collar soldiers, a tellin' thar ain't no smoke, when I seen it!" He was sure of his ability to outsee them even with the aid of field glasses, and he was right![111]

A frontiersman named Vaughn left an account of his introduction to this master guide in 1850:

> ... On they came, a big, strong, broad-shouldered, flaxen-haired, and blue-eyed man in the lead, riding as fine a saddle animal as I ever saw. They were now quite close; they came within a few paces and stopped.
>
> "How?" exclaimed the big man.
>
> "How, how," we exclaimed, shaking hands with him in turn.
>
> "Who are you?" he asked, "free trappers?"
>
> "No," I replied, "we belong to the Company. And you?"
>
> "My name is Bridger," he said, "Jim Bridger. Maybe you've heard of me."
>
> We had. There wasn't a man west of the Mississippi River who did not know him or know of him, for he was the greatest hunter, trapper, and Indian fighter of us all.[112]

Yes, Bridger was the real tobacco chew, "thirty-third degree" mountain man, and he certainly knew his way around. Every ridge and canyon of the Rockies dropped their last shadows of oblivion before his restless energy. He spent his winters in trapping and his summers in exploration. On most of these trips he chose to go alone, relying upon his faithful horse, trusty rifle, and hatchet of the finest steel. One excursion took him so far north that only the North Star served as guide. He followed the McKenzie River to the Arctic Ocean. This journey took eighteen months.[113] The rivers, mountains, and valleys of the Rockies were as one great plantation to him. He knew them all and kept a picture of the whole area in his mind. He was possessed by an insatiable curiosity. In wandering about the untouched West he kept poking into the off-trail corners to feast his eyes on strange wonders of hidden fairylands.

Bridger's services were always in demand. He started with the Missouri Fur Company. Later he became one of Ashley's men. By 1830 he was recognized as one of the most daring and effective trappers of the West. This won him a partnership in the newly organized Rocky Mountain Fur Company. After the disbanding of this firm he became identified with John Jacob Astor's American Fur Company. Naturally he realized the evanescent character of the fur business. In 1843 this insight impelled him to establish Fort Bridger on Black's Fork of Green

River. Here he developed one of the great frontier institutions. It was an oasis in the desert. Here the weary traveler found respite from the toil of his journey. While wagons were being repaired, stock exchanged, and provisions replenished, the wayfarers got acquainted with the gracious host. Bridger generously imparted his valuable mountain information to the public. Frequently he rendered service as a guide, for which he was liberally rewarded. His unerring judgment of distance and contour, together with a photographic memory of detail, enabled him to make nice corrections on the drafts of map makers. There is no gainsaying the fact that Jim Bridger was a man of affairs.

Jim Bridger.

In the autumn of 1824 some of Ashley's men were trapping the headwaters of Bear River. They were uncertain of its course, and Bridger was chosen to explore the stream to settle the bet. When he reached Great Salt Lake he scooped up a handful of its saline water. Spitting and coughing, he is reported to have said, "Hell, I'm on the shores of the Pacific."

Naturally of mild and gracious manner, Bridger possessed a Yankee wit that enabled him to take care of himself. This fact is attested by his ability to get along with the Indians, among whom he was known as Chief "Big Throat." He prided himself in being able to outdo the "sarpints" in every field of action. Bridger's experience with Indians made him very skeptical. This caution is expressed in his warning to Colonel Henry B. Carrington on the Powder River Expedition of 1866:

> Better not go too fur. Thar's Injuns enough lyin' under wolfskins er skulkin' on them cliffs, I'm a-tellin' ye. They foller ye allus. They've seen ye ev'ry day, an' take it frum me—when ye don't see any of 'em that's jest the time to watch out fer their devilment.[114]

However, he was wise in making alliances with them. Three times he married Indian squaws, a Flathead, a Ute, and a Shoshoni. These affiliations gave him greater security in his travels. Upon one occasion, when reference was made to this multiple spouse arrangement, someone asked Jim: "Which is which is which?" Quick as a flash came his rejoinder: "Thar all witches!"

From the Flathead wife two children were born, Josephine and Felix. Both were educated in St. Louis. His Ute wife died at the birth of a daughter, Virginia. Buffalo milk was utilized to nourish the infant, and she later returned her father's care by looking after him in his declining years. His Shoshoni wife also had two children, Mary and William.

During his indefatigable peregrinations Bridger gained intimacy with Yellowstone. He must have had a soul-loving zest for the wonderful and beautiful, or he wouldn't have noticed nature's handiwork in the first place. Early in his experience he noted the disbelief that greeted his relations. Observing that unimaginative people regarded him as a liar, he evidently concluded to adopt the old poacher's proverb about keeping the game when given the name. Why not embroider his tales in proportion to the listener's credulity? Anyway, much entertainment was expected from a guide. Jim was not one to disappoint a tenderfoot. One young unsophisticate, attached to a government party, approached "Old Gabe" (Jim's nickname) in a patronizing manner upon one occasion. "Mr. Bridger, they tell me that you have lived a long time on these plains and in the mountains." "Young feller," said "Gabe," "you see that thar butte yonder? Well, siree, that mountain was nuthin' but a hole in the ground when I come here!" It is said that two robbers entered his room at Fort Bridger. He awoke from sleep and said, "What air ye lookin' fer?" One of the desperados replied, "We are lookin' for your money." Bridger then answered, "Jest a minnit an' I'll git up and help ye." The robbers did not wait.[115]

When asked about some of his extravagant statements he quietly intimated that there was no harm in fooling people who pumped him for information and would not even say "thank ye." Like most of his contemporaries, Jim didn't think it proper to spoil a good story just for the sake of the truth. He could reel off story after story with astonishing spontaneity. These yarns were related in a solemn dead-pan gravity that was very effective.

Some of Bridger's more notable experiences and stories follow a pattern worthy of perpetuation in the literature of the Old West. In October 1832, while hunting in the Beaverhead country, Bridger's party was attacked by the Blackfeet. In this skirmish Jim received two long iron arrowheads in his back, one of which was embedded there for three years. It was removed by Dr. Marcus Whitman under circumstances that showed the strength and endurance of both surgeon and patient.

Perhaps this experience was the basis of the story he told about an encounter with the Blackfeet tribe. Said Jim:

> The pesky devils made a circle all aroun' me, ten Injuns deep. Then they pounce on top of me and hack me with their tommy hawks. The varmints stomp and club me until I faint dead away.[116]

At this point his voice would choke up with emotion. Finally, someone would make bold to inquire, "What did they do next, Jim?" Whereupon he would earnestly reply, "Them danged cussed Induns kilt and sculped me!"

What did Bridger actually know about Yellowstone? Probably his first visit was in 1829. He was also a member of a trapping party that worked the Bighorn Basin north, then passed over to Three Forks, and trapped to their sources during 1830. Therefore, they were in the western part of the Park. Dr. F. V. Hayden called Bridger the best mountain man the West had ever produced and said he learned of the marvels of Yellowstone from him in the early fifties. It is reasonable to believe that the old scout saw and appreciated all of the major features of Wonderland, with the possible exception of the Upper Geyser Basin. His descriptions of spouting springs, strange to say, fall far short of the standard set by the Old Faithful group.[117]

Several of the most famous Bridger yarns were embroidered upon a Yellowstone backdrop. It was this unique element that made them unconscious conservers of fact. A certain residuum of truth seems to be present in each of his tales if one searches carefully enough. There were occasional implications so freighted with the earmarks of reality that genuine curiosity was piqued. Amusement was often tempered by wonder; perhaps there was something in the old mountaineer's ravings!

There was the celebrated Obsidian Cliff fiasco. Its perpendicular volcanic glass properties were advertised in this yarn: "Oncet I camp yonder in a purty meadow. Wantin' meat I went lookin' fer an elk. I seen a beaut a right smart spell yonder. Comin' close, I let him have it. Bejabers, he didn't make a move. I moved nigh onto him—took a dead bead. Same result. Says I, I'll get so darn nigh the report o' the gun'll kill him. So I did. The blame critter didn't look up. O' course, I thought he was deaf, dumb, and blind. I was so bloomin' mad I grab my blunderbuss by the shank an' start runnin' direct fur him, intendin' to smash him slam-bang on the haid. Well siree, ye'd never believe it! What I act'lly hit was the side of a glass mountain ... crawlin' to the top, what do I see but that same elk way yonder, feedin' as peaceable as ye please." Thus he gave a quaint representation of an interesting feature of nature.

Bridger boasted the knowledge of a choice campground hidden among the inner labyrinth of Yellowstone's canyon. The marvel of this place was in its curious delayed-action echoes. "In fact," said Jim, "it's a natural alarm clock which I winds up so: when campin' thar I beds myself down, and jist afor I goes to sleep I raises my haid from the saddle an' hollers, 'Time to get up, you sunuvagun'; an' sure as shootin', the echo comes a bouncin' back at the crack o' dawn!"

Still another extravaganza, with a basis in fact, had a bearing upon the northeast corner of the Park. Jim averred that the entire region was under the curse of an old Crow chieftain. All things became lifeless, plants, animals, rivers, and even the light of sun, moon, and stars had a petrified cast. "Yes, siree, thar's miles o' peetrefied hills, covered with layers o' peetrefied trees, and on 'em trees air peetrefied birds a singin' peetrefied songs!" Sometimes for the sake of spice and variety he used the word putrified instead of peetrefied.

There can be little doubt that he actually knew of a spot in the great lake where a cast hook and line would catch a cutthroat. Then a semicircular swerve would bring him slowly to shore.

Upon taking the fish from the hook it would be found well-cooked and ready for eating!

Jim's Alum Creek episode tips heavily on the ludicrous side. "We was ridin' east o' the river along the side o' a creek. 'Twas boggy an' goin' was slow. When the cañon narrowed we guide our hosses into the stream. 'Twasn't no time till the hosses' feet shrunk to pin points, an', by tarnation, we went twenty miles in a jiffy. Them thar waters was so strong o' alum as to pucker distance itself!"

Is there any wonder that a classic mantle of exaggeration should invest Bridger with an enduring title of Münchausen? However, underneath Jim's tough, frontier-beaten exterior, obvious self-esteem, and braggadocio, there was a genuine and picturesque sincerity. He was not only colorful in acting an interesting frontier role, in which the setting was fully exploited, but he was a reliable geographer as well. Captain J. W. Gunnison received such a precise account of Yellowstone from Bridger as to enable him to write the following vivid description without reference to any other source:

> He [Bridger] gives a picture, most romantic and enticing, of the headwaters of the Yellowstone. A lake, sixty miles long, cold and pellucid, lies embosomed among high precipitous mountains. On the west side is a sloping plain, several miles wide, with clumps of trees and groves of pine. The ground resounds with the tread of horses. Geysers spout up seventy feet high, with a terrific, hissing noise, at regular intervals. Waterfalls are sparkling, leaping and thundering down the precipices, and collect in the lake, and for fifteen miles roars through the perpendicular canyon at the outlet. In this section are the "Great Springs"—so hot that meat is readily cooked in them, and as they descend on the successive terraces, afford at length delightful baths. On the other side is an acid spring, which gushes out in a river torrent; and below is a cave, which supplies "vermillion" for the savages in abundance.[118]

Surely this evidence speaks well of the great scout's capacity to impart the whole truth to those who were prepared to receive it. Bridger was evidently an unconscious believer in the scripture, "I am made all things to all men, that I might by all means save some." He persisted in his way of life among the mountains until late in the seventies. He could not withdraw from the companionship of the free and generous spirits around a campfire. However, his demeanor became more subdued with age. There was upon him much of the dignity of an Indian chief. After all, to the red men he was Chief Big Throat, also the Blanket Chief.

Before retiring, Bridger managed a visit to Washington, D. C., where he was introduced to the President of the United States. After staring at him in amazement for a minute, he turned to the congressman and remarked, "Looks jest like any other man, don't he?"[119]

After many years Bridger retired to a farm near Kansas City, Missouri. In 1884 the uncrowned king of Rocky Mountain scouts passed beyond, and thereby an epoch was ended.

In respect to his Yellowstone explorations, it is worthy of note that long before his death Bridger succeeded in kindling a lively interest among others. In fact, partly due to his efforts a consuming curiosity was preying upon the minds of several leading Montana residents. These citizens proved competent to find and interpret the great features of natural history.

CHAPTER VIII
FINAL DISCOVERY IN 1869 AND 1870

During the year 1867 several garbled accounts of monstrous wonders were reported to the Montana Post at Virginia City by returning prospectors. On July 29 the Post stated that an expedition to the Yellowstone country was being organized to explore the region as far as Yellowstone Lake. The project evidently fell through, but the notice accurately gauged the sentiment of Montana people.

By 1867 a dozen ranking citizens, later to be known as the Washburn-Langford-Doane party, held one common opinion concerning the Yellowstone rumors; namely, that it was high time some reputable authority should ascertain the facts. These men made tentative plans for an exploration that year and also in 1868, but the urge was not strong enough to impel definite preparations until 1869.

THE FOLSOM-COOK-PETERSON EXPLORATION

Even this effort proved abortive, due to Indian unrest and the failure of the military at Fort Ellis to furnish an escort. However, there were several men living at Diamond City on the Missouri River, forty miles below Helena, who were enrolled and waiting to join the Helena party. When word arrived of the postponement they decided to set out by themselves. This little expedition consisted of Hon. David E. Folsom, C. W. Cook, and William Peterson. Folsom and Cook were unusually intelligent men, with large experience in ranching and mining affairs. They were capable of executing a purposeful exploration of this character. Mr. Peterson's precise status is not so well known. He was born in Denmark, served many years as a sailor, came to Montana as a miner, and later made a modest fortune as a stockman in Idaho. He was no doubt a resourceful member of the party, but his educational deficiency prevented him from making any contribution to the literary side of the enterprise.[120]

They left Diamond City on September 6, after making arrangements to be away for six weeks. Their provisions and armaments were adequate for any emergency which three men might be expected to meet and survive. They had three riding horses and two for the packs. Among the usual camping equipment were listed a field glass, a pocket compass, and a thermometer.

Bozeman was their last station of supply. From there they ascended a tributary of the East Gallatin River, and crossed the divide onto the headwaters of Trail Creek, which lies on the Yellowstone drainage. By September 14 they were at the junction of the Yellowstone, near Tower Falls. They followed the East Fork of Yellowstone River (now Lamar) for a day and then doubled back to Tower Creek. The scenery at this point intrigued them:

> ... Yesterday we caught glimpses of scenery surpassing in grandeur anything we have before seen so we concluded to lay over one day and give it a more thorough examination....[121]

They were speaking of the overhanging cliffs and the second canyon of the Yellowstone directly beneath, also of the classic falls on Tower Creek.

They reached Grand Canyon on September 21, after two weeks' travel. From there they journeyed to the extreme west end of the lake and thence to Shoshone Lake, which they mistakenly considered the head of Madison River. Here they saw species of rare aquatic fowl, such as the whistling and trumpeter swans. Crossing the Continental Divide, which they called the "Dike," they emerged into the Lower Geyser Basin. They made precise observations of the geysers and hot springs throughout the area and were enthusiastic over their performance. There was no lack of appreciation in this party.

On the night of October 1, three thoughtful men conversed in their Firehole River camp. William Peterson observed that it would not be long before settlers and prospectors began coming into the district and taking up the land around the geysers and canyons. Charles Cook sincerely hoped that people might have free access to the area to enjoy its beauty, while David Folsom expressed the opinion that the government should not allow anyone to locate in the vicinity.

Fifty-three years later, upon the occasion of the Park's Golden Anniversary, observed on July 14, 1922, at Madison Junction, the matured reflection of Charles W. Cook was recorded:

None of us definitely suggested the idea of a national park. National parks were unknown then. But we knew that as soon as the wonderful character of the country was generally known outside, there would be plenty of people hurrying to get possession, unless something were done.

We all had this thought in mind when we came out a few days later, and told others what we had seen.[122]

Trumpeter Swan, a rare species of aquatic life.

Folsom, in particular, had a lively interest in the idea of preserving the phenomena, and he discussed the subject with H. D. Washburn, N. P. Langford, and others. Indeed, Mr. Peterson later remarked that their own astonishment was so profound that they thought surely no one would believe half of what they could tell. However, upon the solicitation of a friend, Cook and Folsom prepared a joint article from their diaries for publication. The account was rejected by The New York Tribune, Scribner's, and Harper's as "they had a reputation that they could not risk with such unreliable material." Finally it appeared in the July 1870 issue of the Western Monthly of Chicago. The editors deleted the account considerably and printed an emasculated narrative. It is affirmed that among the items left out was the germ of the grand idea advocating the creation of a national park.

Much credit is due these three gentlemen for accomplishing a difficult and dangerous mission without military escort. It was purely a private venture, lasting thirty-six days, and may be considered as having been eminently successful. In fact, it was the first expedition to make a complete and authentic report of its exploration.

THE WASHBURN-LANGFORD-DOANE EXPEDITION

It was these articulate reports of Folsom, Cook, and Peterson that electrified the natural interest of Helena's intellectual leadership. Thereafter, Langford and his associates were burning to effect a grand expedition and achieve conclusive results. General Phil Sheridan gave the project his blessing and the assurance of a military escort.

A congenial personnel was sifted out, consisting of Hon. Nathaniel P. Langford, Hon. Cornelius Hedges, Hon. Truman C. Everts, Hon. Samuel T. Hauser, Walter Trumbull, Benjamin Stickney, Jr., Warren C. Gillette, and Jacob Smith. James Stuart was selected as leader, but he was deprived of that privilege by jury service. Thereupon, Surveyor General Henry D. Washburn was given the honor of taking command. He was a worthy leader, having achieved the rank of Major General in the Civil War. He had also served two terms in Congress. Altogether it was a hand-picked company. The men were uniformly young and energetic, with the exception of Everts who was fifty-four. Several of them had served as Vigilantes. Indeed, they were men of intelligence, action, and high integrity. With one exception the men were serious-minded and mature. They early sensed the hazards of the endeavor and struggled manfully to reduce them to a minimum.

Elaborate preparations were made in point of equipment and provisions. Two packers, Reynolds and Bean, and two colored cooks were employed, and the whole enterprise, although private, took on a semiscientific, quasi-military character from the start. Washburn possessed a copy of the Folsom-Cook diary and a map made by Walter W. DeLacy.[123] In addition, he had numerous conversations with these men, and he was, therefore, the beneficiary of their experience. They left Helena on August 17, 1870. Four days later they were at Fort Ellis. Here they listened to the post order detailing Lieutenant Gustavus C. Doane, one sergeant, and four privates "to escort the Surveyor-General of Montana to the falls and lakes of the Yellowstone and return...." The soldiers in the party were Sergeant William Baker and Privates John Williamson, George W. McConnell, William Leipler, and Charles Moore.

There was no allusion to thermal phenomena or any exotic features whatsoever. Judge Hedges subsequently characterized the general temper of the explorers in respect to those particulars:

> I think a more confirmed set of skeptics never went out into the wilderness than those who composed our party, and never was a party more completely surprised and captivated with the wonders of nature.[124]

The complete expedition now comprehended nineteen men, thirty-five horses and mules, and adequate supplies for a month's journey. Leaving Fort Ellis, they ascended the Yellowstone River to its junction with the Gardner. This brought them within five miles of the Mammoth Hot Springs, but ignorance of the fact precluded their visitation. Instead, they crossed over the plateau and reached Tower Creek where they camped on August 27. All members were delighted with the hot springs and fumaroles in that area.

Around the campfire they evolved a name-giving policy and enjoyed great sport incident to its first application. They adopted a self-sacrificing resolution. Natural features should not be given the names of the present personnel or their relatives and friends. Instead, all wonders must bear the most appropriate cognomens possible. This was a noble gesture, and while it was not strictly observed one wishes that their demonic impressions might have been less vivid. Here was the Devil's Slide; there, Hellbroth Springs; yonder, Brimstone; now, Devil's Hoof, Den, Kitchen, and Ink Well; again, Hells Half Acre and Hell Roaring Mountain. Surely their concepts of Christian theology rendered them acutely conscious of the attributes and environment of His Satanic Majesty.

The first controversy arose over naming the falls. "What shall we name these sentinel-guarded falls?" "Minaret is the proper name," said young Trumbull. "What's a minaret?" queried Jake Smith. Trumbull gave a classical description of Moslem architecture and drew his analogy to this similitude. Sam Hauser objected on the ground that the name was not "fitten" in western America where there weren't any mosques. Hence, he proposed the more expressive name "Tower." The council deliberated, expanded, and talked big. Minaret was the most significant, had a deeper meaning, more symbolical. Therefore, General Washburn christened them "Minaret Falls."[125]

But Sam Hauser was a politician; he later became governor of Montana. During the night he confidentially circulated the rumor that Walter Trumbull had a girl friend by the name of Minnie Rhett. Trumbull denied the statement, said it was a canard, a roarback, a plain lie! However, the seed of doubt had been sown, and at breakfast Hauser's point was won. The name was Tower Falls. Later it transpired that the future governor's girl friend was a Miss Tower! Surely there was genuine political statesmanship in this party, and its genius was clearly manifest before the journey's end.

The party skirted Mount Washburn on the twenty-ninth and spontaneously named it for their honored leader, because he was the first to climb its summit. Said Washburn, "I saw the canyon and the lake. There are unmistakable columns of steam in the distance. This is a glorious region." Whereupon the entire party hustled upward, frightening the resentful bighorn en route. Upon reaching the summit silence prevailed while these subdued men paid unconscious tribute to the Powers That Be. Standing there upon a natural observatory, they looked down upon the whole grand panorama, as does yonder eagle. Their vision darted a hundred miles southward, where the Tetons glittered like purple icebergs. Then nearer they beheld Lake Titicaca's only rival, shimmering in the sun. Lake Yellowstone's deeply sinuous shores, scattered islands, and fingerlike peninsulas gave it a mystic character. Now their gaze followed the Yellowstone River crooking away from the lake and then whirling toward them flashing in its canyon cameo until it seemed to be biting at their very feet. From this central apex the whole mountain-girt plateau conformed to the shape of a mammoth saucer as its distant rim merged with the sky.

Another day found them standing on the brink of an imprisoned river's chasm, enchanted by the ponderous roaring of the awful force below. So vast were the canyon's alternating gulfs and monoliths that lofty pines "dwindle to shrubs in the dizziness of distance!" Bald eagles far below screamed in angry protest upon this invasion of their secret eyries. Fishhawks hovered cautiously above, less fearful of new dangers than old. Nineteen lonely men stood amazed by an environment at once both grand and gloomy, mellow and terrible, an "empire of shadows and turmoil."[126]

Then the sun came out and the whole gorge flamed! They beheld the marvelously variegated volcanic coloring as vivid and broken as the field of a kaleidoscope. It was as though rainbows had fallen from the sky and draped themselves like glorious banners upon the chasm below. How did it all come about?

> All nature's forces conspired to build this temple to her glory. The smooth, sharp tongue of glacial ice first plowed the great furrow deep into the bosom of the earth. Volcanic fires subdued the rigid hardness of the riven rock. Steam from boiling springs tempered to plastic yielding the surface of massive stone. And wind and water came with all their energies and skill to carve and sculpture it to befitting shapes. The air brought all its magic alchemy to bear upon the ingredients of the rock to call thence the gorgeous pigments for its coloring.[127]

Truly, here was a noble river, vibrating like a bundle of quivering electric wires a mile below, yet notching the centuries, revealing a record of geological time, and disclosing to men how God writes history. It was a canyon full of interest even to the most casual observer in the group. External senses were all appropriately appealed to. Indeed, the hidden recesses of the inner self were reached and stirred by the wild beauty and mystery of the scene. The world would surely want to visit such a place.

As they reluctantly journeyed along the river toward the lake, their ears were assailed by a series of resounding thuds. The source was the combined agitations of Mud Volcano and Dragons Mouth. These frightful vents reminded them of two vicious, frothing animals chained in cavernous lairs. There they spewed their foul compounds, as in terrible rage, growling and groaning in their perpetual regurgitations. It was one of the fascinating, if loathsome, sights in the Park.

Bighorn resentful toward invaders.

Later there was Yellowstone Lake, nestled serenely against its buttress-based, snow-capped mountain guardians. Many people have been made happy by its sparkling water. One capable writer has left his impression:

> From a gentle headland, at last we overlooked the lake. It was like the fairest dream which ever came to bless the slumbers of a child. How still it was! What silence reigned! How lovingly it laid its hush upon you![128]

It was the Washburn party that fancied a resemblance between the lake and the human hand. Concerning this analogy Professor R. W. Raymond made an amusing observation:

> The gentleman who first discovered this resemblance must have thought the size and form of fingers quite insignificant, provided the number was complete. The hand in question is afflicted with Elephantiasis in the thumb, dropsy in the little finger, hornet bites on the third finger, and the last stages of starvation in the other two.[129]

What a struggle they had in threading their way through fir and lodgepole forests east of the lake. The tanglewood was nearly impenetrable; no trails to guide them except the dim and devious ways of wild animals, "through which we toiled and swore our way, coming out after several days tattered and torn, ragged, bleeding and sullen."[130] In this welter it was every man for himself after the general course had been determined. It was this circumstance that eventuated in the painful despair of Truman C. Everts.

LOST IN THE WILDERNESS

In Yellowstone even now the wilderness is almost within rifle-shot of the Grand Loop highway. Furthermore, the area's conformation to a vast plateau renders it relatively deficient in accessible landmarks. Hedges and Stickney were inadvertently separated from the party on September 8, but they stumbled upon the camp by nightfall. The very next day Mr. Everts unintentionally drifted away from his associates. By evening he was laboriously embroiled in the forest labyrinth southeast of Lake Yellowstone. Unconcerned the first night, he made himself comfortable, fully assured of an early reunion the next day. From this point on, a chronicle of his experience reveals a record of astonishing incompetency and carelessness on his part. It is amazing that he escaped fatal consequences.

Up bright and early he was retracing the trail; dismounting to survey an engulfing situation, he left his horse untied, and it bolted. Upon its disappearing back was his entire outfit. In his excitement Everts then lost his spectacles, a grievous loss because he was nearsighted. Later on he also lost two knives and one of his shoes. The most valuable article on his person was his field glass. It saved his life.

Another day passed; complacence now turned to frenzy, and Everts fairly ran in circles. His voice gave out; his head whirled. The pangs of hunger were extremely severe, and the close of the second day found him in tears. A cold, dark night added terrors of its own. There were howling coyotes and roaring lions—whether real or fancied made little difference to a timid man.

Still, he reasoned upon his problem and resolved to fight his way through. In his ill-conceived exertions he came upon a beautiful little lake. He named it Bessie for his daughter. On its banks were several hot springs and numerous patches of elk thistles. In an agony of hunger he tasted a root; it was edible, better still when cooked in the boiling water. Then a storm came up. It whipped him both in body and mind. He became lethargic, satisfied to chew thistle roots and bake his backside on warm spring incrustations. Seven days Everts hovered over this location. This indecision on his part put him completely out of reach of salvation by the Washburn party.

Then the skies cleared; the sun glistened upon the water. Its reflection flashed an idea into his mind. "My opera glasses—fire from heaven!" Oh, happy, hope-renewing thought! It worked; he made a fire. With new purpose he bestirred himself; he would make a break, but which way should he go? South to Snake River? Yes, there were frontiersmen in Idaho. After many miles of painful toil among the intricacies of hill and vale his faith weakened. The goal—a notch in the mountain barrier—seemed to recede as if in mockery of his feeble efforts.[131]

"I'll go west into the Madison Valley—that's shorter." So he stumbled off in that direction. A precipitous escarpment obstructed his path; there was no pass. The distraught pilgrim lighted a fire. It got out of control; he fled from its awful devastation. In utter exhaustion he sat down to rest; whereupon, he experienced an hallucination. An old clerical friend seemed to be standing before him. He seemed to say, "Go back immediately, as rapidly as your strength will permit. There is no food here, and the idea of scaling these rocks is madness." Amid serious misgivings Everts decided to retrace the course of ingress. His heart nearly failed him as he envisioned the unending panorama of the Yellowstone River trail. Final resolution was helpful, and he trudged on by day, rested by night, and gnawed on "Everts" thistle betimes.

For two long weeks the party camped along the southwest shore of the lake. From this base position they daily sent out searching details, lighted signal fires, shot guns, posted notices, and cached food. No clues were found, and the time was far spent. They regretfully concluded that their companion was either hopelessly lost or well upon his way toward home. A foot of snow had already fallen. The thirty-day rations had rendered thirty-two days' service. In these circumstances Cornelius Hedges expressed his depression in his diary:

> Had to lie in bed to keep warm, wished I was at home ... stormed all night. We are in for it. Snowed all day ... the season is in our favor, we shall make haste home as soon as the blockade raises.[132]

Therefore, they left the Thumb of the Lake and started toward Firehole Basin on September 17. They were exultant over the exploration; accurate journals were kept. It was generally felt that their observations were of great value and the exploration would be considered important. Allow Langford to describe their reactions:

> Strange and interesting as are the various objects which we have met within this vast field of natural wonders, no camp or place of rest on our journey has afforded our party greater satisfaction than the one we are now occupying, which is our first camp since emerging from the dense forest. Filled with gloom at the loss of our comrade, tired, tattered, browned by exposure and reduced in flesh by our labors, we resemble more a party of organized mendicants, than of men in pursuit of Nature's greatest novelties. But from this point we hope that our journey will be comparatively free from difficulties of travel.[133]

Having finished an assignment, they were thinking of home and their neglected affairs. Notwithstanding the grandeur of nature's wonders in the Yellowstone Lake region they were about to get the surprise of their lives. This marvel of wonders occurred on the evening of September 18. Just as they emerged from the woods into the Upper Geyser Basin, Old Faithful was shyly preening her billowy plume, and as the vanguard shouted, "Look!" she gracefully mounted, wave upon wave, until a mighty torrent vaulted heavenward, where it unfurled like a watery flag, as if in welcome to its known immortalizers. Thus, the Fairy Queen had the honor of first saluting those weary explorers, and never since that eventful day has she failed any visitor.

In that gloryful presence Lieutenant Doane solemnly declared, "The earth affords not its equal. It is the most lovely inanimate object in existence."[134] To General Washburn, the Giantess, when quiet, was like a hallowed fountain and in eruption, grandly magnificent, with "each broken atom shining like so many brilliants with myriads of rainbows dancing in attendance."[135] What ecstasy! A whole kingdom of fairy spirits seemed determined to outdo each other. There ensued an orgy of thermal activity. During the short visit of twenty-two hours, twelve geysers were seen in action. It was then that their experience waxed "more and more wonderful until wonder itself became paralyzed." In this basin they overcame the tendency to apply the wretched Satanic nomenclature so fully employed elsewhere. Instead, the names bestowed bear witness to a profound appreciation. It was for them alone that Old Faithful marked the hours by sending up "a plume of spun glass iridescent and superb, against the sky."[136] When the Giant played, "Our whole party went wild with enthusiasm; many declared it was three hundred feet in height." The picturesque name "Broken Horn" was then proposed; it is most descriptive and worthy of being retained. The Grotto reminded them of

> ... a miniature temple of alabaster whiteness, with arches leading to some interior Holy of Holies, whose sacred places may never be profaned by eye or foot.[137]

Geysers soon to become known as Giantess, Lion, Grand, Turban (or Turk's Head), Splendid, Beehive, Fan, Castle, Rocket, and Grotto performed with unrivaled courtesy. What an array of Titans! Surely the world would also want to know about this.

And then there were the pools, the amazing springs of Yellowstone—thousands of them, all colors, a riot of aquatic pigmentation—Emerald, Sapphire, Gentian, Grand Prismatic, Rainbow, Topaz, and glamorous Morning Glory. The amazing intricacy of color-blend in the water did not then excel in beauty the surrounding border incrustations. Indeed, the most delicate embroidery could not rival them in their wonderful variety and complexity.[138]

How was such symmetry of design created? Species by the score of tiny plants called algae and diatoms thrive in hot water, temperatures ranging from approximately 100° to 170° F. These plants have the capacity to assimilate silica held in solution, and as their lives are short they build sinter formations in the same manner as coral reefs are fashioned. These algae are, therefore, active geological agents in soil building on a considerable scale.[139] However, the intricate mineral incrustations and lacy embroidery surrounding the boiling hot springs and geysers are entirely the product of deposition due to evaporation.

As the party progressed through the hierarchy of basins, Upper, Biscuit, Midway, and Lower, samples were taken and names given to many thermal features. They were leaving the Firehole region, but before an exit was made, or its spell broken, their whole experience was given a proper evaluation, and the greatest natural history idea of a millennium was born.

On the evening of September 19, the explorers were encamped at the junction of the Firehole and Gibbon rivers. The setting was an impressive one. A majestic mountain backdrop cast long shadows upon them. The silvery Madison glided away in the foreground. On center stage, red embers of a neglected fire sparked and glowed in contact with a fanning breeze.

The last scene was being enacted—the curtain was about to fall. It was an hour of recapitulation. Thrills were relived, confidences exchanged, speculations indulged. Then came the inevitable question of Yellowstone's destiny. The question was posed, "Men and brethren, what shall we do?" "Why," said Smith, "we'll fence it in; give me Old Faithful." "I'll take the Falls," echoed another. Serious consideration was given the idea of allowing each explorer to pre-empt a choice section in the most strategic location and pool the income for equal distribution. Whereupon, the inspired mind of Cornelius Hedges proposed and explained an idea that marked him as one of the far-sighted men of his generation. Said he:

> There ought to be no private ownership of any portion of this region. Rather the whole of it should be set apart as a great National Park for all time as a reserve for the use and enjoyment of all the people. Furthermore, each and everyone of us should make every effort to have this purpose accomplished.[140]

The response was instantaneous and all but unanimous. The next day Langford wrote in his diary, "I lay awake half of last night thinking about it;—and if my wakefulness deprived my bed-fellow [Hedges] of any sleep, he has only himself and his disturbing National Park proposition to answer for it."[141]

Within a week the Helena Daily Herald had printed the first of a series of articles on "The Yellowstone Expedition." Washburn, Langford, Hedges, and Trumbull wrote separate accounts, all of which were in general agreement that they had seen "the most interesting country ... where are presented at once the wonders of Iceland, Italy, and South America."

W. S. Chapman
Part of Washburn-Langford-Doane party in camp.

The members were banqueted and feted; specimens of petrifaction, geyserite, and other strange items were displayed. Langford gave a "Grand Lecture" to open the Helena Library Association Lecture Course.

Hedges paid glowing tribute to the memory of Truman C. Everts, thought to be deceased. Indeed, his disappearance did as much as anything else to capture the public interest. Still anxious to do everything possible in his behalf, a searching party was immediately organized and sent off. On October 15, Jack Baronett and George A. Pritchett, two well-known scouts, came upon the prostrate Everts. It was his thirty-seventh day of travail. They found him near the northern boundary of the Park, near a mountain now bearing his name. The day was raw and gusty. Against the prospect of an overcast sky he carried a firebrand in his seared hands. His weight was halved; his whole system was terribly out of order. Actually he was sinking under the conviction that death was near. According to his own report rescue came in the nick of time:

> Groping along the side of the hill, I became suddenly sensible of a sharp reflection, as of burnished steel. Looking up, through half-closed eyes, two rough but kindly faces met my gaze.

"Are you Mr. Everts?"

"Yes. All that is left of him."

"We have come for you."

"Who sent you?"

"Judge Lawrence and other friends."

"God bless him, and them, and you! I am saved!"[142]

Everts fell helpless into the strong arms of his preservers. They carried him to a trapper's cabin, and there he rested after swallowing a pint of bear grease. In time his recovery was complete, and he lived to the ripe age of eighty-five. During these years he experienced much satisfaction over the contribution he had made in the discovery of Yellowstone, even at the high price of "Thirty Seven Days of Peril."

CHAPTER IX
CREATION OF YELLOWSTONE NATIONAL PARK

The return of Everts operated as a springboard for an attempt to get government action. Graphic accounts of the exploration in general filled the columns of the Helena Herald during October. An article written by Cornelius Hedges, which appeared in the issue of November 9, suggested an extension of Montana's southern boundary to include the whole Yellowstone region. He also outlined the proposal for appropriation of the same for public purposes. An excited public interest consumed every issue. Bursting upon national attention, these highly entertaining narratives, spontaneous and vivid like tales from Arabian Nights, carried a large measure of conviction.

Nathaniel P. Langford went east to proclaim the discovery. He first announced the good news to his own people in a public meeting in Minneapolis. They gave him a responsive hearing, which encouraged him for the work ahead.[143] On January 19, 1871, a large crowd listened intently to his delineation at Lincoln Hall in New York City. The people of Washington accorded similar attention. In fact, one of the lectures was presided over by Senator James G. Blaine, and one of the most alert auditors was Dr. Ferdinand V. Hayden who was soon converted to the importance of the project and agreed to conduct a government geological survey the following summer. Hayden's leadership was an important factor in making Yellowstone a live political issue. Sam Hauser also visited Washington, D. C., and he was subsequently joined by Truman C. Everts. Henry D. Washburn started for the national Capitol, but he fell ill on the way and died at his former home in Clinton, Indiana, on January 26, 1871. Walter Trumbull was serving as clerk of the Senate Judiciary Committee, of which his father was chairman. Interesting accounts of Yellowstone's features by Langford and Trumbull appeared in the May and June numbers of Scribner's and the Overland Monthly. The Firehole campfire resolution was bearing fruit.

Dr. Ferdinand V. Hayden

Montana's new but able territorial representative, Hon. William H. Clagett, went assiduously to work upon the members of Congress. In his view there was a great prize to be secured for the benefit of all people and especially his constituents. A wonderland was available for the taking. As yet there were no complications of private ownership to arrest an alert government's purpose. The Congress responded with alacrity by making provision for an official exploration. The sundry civil service act of March 3, 1871, carried an item of $40,000 for the construction of the Hayden Survey, to complete "the season's work about the sources of the Missouri and Yellowstone Rivers." In fact, the bill also provided for a reconnaissance of the upper Yellowstone under Captain J. W. Barlow and Captain D. P. Heap of the Army Engineer Corps. Congress was not entering into the problem halfway; it was actually doubling up.[144]

The chief officer, Dr. Ferdinand V. Hayden, was an unusually capable geologist. In addition, he possessed an inspiring personality and statesmanlike views. There were nineteen scientists directly under his command. The personnel included

James Stevenson, managing director; Henry W. Elliott and Thomas Moran, artists; Professor Cyrus Thomas, agricultural statistician and entomologist; Anton Schonborn, chief topographer; William H. Jackson, photographer; George B. Dixon, assistant photographer; J. W. Beaman, meteorologist; Professor G. N. Allen, botanist; Robert Adams, Jr., assistant botanist; Dr. A. C. Peale, mineralogist; Dr. C. S. Trunbull, physician; Campbell Carrington, in charge of zoological collections; William B. Logan, secretary; F. J. Huse; Chester M. Dawes, son of Representative Henry L. Dawes of Massachusetts; C. De V. Hegley and J. W. Duncan, assistants. Barlow's army detail also had a competent and well-balanced personnel.[145]

A military escort, including Lieutenant Doane, rounded out these expeditions and provided all that could have been desired in point of training and ability. Each detachment had a retinue of helpers. Two technical studies and scientific reports, which not only substantiated but actually enhanced the findings of the previous civilian explorations, resulted from these two expeditions.

Hayden's party left Fort Ellis, near Bozeman, on July 15, 1871. Upon reaching the junction of the Yellowstone and Gardner rivers they elected to ascend the latter. It was a good choice because within the hour they beheld a white mountain which resembled a vast cascade of frozen snow. The Mammoth Hot Springs Terraces "alone surpassed all the descriptions which had been given by former travelers."[146]

As this expedition progressed, the geological record was interpreted. Thereafter, rocks were identified as travertine, gneiss, rhyolite, dacite, basalt, breccia, geyserite, sinter, and obsidian. Trees and plants were likewise classified, and in addition to geysers, springs and pools there were fumaroles and solfataras. Geological speculations were formulated relative to petrified forests, Grand Canyon, the lake's former Snake River outlet, and the relationship of heat, water, and "plumbing" essential for geyser action.

The Hayden expedition in camp

Henry Elliott and Campbell Carrington launched a canvas boat and made a survey of Yellowstone Lake's hundred-mile shoreline. Later the temperatures of over six hundred hot springs were taken. Sketches were made of many features, and significant names were given, such as Architectural Fountain Geyser. Captain Barlow's division paid particular attention to the mapping of Snake River's headwaters. It also made a cursory survey of the Lamar River. Unfortunately most of the data and accompanying photographs were destroyed in the great Chicago fire. This delayed Barlow's official report until six weeks after the Park Bill was enacted. However, an interesting summary appeared in the Chicago Journal for January 13, 1872. Thus, the report and collection of specimens and photographs by Dr. Hayden represented the principal result of the season's endeavor.[147]

The beauty of Jackson's photographs and Moran's paintings could scarcely be denied. Each represented the work of a master. Dr. Hayden's report to Secretary of Interior, Columbus Delano, was received in February, 1872. He also contributed feature articles to the American Journal of Science and Arts and Scribner's. Thus, a number of authorities had taken up the national park cause without reservation. Indeed, after he became intrigued with the idea of government development, Dr. Hayden's efforts were so impressive that many people regarded him as the true originator of the movement. In fact, his own enthusiasm unfortunately caused him to make pretensions for which he was severely criticized by his colleagues in the effort.[148] Although Dr. Hayden's contribution was invaluable, it was not exclusive. It was through the combined effort of the entire Montana delegation, and its powerful friends, that Congress was made receptive and responsive.

On December 18, 1871, a bill to create Yellowstone National Park was introduced simultaneously in both houses of Congress. The direct sponsors were Delegate William H. Clagett of Montana and Senator Samuel C. Pomeroy of Kansas. A thorough canvass was made; photographs, specimens, and testimonials did heavy duty in both the Senate and the House. Four hundred copies of Scribner's containing Langford's articles were distributed among the congressmen, and all were personally interviewed. The advocates were few, but effective, and there was never any doubt as to the outcome. In the Senate, Pomeroy's efforts were backed by George F. Edmunds, H. B. Anthony, and Lyman Trumbull. They made an unsuccessful attempt to bring the bill, S392, to a vote on January 22 and 23, but objections were raised, and it came up in calendar order on the thirtieth. Senator Edmunds appealed for unanimous support for the bill. Senators Cameron of Pennsylvania and Morton of Indiana were curious about the number of square miles in the proposed reservation. Senator Pomeroy assured them that, although it was a large tract, there were no arable lands therein because of the elevation.

The advocates were puzzled by the opposition exhibited by Senator Cornelius Cole of California. He entertained grave doubts as to the value of the bill. Settlers should not be excluded from such a large area. As to the natural curiosities, they would remain. Edmunds replied that the region was north of 40° and about seven thousand feet elevation. Pomeroy affirmed that:

> ... the only object of the bill is to take early possession of it by the United States, and set it apart, so that it cannot be included in any claims or occupied by any settlers.[149]

Opposition was removed from the discussion by the forceful and tactful speech made by Senator Trumbull. He reviewed the history of Yosemite and the Big Trees in California:

> I think our experience with the wonderful natural curiosity, if I may so call it, in the Senator's own State, should admonish us of the propriety of passing such a bill as this.... Here is a

region of country away up in the Rocky Mountains, where there are the most wonderful geysers on the face of the earth.... It is possible that some person may go there and plant himself right across the only path that leads to these wonders, and charge every man that passes along ... the gorges of these mountains a fee of a dollar or five dollars....

I think it is a very proper bill to pass, and now is the time to enact it.... Now, before there is any dispute as to this wonderful country, I hope we shall except it from the general disposition of the public lands, and reserve it to the Government.... At some future time, if we desire to do so, we can repeal this law, if it is in anybody's way; but now I think it a very appropriate bill to pass.[150]

The matter was then presented for a vote, and it passed without a call for the ayes and noes.

The progress of the Park Bill, H.R. 764, through the House was just as sure, if not so speedy, as in the Senate. On February 27 Chairman Mark H. Dunnell of the Public Lands Committee brought out a favorable report. He personally was convinced by careful investigation that the bill should pass. Henry L. Dawes clearly and forcibly explained its purpose and observed that it went a step further than the Yosemite precedent. In this case "the title will still remain in the United States.... This bill treads upon no rights of the settler ... and it receives the urgent and ardent support of the legislature of that Territory [Montana], and of the Delegate himself...."[151]

The roll call on February 28, 1872, showed 115 ayes, 65 noes, and 60 not voting. George W. Morgan, the minority leader, was opposed to the bill on partisan principles in general and his personal dislike for Secretary Delano in particular. Within ten weeks the measure had passed both houses by large majorities, and on March 1, 1872, it received the signature of President Ulysses S. Grant.

Upon passage of the act the Helena Herald printed a laudatory editorial on "Our National Park," while the Helena Rocky Mountain Gazette considered the bill "as a great blow struck at the prosperity of the towns of Bozeman and Virginia City ... if it were thrown open to a curious but comfort-loving public." Other local papers joined the Herald's side of the controversy.[152]

A mild national reaction was generally favorable to the reservation idea. The bill even attracted attention abroad, as evidenced by an article in the London Times, April 10, 1873, under the caption, "A Very National Park."

Who should receive the credit for this eminent accomplishment? A careful examination of the facts warrants the conclusion that the idea of establishing Yellowstone as a public reservation had a dual birth. It was independently conceived in the minds of two men. This view is attested by the deliberate statement of N. P. Langford:

> It is true that Professor Hayden joined with Mr. Clagett and myself in working for the passage of the act of dedication, but no person can divide with Cornelius Hedges and David E. Folsom the honor of originating the idea of creating the Yellowstone Park.[153]

W. S. Chapman
President Ulysses S. Grant signing the Yellowstone National Park Bill.

In his Westward America, Howard R. Driggs states that the pioneer artist, George Catlin, made a similar observation about other parts of the Old West in the eighteen thirties. Surely it was Hedges' suggestion at Madison Junction campfire that initiated the conception of a program which other men were well conditioned to execute. N. P. Langford was the enthusiast, the zealous crusader. William H. Clagett was the man at the helm, but he was ably supported by the sage advice of Henry L. Dawes, representative from Massachusetts, who probably formulated the general principles of the measure.[154] Dr. F. V. Hayden's scientific reports and unstinted support must be weighed heavily in the scale. Senators Samuel C. Pomeroy and Lyman Trumbull gave strength to the movement. The good will of General Phil Sheridan was a constant factor. Beyond this spearhead of ability and integrity the number of contributors broadens. It was an altogether democratic effort, and little injustice results from the omission of other efforts toward the cause. Most of them would probably have had it so. It was a program for the benefit and enjoyment of all people, rather than the personal aggrandizement of a few.

The rapidity that characterized the government's action in this matter will always stand as a tribute to the common sense and natural idealism of the Forty-second Congress. Judge Hedges' idea had found ready acceptance as it journeyed along the legislative course. The "Dedicatory Act," as it is now called, was a remarkably well-drawn bill, especially when it is remembered that the issues involved were not only new in America but to the entire world. It was a pioneer measure in the field of conserving natural phenomena for recreational and spiritual appreciation. John Muir has cogently expressed the significance of the endeavor:

> Fortunately, almost as soon as it—the Yellowstone region—was discovered it was dedicated and set apart for the benefit of the people, a piece of legislation that shines benignly amid the common dust-and-ashes history of the public domain.[155]

The philosophy in the statement of the purpose was both unique and basic. The reservation was "dedicated and set apart as a public park or pleasuring ground for the benefit and enjoyment of the people." Conservation was keynoted in "the preservation from injury or spoliation of all timber, mineral deposits, natural curiosities or wonders within said park and for retention in their natural condition." There was a declaration against "the wanton destruction of fish and game—and the capture or destruction for the purpose of merchandise or profit." Senators Anthony and Tipton wanted to strike out the last phrase so there would be no destruction of game for any purpose. Anthony said, "We do not want sportsmen going over there with their guns," and Mr. Tipton, "... if the door is once opened I fear there will ultimately be an entire destruction of all the game in the Park."[156] Within a score of years their fears were fully vindicated, and their wishes realized in the passage of a Protective Act on May 7, 1894.

Altogether, the Yellowstone National Park bill represents a comprehensive glance into the principle of use without abuse. Nature was to be preserved, protected, and not improved. Art could not embellish what God had wrought in Yellowstone. The Act of Dedication became the touchstone of a national conservation policy whose blessings are legion. The bill did not carry an appropriation. It appears that the program was to be implemented entirely by voluntary service. In the years that followed there was a noble devotion which burned brightly, then waned, and almost died before resuscitation came. Eventually Yellowstone administrative experience evolved a program of surpassing merit which served as an example for the whole nation in the matter of managing certain phases of natural resources.

CHAPTER X
THE LAST ROUNDUP

Before Yellowstone could become accessible as a national playground a certain evolution of security had to take place. Indian tribes and buffalo herds were hindrances to both colonization and travel. A double-action roundup was needed to clear the way for an ephemeral phase, known as cattle days on the open range, and ultimate colonization within the approaches of the Park.

The early clash of white trappers and Indians has been reviewed. Passing of time worked no respite. Indeed, occasional friction swelled into almost constant strife. As settlers multiplied, the accumulation of past mutual grievances and suspicions rolled in from other scenes of combat like a moving tide and then broke into smaller waves, backwashing among the Rockies.[157] What was regarded as the natives' overbearing superiority was well matched by similar attitudes among the whites, but more important was the latter's greater strength.

Racial antagonisms and cultural conflicts swept every tribe into the whirlpool. Each in turn wrecked itself against the might of federal power. Finally, a crimson trail was stretched toward Yellowstone when Nez Percé Joseph chose to make it a part of his escape route.[158] The Park area and its environs was by way of becoming the Indians' last refuge. Therefore, the destiny of Yellowstone itself was contingent upon a solution of the Indian problem. Few people have the hardihood to seek pleasure at their peril, and that was precisely the condition until 1880. Only through complete Indian submission was the security issue brought to rest. How the events unfolded in this conflict between the settlers and the natives is a tale worth telling. Perhaps a brief exploration of the mutual opinions of disrespect will help give one a more balanced judgment of the factors that marshaled the two races into almost perpetual strife. It is an appropriate setting for the wind-up Indian scene, as narrated in the chapter on Chief Joseph's flight and surrender.

In the outset, English colonial charters granted belts of land to companies, or proprietors, without reference to Indian occupation. Still, a native people was found almost everywhere, but these savages were generally interested only in what might be had for the taking, whether from nature's bounty or an enemy tribe. Here was a land with resources for the sustenance of a thousand times their number. White men were given a generous reception at first. Indians generally displayed an Arabian type of hospitality and enjoyed showing homage to important visitors.

However, it became increasingly apparent that white and red men had little in common. The former were quick to recognize the Indians' simplicity and to exploit it. If judged by civilized standards, they were a people living as children, naïve and simple. They roamed about seeking game and plunder. Something to eat, a shred of clothing, a partial shelter, and a touch of adornment sufficed. They would exchange much corn, meat, beaver, and deerskins for a handful of beads, an iron hatchet, knife, ax, awl, or—best of all—fire water. Articles of real value were first given cheaply for items of scarcely any value at all. Mere curiosity led them into many commercial pitfalls. Ross, the trader, said, "Our people might have loaded a seventy-five-gun ship with provisions bought with buttons and rings."[159]

In the opinion of the Indians, palefaces were weaklings under torture. Still, white folks possessed strong medicine capable of moving great boats upon water without paddles. They also set great store upon boundaries on land and upon scratches on paper, which they said meant the same thing yesterday, today, and forever, and when a chief touched the quill to make his mark at the end of a writing it might bring trouble for years to come. Of course, the whites then said it was a treaty of cession by which the tribe had agreed to move the Indian village away and leave the settlers alone. These strange white people had a passion for killing trees continually, for making more tobacco than they could smoke, and for sending most of it away in their ships. White men were always working, mostly at tasks fit only for squaws, and they were fond of getting other white men and black men, and even trying to get red men, to work for them. Palefaces rarely moved their houses or changed their wives, and they would eat little more in harvest, or after a kill, than at any other time. Their restraints and their lack of restraint were equally unaccountable; and their numbers were ever swelling and their demands ever continuing for more and more land. They were, in truth, unfriendly neighbors, unwilling to blend the colony with the tribe; but they were firm, and on occasion impolite, in living their own lives and crowding the red men out. This brought battle now and then and a few blond scalps to dangle, but in war, too, the whites were unreasonable. They would not wait for Indian summer to do battle, and when once they took the path they were not content with raids, ambushes, and surprise attacks, but they would persist in a campaign under staunch command long after sensible, spasmodic Indian folk had grown weary.[160]

Thus, we may fancy, thought the Algonquins, Iroquois, Mohicans, Tuscaroras, and the Cherokees, the more sedentary eastern tribes early to experience the white man's aggression. At length they concluded that their first welcome had been unwise and wrecked themselves in efforts to drive the invaders out, but even in this purpose the tribes could not unite. Alliances reluctantly made between them were carelessly broken in the hour of peril. There is record of few confederations of Indian tribes that acted with any degree of unity. The ordinary tribal relationships were hostile. Indeed, every Indian tribe had at least one implacable enemy. As Chief Little Plume once said, "As long as there remains a Crow and a Piegan, so long will there be war."[161] Even in their campaigns with the white men they were inconstant and uncertain and quite as much the victims of treachery and double dealing as they were perpetrators of such offenses.

In what light was the Indian held by the white settlers of America? It has already been noted that Europe's Christian sovereigns and their governors disregarded the Indians' tribal ownership. They were primitive, pagan, and of ill repute. Human beings they were, perhaps, but with a hazy past, precarious present, and reckless future. If they could be converted to Christianity, well and good. That blessing would adequately compensate for the loss of their hunting grounds. Salvation in heaven was far better than savagery on earth.

Hence, we learn that the Pilgrim Fathers first "fell upon their knees and then upon the aborigines." Roger Williams, William Penn, Zebulon Pike, John C. Calhoun, and Brigham Young raised dissenting views, but theirs were as voices crying in the wilderness. Other more self-seeking councils prevailed. Many were the voices raised in condemnation.

General Phil Sheridan, in his oft-quoted comment, said, "There is no good Indian but a dead Indian.... If a white man steals, we put him in prison; if an Indian steals, we give him a blanket. If a white man kills, we hang him; if an Indian kills, we give him a horse to put the blanket on."[162]

Another characterization from a Montana frontiersman goes, "An Indian's heart is never good until he is hungry and cold."

Jim Stuart, than whom no man had more occasion to harshly judge Indians about Yellowstone, made the following observation:

> "Arro-Ka-Kee" or The Big Rogue [eminently appropriate, that name], stood six and a half feet high in his moccasins and weighed two hundred and seventy-five pounds. He was accompanied by "Saw-a-bee Win-an," who was a good Indian, although not dead, which I note as an exception to the general rule.[163]

The Earl of Dunraven professed to express the Sportsman's viewpoint when he said that Buffalo Bill and Texas Jack had the same feeling for Indians that they entertained toward game. That is to say, "They love them, and they slay them."

To the typical frontiersman, the Indian was a savage, ready to pounce on careless settlers, scalp them, burn their homes, and carry off their loved ones—in short, a "varmint." To the romantic writers, the Indians were children of nature, dwellers in shady forests and peaceful plains, earth's true nobility! Of course, the romantic writers seldom saw the natives and never lived with them. These errors, and many others, have been accepted as first-hand accurate observations. Indeed, the whole American Indian policy has been called a tragedy of errors, beginning with the naming of the race "Indian."[164]

Given this background of Indian ways, what might reasonably have been expected in the way of biracial adjustment? So little was the question of Indian welfare considered before 1880 that one cannot yet determine just what course might have solved the problem and brought about successful assimilation. First the English, and then the Americans, just muddled along, bribing here, cajoling there, and ultimately forcing everywhere, until this once proud and militant race was reduced to an inconsolable remnant, broken, defeated, and forlorn, but not forsaken.

Even when the white man's heart was good toward his red brother there was conflict in policies. Some thought his only salvation was in the adoption of agriculture and stock raising, but such a program was ruinous to the fur traders. The natives were the sinews of that business. The contrast in economy and culture, rival claims to land, and mutual feelings of superiority presented a gulf too vast for peaceful desires to overcome. It was the realization of this fact that impelled the wise Alexander Ross to say, "Peace in reality was beyond our power; it was but an empty name."[165] White men's activities and aggressions, under whatever guise, progressively deranged the Indians' economy. From every frontier came incessant demands for the reduction of Indian lands. Memorials to Congress, complaints to Indian commissioners, blistering editorials in local newspapers, all mark a stage in frontier development. Settlers were intolerant of checks upon their expansion, and few, indeed, were the officials who had the temerity to "arrest the tide of empire in the Territories."

Against this ominous force the Indians could only writhe and twist. The uneven contest waged for two and a half centuries, extending from Jamestown to the Pequot War and from Tippecanoe to Custer's defeat in the battle of the Little Bighorn in 1876. It is a tale of red fury and white vengeance such as might properly appertain to an age of barbarism but which presents an incongruous picture in a Christian land. It is correct to say that Indian-American relations were never improved but always embittered until the natives were reduced to the point of decimation.

Actually, the activities of fur trappers were not bitterly resented by the natives. Notwithstanding their excessive exploitation of the game there were compensations. A measure of accommodation resulted, which does not imply that there was any lack of violence. Theft, rivalry, and sheer joy of conflict were motives always operating. But there was a community of interest existing between the trapper and Indian which was impossible between the settler and Indian. Primitive existence was based upon tribal land and native game; both of these methods were denied by white settlers. Two types of economy were in conflict, and the red man's sun was already beginning to set. The clash is brought into clear relief in the story of the buffalo.

The bison is America's largest game animal, and for centuries it was most plentiful. Native to both plains and mountains it was a truly monarchial beast. A Spanish conquistador, Cabeza de Vaca, left an account of his observation upon the Texas plains in 1532: "The cows came from the north, and are found all over the land for over four hundred leagues."[166]

Several years later Coronado's report stated that they "had seen nothing but cows and sky." Ample supporting evidence sustains the fact that the number was legion. In 1832, Captain Bonneville stated, "As far as the eye could reach the country seemed absolutely blackened by innumerable herds." No census was ever taken, but competent authority suggests that sixty million head was a conservative estimate for the American plains in the early nineteenth century. Dependable calculations place the number persisting until 1870 at one fourth that number. At the end of the century the species was on the verge of extinction.

How did this remarkable diminution transpire? Here, indeed, is a roundup of mammoth proportions and far-reaching consequences. Bison were the natives' base of life, their tribal grubstake, a divine heritage. Only by wise conservation of this wild animal wealth were they enabled to maintain such a free and easy life.

After the Civil War railroads were projected into the buffalo country. Construction camps employed professional hunters to provide fresh meat. William F. Cody held a contract for the Union Pacific. It was this circumstance that gave him the name "Buffalo Bill." Such hunters set amazing records for a day's slaughter. Wasteful as this practice was, much greater prodigality emanated from the camps of certain foreign and American sportsmen and celebrities. Russian grand dukes, English lords, German counts, and American "no-a-counts" were alike in their insatiable instinct of destruction.[167] In way of extenuation it is fair to state that the emotional strain of bison chasing was overpowering.

However, it was the railroad itself that dealt the deadliest blow. Bison robes were too bulky to be handled by pack train, and only marginal profits accrued to wagon masters, but the effect of the iron horse was revolutionary. During the early seventies several lines conducted hunting excursions at low rates, guaranteeing shots from the windows. These facilities, supplemented by horse-and-wagon outfits, made the conquest of buffalo easy, especially when a definite profit was in view. That condition developed when the tanneries discovered bison hides could be used in leather wear. Thereafter, hides sold from $1.00 to $4.00 each, and a party of six hunters could kill and skin fifty or more in a day. In 1873, the Santa Fe alone carried 754,529 hides to eastern markets.[168] The traffic in buffalo hides grew and prospered and finally degenerated into debauching butchery.

Courtesy Union Pacific Ry.
The iron horse in Buffalo country—an early Wyoming scene

Thus, for a score of years, hundreds of expert riflemen combed the plains. They were armed with heavy Sharps and Winchester rifles, which boomed relentlessly at the ponderous bellowing herds. They took away the hides, brains, and tongues, leaving the rest to waste. It was wanton business written in crimson carcasses that dissolved into whitened bones. The railroad, therefore, destroyed frontier isolation and quickened the process of transforming a wilderness into a settled community. This increase in the tempo of frontier life was most apparent in the solution of the Indian problem.

As the great train, piled high with hides, rumbled away its reverberations were echoed by a more ominous rumble in the disconsolate camps of the red men. This was the final aggression, the ultimate grievance, and it set the people's teeth on edge. This inexorable white advance broke the natives' hearts. Once again, it was demonstrated that Indians and white men could not live together. It meant the annihilation of their way of life—their very existence—and a tragic fate—starvation.

Why did the government wink at this great imposition? Because after the railroad came colonization was imminent, but land overrun by wild Indians and buffalo could not be occupied. The herds had to be greatly diminished and the Indians, confined. The destruction of the bison was the most expedient means of bringing a recalcitrant race into subjection.[169] The nomads cagily rejected federal treaties until the bison commissary was destroyed. Then it was either fight or surrender. Several tribes elected to fight, to try to drive the white man back across the Missouri River. How much chance did they have in this belated effort? Indians were able warriors. They were slow to project, cautious to proceed, and firm to execute. Always cunning in strategy and subtle in ambush, they were certain to surprise.[170] An awareness of their limited numbers made them expert in decoy tactics and careful of their lives. Vigilant and watchful, they waited patiently for the advantage in time. They were quick and precise in estimating the strength of an enemy. Their code did not require a fight on equal terms. Indians, as a class, never equaled white men in the use of the rifle; however, they soon learned to improve the interval between firing and reloading.

Extremely superstitious, they carried certain charms about their persons, the efficacy of which was never doubted. Thus protected, they charged fearlessly into an affray. Too, youth was considered the proper time to die, and young men sometimes sought death, lending an air of fanaticism to the attacks.

Red men were greatly exhilarated by victory. They would vault and yell in fiendish glee as they flourished the gory scalps of their victims. By 1850, however, the destiny of Indian folk was established. Thereafter, their cries seldom bore the shrill staccato notes of victory but rather the mournful wail of defeat.

The legend of "Big Foot," great chief of the Flathead tribe, had been fulfilled. In 1804 he is supposed to have assembled his warriors in council and related this message:

> My heart tells me that the Great Spirit has forsaken us; he has furnished our enemies with his thunder to destroy us, yet something whispers to me, that we may fly to the mountains and avoid a fate, which, if we remain here, is inevitable. The lips of our women are white with dread, there are no smiles on the lips of our children. Our joyous sports are no more,

glad tales are gone from the evening fires of our lodges. I see no face but is sad, silent, and thoughtful; nothing meets my ears but wild lamentations for departed heroes. Arise, let us fly to the mountains, let us seek their deepest recesses where unknown to our destroyers, we may hunt the deer and bighorn, and bring gladness back to the hearts of our wives and our children![171]

Flight of the Indians to the mountains delayed, but did not preclude, the final conquest of their domain. They were only reserved for the last roundup. Eventually each tribe was brought to its respective day of reckoning. The government's policy was not always crystal clear. It fluctuated between the extremes of the "Quaker Peace Policy" and "Fire and the Sword Practice." However, the goal was the same; "blanket" Indians were to become "farmers," live in fixed abodes, and "walk the white man's road."[172]

After the Civil War the execution of this business was taken in hand by resolute fighting men. Hence, the military spirit was hardened toward the red men. Inexorably the race was pressed toward the appointed end. This work was accomplished by a series of military actions during the sixties and seventies.

In eastern Idaho Colonel Patrick Connor wrought swift vengeance on the Bannock nation in 1863. More than two hundred Indians were killed, a loss which forever broke down their force and effectiveness. This tribe was guilty of many depredations against migrants, miners, and Mormon settlers. Its forlorn remnants were assigned to the Fort Hall Reservation.

The plains tribes went on the war path in 1864. Colonel Chivington's command surprised and almost annihilated a peaceful band of Arapahos and Cheyennes in the Sand Creek massacre. What Chivington neglected General Custer completed four years later in the destruction of Black Kettle's village. In frontier parlance there was always battle when the Indians were killed and a massacre when the whites were the victims.[173]

In 1871 Generals Sherman and Sheridan projected a plan that eventuated in the complete conquest of the Kiowa and Comanche nations, but the Sioux were the most formidable obstacle to the colonization of Wyoming and Montana. They stood immovable astride the country lying between the headwaters of the Powder and Yellowstone rivers. This was the heart of the Sioux country—their last and favorite retreat. There, grass grew lush, and cool, sweet streams teemed with trout. Wild berries flourished, and a hunter could take his pick of buffalo, bear, elk, deer, antelope, and sheep. The great Sioux Chieftains, Red Cloud and Crazy Horse, together with Sitting Bull, the medicine man, protested bitterly in 1864 when John Bozeman, John Jacobs, and others began traveling across these lands.[174]

Federal ultimatums to assemble upon designated reservations were spurned by the Sioux, and a campaign of coercion was invoked with Brigadier Generals Alfred H. Terry and George Crook on far-flung phalanx and Colonel George A. Custer as the spearhead of the advance. Whether through reckless bravery, error of judgment, or necessity, Custer rushed into a treacherous situation, and his entire command (265 men) was annihilated. The day was June 25, 1876; the place, Little Bighorn River. It was a red letter event in the history of the Sioux, but it was a fleeting victory because the military, ably led by Colonel Nelson A. Miles, persisted in the campaign, and within a few months the mighty Sioux were either upon their appointed reservations or in exile. One of the last scenes in this solemn drama was enacted in June, 1881, at Miles City, Montana. Sixteen hundred Sioux, formerly under the leadership of Chief Rain-in-the-Face, were loaded on government steamboats for the Standing Rock Reservation in Dakota. Deep mourning issued from their camp on Tongue River:

> For two days and nights the Indians, and more especially the squaws, kept up their dismal howlings on taking farewell of their beloved homes and hunting grounds.[175]

Courtesy Union Pacific Ry.
Strong medicine against the Indians

As the buffalo and Indian went out, the Texas longhorn and "long drive" came in. The long drive lay across the tablelands of western Texas into Kansas, crossed the Santa Fe Trail at Dodge City, passed over the headwaters of the Salmon and across the Republican, and reached the South Platte at Ogallala. From this camp it followed the Oregon Trail to Fort Laramie, and then veered north over the Bozeman road.[176] The Texas Longhorn rolled up from the Southwest like a tidal wave once the way was opened. In fact, wild "speckled cattle" had been sharing part of the Texas plains for generations. Now, cattle raising became the great bonanza for a period.

The American cattle industry started back in 1521 when seven calves of Andalusian breed landed in Mexico. Gregorio was the pioneer ranchman on the continent. His flocks literally covered "a thousand hills." In spite of his vaquero's diligence, some of his stock strayed and formed the nucleus of a mighty herd.[177] From buffalo to range cattle is not a wide step; it was the capacity of the winter range to carry bison that suggested the cattle industry.

Conditions for stock raising were ideal in Texas. Millions of acres were plush carpeted with grama, mesquite, buffalo, and bluestem grasses. Early settlers gathered this wild stock into princely domains, and a new industry was born. The greatest problem was getting the cattle to market. New Orleans, Mobile, and Cuba were reached from Shreveport by boat. Still, there were the thriving northern cities where prices doubled those in Texas.

The first authenticated northern drive came in 1846 when Edward Piper drove one thousand Texas steers to Ohio. By 1865 Texas boasted one-eighth of all the cattle in America, as against a local population of less than half a million people. Somehow these cattle had to be gotten to market.

Returning Confederate veterans, broke but adventurous, saw the challenge of the open range and seized it. Loose, wild stock and "mavericks" were soon in the clutches of men and mustangs as wild as they. The first cowboys to make the long drive had need to be tough. There were many hazards menacing their way—non-treaty Indians, white thieves, floods, cyclones, and ever threatening stampedes. Sometimes the distance between water was more than a day's travel.

Cattle kings were men of great energy and enterprise. They took big risks, sometimes winning large profits and occasionally losing just as handsomely. Chisum, Hittson, Kennedy, O'Connor, and King were charmed names in the cattle fraternity. They nurtured their stock on hundred-thousand-acre ranches and then sent them forth to forage upon the public domain. It is estimated that six million head grazed their way to market over the Chisholm, Great Western, Shawnee, and other trails.

This wealth of the cloven hoof was entrusted to young athletes equally adept in forking a hoss, shooting a gun, and hurling a lariat. Cowboys were capable of both long, patient application to duty and vigorous relaxation when opportunity afforded. As a class they were steady and dependable. They delivered their charges in good condition at such shipping points as Sedalia, Abilene, Wichita, Ogallala, Glendive, and Miles City. This migration of cowmen and their herds was a strong, tremendous movement. It came with a rush and a surge, and in ten years it had subsided.

Even as the iron horse gave birth to the long drive, just so surely did it eventually destroy the big cattle business itself. Homesteaders came with the advance in transportation. There was a gradual, but irresistible, invasion of the open range. The "nesters" enclosed public domains. Thus, as the Indian gave way before the soldier and the hunter, so the cowboy yielded to the farmer. Ranches soon absorbed the eight million acres formerly overrun by bison and cattle.

There were still several regions ideally suited for stock raising—Montana, Wyoming, and Idaho. Toward these remote areas men looking for new, free grassland, timber, and water headed their cattle. The quest led them into the several great valley approaches to the Yellowstone Plateau. On both slopes of the great divide plants and grass grow steadily during summer, and the dry atmosphere cures and ripens them as they mature. This type of feed is highly nutritious and conducive to the development or perfection of form and strength of bone and muscle.

Among the pioneer ranchmen of the Rockies was Nelson Story. He netted more than ten thousand dollars in the placer mines of Alder Gulch. This sum he invested in a thousand Texas longhorns in 1866. With twenty-seven trail-hardened cowboys he brought the cattle to Montana. It was a tremendous undertaking to get them through a veritable gauntlet of hostile Indians and desperate white thieves. Three of his men were killed before they reached the end of Bozeman Trail.[178] Gold dust in exchange for beef proved more profitable than taking it from the placers themselves. Even the poorest ox would bring a hundred dollars, and so the traffic increased.

At this time the able Sioux chief, Red Cloud, served notice upon the government that he would kill every white man who traveled along that trail. It was not an idle boast; the record shows nearly two hundred casualties in the last six months of 1866. In fact, the Bozeman Trail became one long battleground, scene of such Sioux victories as the Fetterman and Wagon Box massacres. However, the military persisted, and with constant operations stemming from Forts Kearney and Smith the trail was kept open.[179]

In 1870 more than 40,000 Texas cattle reached Wyoming, Montana, and Idaho. Six years later the mountain Indians were largely liquidated. The removal of Red Cloud, Crazy Horse, and Sitting Bull opened the way for new cattle commonwealths. By 1880 the federal census reported 428,279 head in Montana and 521,213, in Wyoming. Soon the stockmen evolved a considerable network of mountain trails. The main artery went up the Yellowstone to Fort Custer and thence into Wyoming via Forts McKinney, Reno, and Fetterman to Cheyenne for shipping.

New names entered the stage with the growth of the cattle business such as Granville Stuart, James Fergus, A. J. Davis, John Ming, John Grant, Conrad Kohrs, R. S. Ford, Ancenny, Poindexter, Iliff, Flowerree, and George Searight.[180] Then there were the famous companies, The Union Cattle Company, The Swan Land and Cattle Company, North American, Powder River, Prairie, and Horseshoe being among the major names. Professor Dan E. Clark states that twenty Wyoming companies were organized in 1883, with individual capitalization from ten thousand to three million and a combined value of twelve million dollars.[181] In Montana, though, the Stock Growers Association represented an ownership of half a million head of cattle in 1884. The Eastern Montana Stock Growers Association of the same state claimed a capital investment of thirty-five million dollars.[182]

Under the impetus of such flourishing activity, the great river valleys stemming out of the Yellowstone Plateau were soon dotted by ranches. Wind, Snake, Madison, Gallatin, and Yellowstone valleys each received its quota. None of them quite reached the Park land, but Frederick Bottler's range almost impinged upon the northern border. It is probable that rancher invasion of the actual Park area was minor, if there was any. However, there was a rustler element that quite assuredly knew part of Yellowstone country.

The decade overlapping the sixties and seventies was the twilight period in frontier history. A transition was progressing from semi-lawlessness to orderly government. The arrogant Henry Plummer and his wicked gang of Innocents were liquidated by Montana Vigilantes in 1864, but another nefarious activity was taking heavy toll from the cattlemen. Horse and cattle rustlers found a lucrative business in preying upon the large herds grazing the open range. These cunning men would establish a rendezvous in some sequestered place like Teton Basin or the upper Madison Valley. From such a position they would make forays upon the stock owned by the big interests. The worst offenders, and those most difficult to apprehend, were men who at some time had been connected with the cattle business. Sometimes they altered the brands, but often a crisscross plan of shipment was followed; that is, Wyoming and Montana stock was whisked down to the Utah market; while Idaho material went east to Cheyenne. Men such as "Teton" Jackson, Ed Harrington, and Bob Tarter worked both sides of the Divide. The high meadows in and near Yellowstone were ideal for their purpose. It is also claimed that the notorious Butch Cassidy gang, long ensconced upon the Green River, made occasional forays among stock ranging near the southeastern borders of the Park.

It is a fact that the Washburn-Langford-Doane party encountered representatives of the rustler element upon their last day in the Park area. Mr. Langford left this account:

> Mr. Hauser and Mr. Stickney all through the day were a few miles in advance of the rest of the party, and just below the mouth of the canyon they met two men who manifested some alarm at the sight of them. They had a supply of provisions packed on riding saddles and were walking beside their horses. Mr. Hauser told them that they would meet a large party up the canyon, but we did not see them, and they evidently cached themselves as we went by. The Upper Madison in this vicinity is said to be a rendezvous for horse thieves.[183]

It was actually an area of operation for the Murphy and Edmonson gang of desperadoes. Langford and Doane came upon three of their horses which they caught and pressed into service during the rest of the journey.[184] In 1874 the Earl of Dunraven remarked that the Yellowstone traveler had to keep a sharper lookout for white horse thieves than for redskin robbers.

By 1873 stock losses by rustling were so great as to force counter measures. The Wyoming Stock Growers Association hired a large force of detectives and inspectors. The movements of every newcomer were watched with suspicious vigilance; blacklists were circulated. The penalties for mis-branding and marking were doubled, and prosecution was swift and vigorous. These hard-hitting policies soon brought the problem under control.

Thus ended the major evil of another era, and the rustlers were hustled into that Shangri-la of frontier romance where "happy ghosts," as Professor Paxson has said, "will endure forever, a happy heritage for the American mind."[185]

By 1880 the hostile human barriers, red and white, had been removed from the way. The West's unsettled areas were so broken as to destroy the frontier line. Yellowstone was still a wilderness, but it was accessible to man.

CHAPTER XI
CHIEF JOSEPH'S TRAIL OF BLOOD

The Nez Percé Indians were first encountered in 1805 by the Lewis and Clark Expedition. They were at home in the region of eastern Oregon and western Idaho. The Wallowa Valley, "land of winding water," was their especial habitat. They referred to themselves as "Nim-i-pu," "the real people." The name Nez Percé or "pierced noses" was a French cognomen of doubtful validity.

The Nez Percé were not highly centralized in tribal organization. There were several factions, but in the third quarter of the 19th century, Tu-eka-kas, or Old Joseph, as the Reverend Henry H. Spaulding called him, was a ranking chief. The Nez Percé befriended the Lewis and Clark party by taking care of their horses. Thenceforth their policy was one of cooperation and friendship with the white man, combined with a stern insistence upon their rights. Joseph hoped for biracial adjustment. To this end he always befriended the government, but it was understood that his domain should never be invaded.

Federal Indian treaties made after 1855 brought white settlers ever closer to the Nez Percé domain. Certain unprincipled Oregon people looked greedily upon the choice lands of Wallowa. As the pressure increased there was neither political will nor honor to curb the aggressors. Hence, the noble Nez Percé, like all red men before them, were thrown on the defensive.

Old Joseph sensed the impending issue, and before his death in 1871 he exacted a promise from his son, Young Joseph, that he would never give up Wallowa.[186] Years of increasing pressure brought a full vindication of Old Joseph's fears and a realization of responsibility to his son.

By 1876 the federal government was yielding to local demands for Nez Percé evacuation, and a commission brought in the usual report. The non-treaty Indians had no standing and should be made to conform. They should be required to join the other tribes on the Lapwai Reservation.

General O. O. Howard was directed to enforce the decree. The Nez Percé were greatly distressed. Several conferences were held. Young Joseph resisted manfully. By this time he was in his thirty-seventh year. Fully mature, he stood six feet tall, and his rugged body disclosed tremendous energy and sinew. His mind was keen, but his spirit was disciplined. He was ready for his work.

The military authority gave Chief Joseph thirty days to get his people on the reservation; June 14, 1877 was the deadline.[187] In vain Joseph pleaded for an extension of time until fall. Orders had been given by the military. Joseph also gave orders. His people gathered in their stock and prepared for the migration; it was better for deer to be penned up than to fight the grizzly. There were many soldiers at Howard's back; the odds were too great. They must surely obey or perish.

Other Nez Percé leaders were not so wise. Chiefs Tu-hul-hul-sote and White Bird wanted to fight. They were chiefs in their own right and had large followings. Still, Joseph was willing to sacrifice honor and prestige by resisting war.[188] He valued his people's blood above his own pride. While the great man humbly revealed his integrity, trouble brewed in darker minds.

Courtesy of Haynes, Inc.
Chief Joseph, war chief of the Nez Percé.

An old man in White Bird's band was taunting young Wal-ait-its, whose father, Eagle Blanket, had been slain by a white settler in 1876. "You are brave! Why don't you go and show it by killing the man who killed your father?" The goad fired him to a fever of revenge. He and two companions sprang upon their horses. When they returned to the council, four white men had answered the last call. Wal-ait-its shouted, "Why do you sit here like women? The war has begun already." Tu-hul-hul-sote had organized a war party. Joseph still hoped for a peaceful settlement. It could not be. The war fever spread, and Indian blood was on fire. He must either lead or step aside. He chose to defend his people and their cause.[189]

On the morning of June 17 a battle took place in White Bird's Canyon. Captain Perry, assisted by Lieutenants Theller and Parnell, was approaching with two troops of cavalry. Joseph had taken command. He quickly conceived of a daring triple-action assault. With instinctive judgment he chose strategic positions and gave brisk orders. He moved among his men, encouraging them, and directing them from place to place. He seemed an all-pervading, dominating force. He deployed his braves upon the heights. Protected by rocks and brush, they threaded a bobbing course upon the beleaguered cavalry. Dismounting and aiming deliberately, they decimated the ranks of soldiery.[190]

White Bird Canyon stands next to the Custer and Fetterman massacres as the Waterloo of white troops before Indians, but the conditions were in no way identical. The advantages were equally balanced at White Bird.

Young Joseph had proved himself a great war chief in a single engagement. From this time forth his destiny was with him. He was the last mighty Indian, and his name was Hin-mut-too-yah-lat-kekht, meaning "Thunder strikes out of water and travels to loftier heights." Wherever one touches him he is great; every incident and circumstance discloses a big man. He exercised unerring judgment in strategy and tactics. Years afterward Joseph said, "The Great Spirit puts it into the heart of man to know how to defend himself."

The defeat of Perry threw General Howard's command into a frenzy of activity. Orders went out for reinforcements, and troops moved toward Lewiston from every direction. By the last of June, Howard was in the field. The wily Indian leader had moved his entire nation beyond the raging Salmon River where he made a stand. Said Howard, "A safer position was unchoosable, nor one more puzzling and obstructive."[191]

Howard's soldiers experienced great difficulty in going where Joseph's whole band had gone. This was just the prelude to a game of hide and seek that lasted from late June to early October and lengthened into a dozen engagements as the two forces moved eastward for the space of sixteen hundred miles.

In the weeks that followed, General Howard learned to respect his adroit and formidable foe. Joseph's forces never exceeded three hundred warriors. The whole band numbered about seven hundred. General Howard's command numbered five hundred and eighty regulars, and it was later augmented by four separate commands in the course of the pursuit. The forces of Joseph and Howard came to grips on the banks of Clearwater River. There the Nez Percé fought with such courage and precision that the battle must be written up as a draw.[192]

Joseph was now ready to fight to a finish, but his captains voted for a retreat. Again he bowed to the will of the majority. They were destined to pursue a "trail of tears" during the next three months. It was a march as dramatic as the "flight of a Tartar tribe."[193] The band was on the move, over the Lolo Trail—a terrific route. They lived on the country—roots, berries, and game.

Joseph could cope with one enemy, but the military resources of the whole Western Department baffled him. He found his exit from the Bitter Roots obstructed by Captain Charles C. Rawn from Fort Missoula. Rawn demanded surrender; Joseph parleyed until his forces outflanked Rawn's position and escaped. At this juncture we see his humanity in making a treaty of forbearance with the settlers in Bitter Root Valley.

The entire Nez Percé tribe was overtaken and attacked at daybreak, on the Big Hole, by General John Gibbon's force of one hundred and eighty soldiers, augmented by some of the erstwhile peaceful settlers. The slaughter on both sides was: whites, twenty-nine killed, forty wounded; Indians, eighty-three dead, wounded undetermined (fifty-three of the dead were women and children).[194] Joseph commented bitterly, "The Nez Percé never make war on women and children." Notwithstanding the confusion of this surprise attack, Joseph's band recovered and moved on. Howard was still on their trail.

Several Salmon City, Idaho, freighters fell before the drunken wrath of some of Joseph's braves on Birch Creek. In Camas Meadows Howard maneuvered for a stand. The result was the loss of many mules and horses. Worse still was the mortal wounding of three soldiers and serious injury of five others. Just as Howard was expecting to pounce upon his prey, the crafty chief whirled around and inflicted a surprising blow, escaping almost scot free.

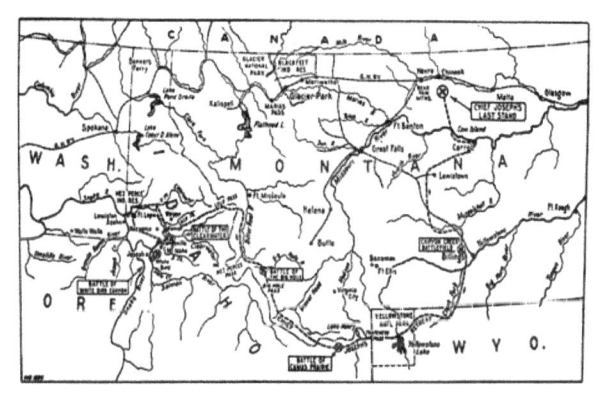

A general map of Chief Joseph's flight.

Several days later the Nez Percé were trailing up the Madison River within the Park. They were strangers in Yellowstone and the most unwelcome tourists it has ever known. Within this identical week Secretary of War William T. Sherman and an escort of five concluded a tour and left for Fort Ellis. They did not see "any signs of Indians, and felt at no moment more sense of danger than we do here."[195] A few days later they were cognizant of their lucky break. Near Madison Junction the Nez Percé met a prospector named Shively whom they pressed into service as a guide. A few days later they seized another miner named Irwin, and held him for a while.

THE RADERSBURG TOURISTS

The Nez Percé spent the night of August 23 in camp on the banks of the Firehole River, above the narrows. At daybreak the next morning several Indians appeared in the camp of some tourists from Radersburg, Montana. The personnel of this party were Mr. and Mrs. George F. Cowan; Mrs. Cowan's brother and sister, Frank and Ida Carpenter; Charles Mann; William Dingee; Albert Oldham; A. J. Arnold; and Henry Myers. A prospector, named Harmon, was also associated with the Cowan party at this time.

These people were just preparing to break up the "home" camp located at this terminus of the wagon road. For the past week they had been enjoying themselves on horseback visits to the geyser basins, and several of them had been to the lake and canyon.

Dingee asked the Indians, "What are you?" "Snake Injun," one replied. Later they admitted they were Nez Percé and made a demand for coffee and bacon. Cowan refused to give them any, and as one who called himself "Charley" attempted to give a signal the stern Cowan peremptorily ordered him to "keep hands down!" Right there a special resentment was engendered toward the "older man." Frank Carpenter asked them if any harm was in store for the party. The spokesman said, "Don't know, maybe so." He gave them to understand that since the Big Hole Battle the Nez Percé were double-minded toward the white man.[196]

The worried little party held a hasty consultation, and in view of their limited arms and ammunition they decided, with serious misgivings, to make an appeal to the chiefs for their deliverance.

They, therefore, hooked up the team, saddled their horses, and joined the Indian caravan, which turned eastward and journeyed up Nez Percé Creek. After proceeding a couple of miles the wagon was abandoned, its contents rifled, and the spokes knocked out for whip handles. By midday the Radersburg case had come to the attention of the chiefs. A council was held at the base of Mary Mountain in which it was decided that the tourists were to be liberated. Poker Joe spoke for the chiefs:

> Some of our people knew Mrs. Cowan and her sister at Spokane House. The soldiers killed many Nez Percé women and children on the Big Hole. But we do not hurt Montana people. You may go. Take old horses and do not spy.[197]

They were relieved of their saddles, guns, and horses, worn-out animals being substituted for the latter. The white men nodded acceptance of these extraordinary terms. They were glad to part with the tribe and retrace their course. Within a half hour, two of the white men, Arnold and Dingee, abandoned their horses and ducked into the forest. Hidden Indian scouts were obviously expecting just such behavior. A few minutes later seventy-five braves swooped upon Cowan's party, demanding the missing members. Cowan could only plead ignorance.

Whereupon, Charley said, "You will have to come back." The little band again turned eastward with leaden spirits.

Angry Indians were milling around on all sides, each waiting for the other to start an attack. Suddenly Um-till-lilp-cown, one of the three Idaho murderers, fired at Cowan, hitting him in the thigh.[198] At the same time Oldham felt a twinge on both cheeks as a bullet passed through his face. Carpenter saw an Indian aiming at him, and thinking some of the Nez Percé might be Catholics he made the sign of the cross. His act may have disconcerted the warrior for he did not fire. Oldham managed to get away through a thicket, while Cowan was so stunned he fell to the earth. His wife jumped down from her horse and clasped him to her bosom, but they dragged her away. Another shot, from close range, struck him in the forehead. His wounds were considered fatal, and he was left to die. At this juncture Poker Joe arrived from the chiefs, who had got word of the attack, and he stopped the onslaught.

In the shuffle and commotion that ensued, Myers, Harmon, and Mann made their getaway. Mann felt a bullet whiz through his hat as he ran among the trees. Each man went in a different direction and carried the impression that he was the sole survivor. This was the opinion of each of the separated contingents. Each considered all missing ones as obviously dead.

The unscattered survivors, including Mrs. Cowan, her brother Frank, and sister Ida, were again taken captives. Although their treatment during the next twenty-four hours was considerate, it was a period of great mental anguish for them. They spent the night by Chief Joseph's campfire, and considering the circumstances their attitude toward him was most interesting. Mrs. Cowan said of him:

> My brother tried to converse with Chief Joseph, but without avail. The Chief sat by the fire, sombre and silent, foreseeing in his gloomy meditations possibly the unhappy ending of his campaign. The "noble red man" we read of was more nearly impersonated in this Indian than in any I have ever met. Grave and dignified, he looked a chief.[199]

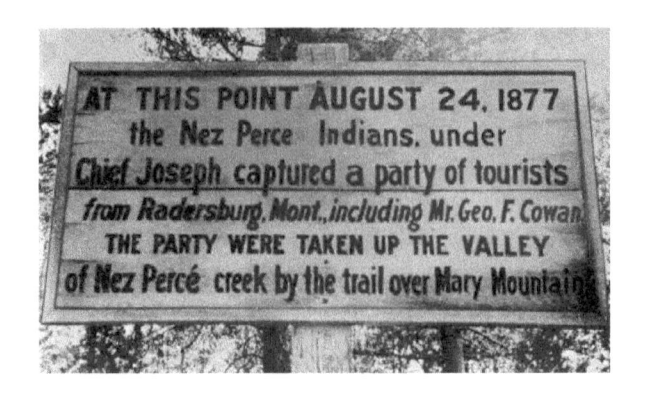

Radersburg tourist party marker

W. S. Chapman
George F. Cowan stands up to Nez Percé warriors.

On the evening of the twenty-fifth the captives were provided with two horses and released near the Mud Volcano. "They must not go too fast"; therefore no saddle for Ida or horse for Frank were provided. Poker Joe directed them to go down the river "quick." This they did as rapidly as their broken-down ponies would carry them. Burdened with grief and care, they made their way over Mount Washburn and beyond Tower Falls where they came upon a detail of soldiers who supplied their most urgent necessities and found them a ride to Bozeman.

In going down Yellowstone Valley they were the recipients of much sympathy from the settlers. As they entered Bozeman,

Lieutenant Doane and a considerable number of Crow Indian scouts and soldiers were leaving for the Park. Carpenter joined Doane's command, with the intention of returning to the scene of the attack and attending to the burial of his brother-in-law. In mourning, Mrs. Cowan and her sister continued on to Radersburg.

But Cowan was a sturdy being; he would not die. It was nearly sundown when he regained consciousness. Wounded in thigh and head, he yet pulled himself up from his rocky "grave." Unfortunately an Indian sentinel observed his movement, drew a bead, and fired. Cowan dropped with a fresh wound in his left side. He now felt that they had "fixed" him beyond all hope of recovery. However, he remained conscious and lay motionless until darkness settled.

Then he started a crawling retreat toward Lower Geyser Basin, nine miles away.[200] What an eternity August 24 must have seemed! Were his wife and friends safe? He had little basis for hoping so. Could he make a getaway, and was it worth the effort? About midnight he apprehended motion among the cinquefoil. It was an Indian scout, raised to elbow posture, listening. Cowan remained perfectly quiet until the watchman relaxed; then he circled the danger zone by more than a mile. Onward he dragged his tortured body, alternately resting and crawling. He finally reached the deserted wagon where his bird dog faithfully waited. She growled and menaced until recognition dawned, then hovered over him like a protecting mother. There was no food anywhere to be found, but he gathered up the sheets of Carpenter's diary. Cowan pressed doggedly on toward the campground in the Lower Geyser Basin. During the third day a band of Indians came by his hiding place. They were friendly Bannocks of Howard's command, but he did not know and took no chance.

On the twenty-seventh he reached the old camp, found matches, and gathered spilled coffee grains and an empty can. These netted him a cup of coffee. He passed the night there. The following day he crawled over by the road, and that effort taxed his strength to the limit. It was enough, as relief came in the form of two of Howard's scouts, Captain S. G. Fisher and J. W. Redington. The latter said, "Who in hell are you?"

"I'm George Cowan of Radersburg."

"You don't say! We've come to bury you."

They rendered first aid, provided food, and left Cowan by a roaring fire with the assurance that the main force would gather him up within two days. Mr. Fee has deftly described the abrupt termination of that hard earned felicity:

> Cowan ate enough to keep himself alive and lay down in silent joy to sleep the night through. Towards morning he was awakened by awful heat, and found to his dismay that the vegetable mold he was lying on had taken fire and encircled him with flames. He rose on hands and knees and suffering terribly, crawled across the charred area to safety. His hands and legs were badly burned.[201]

In the meantime his scattered companions were being united. Mr. Harmon was the first to reach General Howard's encampment at Henrys Lake. Arnold and Dingee arrived after several days and nights of hardship. Myers and Oldham were encountered by Howard's scouts. The latter was in a pitiful state. His tongue was so swollen, as a result of his wound, that he could not speak. Shock and exposure to the cold nights, together with lack of food for four days, had left its mark upon them all.

Howard reluctantly took the whole delegation along, and on August 29 they joined Cowan in the Lower Geyser Basin. Arnold said Cowan was a "most pitiful looking object. He was covered with blood, which had dried on him, and he was as black as a negro." Here Cowan learned of his wife's safety, and that news, together with his friend Arnold's "unremitting attentions," pulled him through. The army surgeon ministered to the physical wounds of the men but no sympathy was forthcoming. The Radersburg men desired to return home by way of Henrys Lake, but they were bundled along with the command, over roads that were:

> simply horrible and almost impassable for wagons. At times we were compelled to lower them over precipices with ropes, and again we would hitch a rope to a wagon and pull it up the hill by man power.[202]

In the meantime Frank Carpenter, along with Lieutenant Doane's command, pressed toward the Park. They found Henderson's ranch buildings in flames. A band of renegade Nez Percé were spreading terror in their wake. Camp was established there anyway, and a courier arrived, directing Lieutenant Doane to mark time until joined by Colonel Charles C. Gilbert and the

Seventh Infantry. Carpenter's plan to return and bury Cowan was again frustrated. A promise to perform that function, given by a frontiersman named Houston induced Carpenter to return to Bozeman. There he learned that all members of the party were safe and accounted for except Cowan. The news that Cowan was still alive reached him a few days later when he met the two scouts who had found Cowan just a week before. Perhaps no one else could have convinced him his friend was alive.

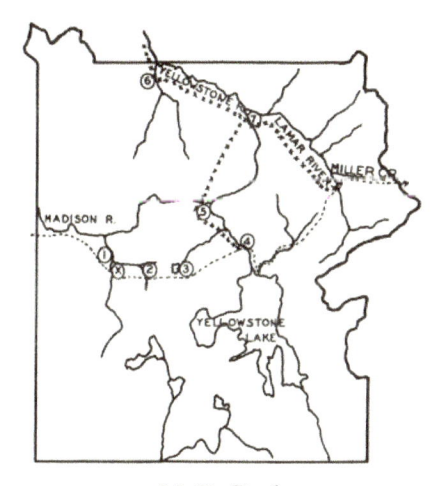

M. D. Beal
Detail map showing Nez Percé movements in Yellowstone Park.

Legend:

- - - - - - Route of main band of Nez Percé Indians.

x x x x x Route of marauding band to the north and back to main
   x   band.

   X   Cowan party camp west of Fountain Geyser.

   1   Nez Percé camp in lower Geyser Basin.

   2   Where Cowan party was attacked and Cowan shot.

   3   Mary Lake and Mary Mountain.

   4   Nez Percé camp and crossing of Yellowstone River near

                Mud Volcano.

    5   Helena party camp on Otter Creek where Indians attacked.

    6   Mammoth Hot Springs.

    7   Baronett's Bridge across Yellowstone River.

A telegram to Mrs. Cowan brought her posthaste from Radersburg. She reached Bottler's ranch, a distance of one hundred and seventy-five miles, in thirty-one hours. The reunion was effected on September 24, exactly one month from the date of the attack.

THE HELENA TOURIST PARTY

Other Yellowstone visitors were caught in the Nez Percé net as it rolled across the Park. It has been sufficiently indicated that Chief Joseph maintained a role of dignified restraint, but there were unprincipled factions under less responsible leadership which he could not keep under his thumb. While the main tribe was slowly weaving its course through the Park some of the reckless young men were foraging far and wide. It is also correct to observe that bitter resentment had been smoldering toward the entire white race since the battle of Big Hole. The Nez Percé were inclined to regard every white man as an enemy.

This Indian psychology, or "bad heart," helps account for the conduct of a marauding band of White Bird's "bucks" toward a party of Helena tourists north of Hayden Valley. There were ten men in this company: A. J. Weikert, Richard Dietrich, Frederick Pfister, Joseph Roberts, Charles Kenck, Jack Stewart, August Foller, Leslie Wilkie, L. Duncan, and a negro cook named Benjamin Stone.

On the morning of August 25 this party was traveling along between Sulphur Mountain and Mud Volcano when they observed a body of horsemen fording the river. They correctly apprehended that the mounted men were hostile Nez Percé.[203] Thereupon, the tourists hastily repaired to the timber near the forks of Otter Creek and formed camp. It was a well-chosen position and might have been defended effectively if the natural advantages had been utilized.

However, no harm came to them that day or night. The next morning Weikert and Wilkie went reconnoitering in the vicinity of Alum Creek where they encountered a detail of the marauders. The white men retreated speedily, but Weikert was hit in the shoulder in the exchange of fire.

In the meantime the camp on Otter Creek was raided. Instead of posting a lookout the campers were huddled together, waiting for dinner, and hoping they would continue to escape notice. Mr. Kenck's mind was active with forebodings; addressing the elderly colored cook, he said, "Stone, what would you do if the Indians should jump us?" Stone laconically replied, "You all take care ob yoursel' and I'll take care ob me."[204] In that instant the Nez Percé struck. The eight tourists scattered like surprised deer. Kenck was hit and killed; Stewart was shot, fell, and was overtaken. He pleaded so earnestly for his life that he charmed their savage impulse and was spared. Dietrich fell in the creek and remained there four hours.

Ben Stone ran as fast as his old legs would carry him, but in midstream they gave out, and he lay prone in the water. The red men left as suddenly as they came. When Wilkie and Weikert arrived they fell in with some of the others and started for Mammoth. Joseph Roberts and August Foller had slipped away, and as it later transpired they went west to Madison River and thence to Virginia City and home. The other seven reached Mammoth, where Dietrich and Stone unfortunately decided to remain pending the arrival of Roberts and Foller. Dietrich had promised young Roberts' mother that he would be responsible for his safe return.

On August 31, Weikert and McCartney, the "hotel" owner, left for the Otter Creek campground to look for the two missing men and to inter the remains of Mr. Kenck. The latter business accomplished, they were returning when the renegades, who had just committed a fresh deed of vengeance at Mammoth, met them at the falls of East Gardner River. A lively skirmish ensued, in which Weikert's horse was killed and the others got away, before a sheltered position was reached. The desperadoes withdrew, and the white men pursued a cautious course to Mammoth. It was in this stage of their journey when McCartney, observing that Weikert was pale as a ghost, asked, "Do I look pale?" "No," replied his friend, "Do I?" McCartney answered, "No." Each was trying hard to "buck up" the other's morale.[205]

Upon reaching Mammoth they learned about Dietrich's fate. On August 31 he and Stone saw a band of Indians pass McCartney's place. They were Nez Percé on their way to Henderson's ranch which they ransacked and burned. The next day, when they returned, Ben Stone made a precipitous exit from the cabin and ran up Clematis Gulch. Dietrich, evidently believing the Indians friendly, stood in the doorway. They shot and killed him. Several days before he had expressed a premonition of death to Weikert. In view of this condition his conduct was attributed to inexperience.

Ben Stone, it will be remembered, was the colored cook who had a narrow call in the Otter Creek melee. This second escapade was even a closer shave. Stone evidently possessed sufficient of the quaint humor characteristic of his race to warrant the perpetuation of an amusing frontier tale.

Following is the story, as related by Stone to the men at Henderson's ranch, before he had fully recovered from his scare. The account begins at the end, wherein the negro was challenged by a sentry as he approached the camp:

"'Halt, who comes dar?' 'Ben Stone.' 'Come in, Ben Stone.' An' you bet I come a-runnin'." Then he rehearsed the day's activities in this wise:

"I seed de Injuns comin' aroun' in de foah-noon dis mornin'. I tole Dietrich we had better be a gettin' out ob dis, but he kept a sayin' 'I'll neber go back to Mrs. Roberts widout Joe.' 'Bout 'leven or twelve o'clock Dietrich says, 'I'll go down an' change de hosses, re-picket dem, while you git dinnah, Ben.' 'I say "all right."

"Well, while he was gone a changin' ob de hosses, I looked out ob de doah an' seed a Injun stick his head up ober a rock out in front ob de house. I didn't wait for no lebe, I didn't, an' dropped eberyting an' bolted trew de back doah, I did, up into de timbah an' laid down awaitin' for somethin' to do next. I seed de Injuns all 'bout de house an' pears like dey was mighty anxious to fine me, but I wasen't anxious to fine dem. It war gettin' along towards night, and I clim a tree. Purty soon a big Injun rode right down under de tree a searchin' aroun' for me. I jes hel' my bref an' say to myself, 'Oh Mr. Injun; good Mr. Injun, don't look up dis way!' Boys, I 'clare to goodness I could hab touched dat Injun's head wif my foot—but I didn't!

"Bye'm-bye de Injun go away down towards de springs an' I got down on to de ground an' strike for de side ob de mountain whar I laid down. I was a layin' in de brush, when all ob a sudden I heerd a crackin' in de brush. Den, boys, I got right down on my knees an' prayed (an' I hope de God Almighty forgive me, I neber prayed before sense I lef' my modder's knee), but I jes got down an' say 'O Lod God A'mighty, jes help me out ob dis scrape an' I will neber interfere wid you no moah!' I heerd dis noise an' a crashin' in de bushes again, an' I jes laid down wid my face to de ground an' I spected to feel de tom hawk in de back of my head. All ob a sudden I turned ober and dar I seed a big black bar a lookin' at me. Boys, I neber was so glad to see a bar afore in all my life. De bar he got up an' run, an' I got up an' run to de top ob de mountain when I saw youah camp fire an' heah I' is—bress de Lod!"[206]

At the conclusion of this delineation two of Lieutenant Doane's friendly Indian scouts rushed toward Stone with arms extended, exclaiming "How, how!" The distraught negro nearly fainted from a fresh attack of fright. No amount of explanation could convince him they were not after his scalp. Indeed, he was certain that the larger buck was Chief Joseph himself![207]

Finally his friends Weikert and McCartney arrived, and thereafter his emotions switched around to unrestrained gratitude to his maker. The rest of the night was given over to lusty expressions of praise and hallelujahs. When objections were raised Stone replied that God had saved his life twice and he was going to thank Him as long and loud as he liked. Lieutenant Doane was forced to post a guard to maintain the peace.

At this time word arrived that Roberts and Foller were in Virginia City. The remains of poor Dietrich, who had been sacrificed so unnecessarily, were taken to Helena by Weikert. He also took the remains of Charles Kenck there for final interment.

General Howard leisurely pursued the fleeing Nez Percé marauders up the Lamar Valley after repairing Baronett's bridge which they had partially burned. In the meantime, Joseph's main band had crossed Yellowstone River, near Mud Volcano, and followed the east bank toward the lake. Shively, their captive guide, directed them up Pelican Creek to its source. Here

Joseph's scouts reported the presence of miners on the Lamar and Howard's spies in the area. The scouts further noted that Colonel Sturgis and eight troops of the Seventh Cavalry from the Crow Agency on the Little Rosebud were in position astride the regular Absaroka Pass near Hart (Heart) Mountain. Joseph was now cut off between the commands of Howard and Sturgis.

This situation demanded desperate action. The threat of interception brought forth a masterful stratagem from the Red Napoleon. Upon reaching the Lamar-Shoshone Divide, Joseph turned abruptly southward. Was he striking for Stinking Water? Sturgis could not risk this chance. He, therefore, whirled in that direction, pursuing a parallel course—the summit dividing their forces.

Joseph's feint worked; he passed by Sturgis' right flank. He now doubled back beyond the main Absaroka gateway, toward Clarks Fork, and plunged through a "hidden" pass located by his feverish scouts. He fairly hurled his people over the rocky barrier and dropped them pell-mell down to Clarks Fork.[208] It was his task to get the protection of the Crow Indians, cross the Buffalo country, and reach Canada and safety.

By the time Colonel Sturgis had discovered the deception General Howard arrived. Indeed, he was already painfully pursuing the elusive foe through the awful earth gash Joseph had taken. When the two officers met there was an impressive demonstration of cussing. Wasn't there a unit in the whole United States' Army that could outwit this red devil?

Spurred by the barbed goad of frustration and anger, Sturgis pressed on in hot pursuit. On September 13, his troops were in their saddles at 5 A.M. When they drew rein at 12 P.M. sixty miles had been negotiated. Joseph's band was still ahead! By daybreak the soldiers were on the trail again. They halted on the lower Yellowstone, near Billings. Discouragement pervaded their ranks; by common consent the Seventh Cavalry was ready to quit.[209] They felt a comrade's compassion for General Howard's command.

Two miles away the Nez Percé were headed for the mouth of Canyon Creek. "Let's beat 'em to it," and away they sped. The Indians gained the protection first. Officers Benteen, Otis, French, and Merrill's battalions maneuvered bravely and well, but the watchful Nez Percé kept them back. There was rapid sharp shooting on both sides. When they finally broke through the Indians had disappeared.

> Strewn upon the dusty battlefield were a dozen dead horses, five soldiers dead and eleven wounded. Night fell, and a cool wind drummed a funeral dirge upon the mind of many a restless soldier. When General Howard arrived the next day Sturgis was still on the trail. A band of Crow Indians had joined the white forces and were spoiling for a fight, but Sturgis had already wind-broken his horse and run out of rations. The Indian pace was too fast for him, but the rapidity of this flight forced them to abandon nine hundred horses.[210] However, Chief Joseph's pony supply was augmented by a wholesale seizure from the Crows. He had crossed the Musselshell; next he would ford the Missouri which would bring them within the protection of Montana's northern wastelands. Canada was not far away. Howard could never catch him now. Perhaps there would be time to kill some buffalo, feed their weary ponies, and rest their squaws.

He was reckoning without the telegraph and the ambitious interest of Colonel Nelson A. Miles at Fort Keogh on Tongue River. On September 17, a rider brought Howard's S. O. S.; immediately Colonel Miles was all action. That very day he had three hundred and eighty-three men across Tongue River and on the march. Twenty-four hours later they were fifty miles away. They crossed the Musselshell River and marched on to the Missouri, where a steamboat ferried them across. Ever crowding men and beasts, he caught up with the Nez Percé on the twenty-ninth of September.

Joseph had made sure that Howard and Sturgis were far behind. In fact, they were deliberately slow. "We must not move too fast lest we flush the game." Actually both of their commands were much depleted. The real job was up to Miles; they were providing the decoy. This time it worked.

Again, as at Big Hole, Joseph failed to anticipate trouble from other quarters than Howard's. The one-armed general was six days' march in the rear. Surely they could relax now. Upon reaching the Bear Paw Mountains he considered his position secure. He posted no scouts. Joseph obviously believed they had crossed the international boundary. Later, as he looked back in retrospection, he said:

I sat down in a fat and beautiful country. I had won my freedom and the freedom of my people. There were many empty places in the lodges and the council, but we were in a land where we would not be forced to live in a place we did not want. I believed that if I could remain safe at a distance and talk straight to the men that would be sent by the Great Father, I could get back to the Wallowa Valley and remain in peace. That is why I did not allow my young men to kill and destroy the white settlers after I began to fight. I wanted to leave a clean trail, and if there were dead soldiers on that trail, I could not be to blame. I had sent out runners to Sitting Bull to tell him that another band of red men had been forced to run from the soldiers of the Great Father, and to propose that we join forces if we were attacked. My people were recovering their health and the wounded getting better of their hurts.[211]

Joseph's coveted felicity was roughly arrested on the dawn of September 30. His brief respite was assailed by the dual forces of nature and men. Snow flurries whipped the lodge flaps. Horses milled restlessly. An Indian youth slipped out to reconnoiter. He perceived the rapid approach of a formidable force of cavalry. The alarm was given.

Instantly the Nez Percé camp was churning with commotion. A hundred ponies were laden with squaws and papooses. They fled north under an escort of sixty braves. The balance of the encampment fairly clawed out positions of defense along a crescent-shaped ravine called Snake Creek.

By this time the military was in position. Colonel Miles sized up the situation at a glance and barked commands: "Captain Hale, draw up on the south flank." "McHugh, mount the Hotchkiss and wheel forward." "Infantry, deploy and follow cavalry charge; swing the four-pound howitzer to north." "Troops of Second Cavalry, surround enemy pony herd." "Lieutenant McClernand, retrieve the fleeing train." "Main cavalry, ready for frontal assault." He surveyed the resulting formation, raised his arm, and shouted, "Attack!"[212]

Reins were loosed, spurs clicked, and away rolled a thundering avalanche of mounted might. The charging line raced headlong toward the Indian camp. It was the same speed and precision that had broken the power of the Sioux and Cheyenne nations.

The Nez Percé grimly waited. At a hundred yards they opened fire, and the battle broke with a roar.

In the wake of the charge were fifty-three soldiers dead or wounded. K Troop lost over sixty per cent of their complement. Joseph's camp was cut in twain, but the position could not be forced, and the cavalry passed through. The Nez Percé settled deeper into their entrenchments, and a state of siege ensued. However, the Colonel's pony detail succeeded in rounding up the Indian ponies. The Nez Percé were now on foot. That night a six-inch mantle of snow fell. Continuous fire was sustained the next day. Then a parley was arranged. Joseph was promised a safe conduct. He accepted but was made a prisoner. However, the Nez Percé captured an officer named Jerome and held him as hostage for Joseph. Terms were proposed. Miles demanded unconditional surrender, but Chief Joseph exacted a promise to return his people to the Lapwai Reservation. This Miles granted.[213]

On October 4, the fifth day of the siege, Joseph led his haggard people out of their camp. His head was bowed in awful solemnity. As he approached a cluster of officers, including General Howard, he straightened up and dismounted with dignity. Impulsively he presented his rifle to Howard, but the general motioned him to "Bear Coat" Miles.

After disarmament the great chief stepped forward, raised his arm in a sweeping motion toward the reddening sun, and intoned the requiem of a dying race:

> Tell General Howard that I know his heart. What he told me before I have in my heart. I am tired of fighting. Our chiefs are killed. Looking Glass is dead, Tu-hul-hul-sote is dead. The old men are all dead. It is the young men who now say yes or no. He who led the young men is dead. It is cold and we have no blankets. The little children are freezing to death. My people—some of them have run away to the hills and have no blankets and no food. No one knows where they are— perhaps freezing to death. I want to have time to look for my children and see how many of them I can find. Maybe I shall find them among the dead. Hear me, my chiefs, my heart is sick and sad. From where the sun now stands I will fight no more forever.[214]

The Montana sun was going down; Hin-mut-too-yah-lat-kekht had spoken as its rays flickered.

The officers came forward and shook his hand. As he turned away, drawing his blanket over his head, the white soldiers discerned five bullet holes in his blanket and wounds on his forehead and wrist.

There was something about this leader that tugged at their heart strings as he beckoned his children toward their prison camp. There were four hundred and twelve survivors, including forty-six wounded. Twenty-six Indians and twenty-seven white men (plus Miles' two Indian scouts) had been slain. Joseph's conduct in burying the dead and in ministering to his half-starved and freezing people elicited the admiration of all. As the handsome, plucky chieftain assuaged their sorrow he seemed greater than any one man. Surely, here was the embodiment of the Nez Percé, indeed, of all Indian people. In his person were combined elements both noble and tragic. He was the last best specimen of a truly native race.

By nature Joseph was a modest man and inclined toward peace and good will. Events forced him into a role that has won eternal fame. Even General Sherman, who entertained no high sentiments for Indians, could not withhold his meed of praise:

> Thus has terminated one of the most extraordinary Indian wars of which there is any record. The Indians throughout displayed a courage and skill that elicited universal praise; they abstained from scalping; let captive women go free; did not commit indiscriminate murders of peaceful families and fought with almost scientific skill, using advance and rear guards, skirmish lines and field fortifications.[215]

Other competent authorities have gone further. One ventured the asseveration that:

> Had Joseph led thousands and had he been born of a people and in a place less remote from the main currents of history, his name would resound in our ears like thunder.[216]

As it is, the tale of the Nez Percé retreat, surrender, and burning years of their exile strike a mournful note upon the ears of men.

At Bear Paw a long "trail of tears" began for Joseph and his people. There was the solemn trek to Fort Keogh, thence to Bismarck, on to Fort Leavenworth, and finally to a small Oklahoma reserve. This was virtually a sentence of death for these mountain-bred people.[217] Miles could not make his promise good. Joseph was depressed by the increasing time and distance. Said he, "The Great Spirit Chief who rules above seemed to be looking some other way and did not see what was happening to my people."

Many government officials called upon Joseph ("White men have too many chiefs"). Promises were lightly made ("Look twice at a two-faced man"). Resolutions were circulated ("Big name often on small legs"). The wise chief was learning the ways of his masters.

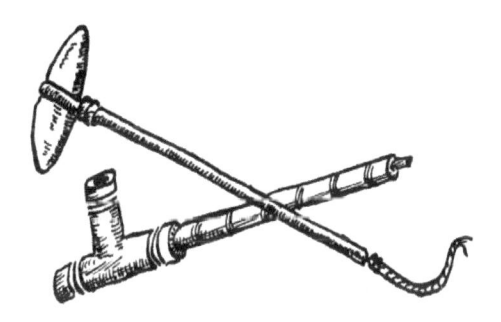

W. S. Chapman
Indian war club and peace pipe.

Joseph's conqueror became his truest friend. Miles, a general now, kept working to fulfill his vow. Said he:

> I frequently and persistently, for seven long years, urged that they be sent home to their own country but not until 1884, when I was in command of the Department of the Columbia, did I succeed in having them returned west of the mountains near their own country.[218]

In 1885, after they had been ravaged by sickness and death, the remnant of the Nez Percé tribe was established on the Colville Reservation in Washington state. Here Joseph's declining years were spent in the companionship of his wives and children, until his death on September 21, 1904. There, among a vast concourse of white and Indian people, Thunder-Traveling-to-Loftier-Heights was gathered to his fathers.

CHAPTER XII
TRAVEL AND ACCOMMODATIONS—
NEW BUSINESSES

The narration of trapper and miner visits and the account of final discovery have already described the difficulties of early travel in Yellowstone. Little segments of animal and Indian trails were all that broke the untraveled wilderness. Since no funds were available for any purpose before 1877, the trail building progress made before that date was negligible.[219] Until that time all visitors came on horseback, but while they generally went to the same places their approaches were different. Each outfit carried axes, and at least a modicum of effort had to be expended along the way. Such had been the way of mountain men. They did not expect someone else to build their roads; neither did they expect anyone to tell them where to go or camp. Therefore, it was every outfit to itself; still, companionship claimed its due, and groups sometimes fell into line and traveled together.

A perusal of old journals shows that packsaddle trips were always thrilling. It was by pack horse that the presidential party of August, 1883 visited the Park. It traveled three hundred and fifty miles, making nineteen camps during its sojourn. The personnel included the following: President Chester A. Arthur, Secretary of War Robert T. Lincoln, Senator George Graham Vest, General Phil H. Sheridan, General Anson Stager, Colonel Michael V. Sheridan, Colonel J. F. Gregory, Captain Philo Clark, Governor Schuyler Crosby (Montana), Judge Rawlins, and Official Photographer Frank Jay Haynes.[220] They had a grand time, and thereafter Yellowstone never lacked friends in high places.

One account tells of traveling three hundred and fifty miles in twenty-four days. Fish were caught in handfuls, horses caved in geyser formations, and Indians were seen. All of these activities were duly reported to a keenly interested American public. Indeed, a general concern for the President's security was aroused. This natural anxiety gave occasion for a rumor that the President's safety was in jeopardy, not from accident, wild animals, or Indians, but rather from a gang of desperadoes. A dispatch bearing the postmark of Hailey, Idaho, stated that a large band of Texas criminals had been observed in a mysterious ceremonial at Willow Park in Yellowstone. According to the report, each man swore by his dagger to do his duty, which was no less than the capture of the President of the United States and his entire party. The captives would then be held in a wilderness cavern until a ransom of one million dollars had been paid!

W. S. Chapman Stagecoach.

The alarming report that "They are after Arthur!" was followed by the reassuring word that Sheriff Farcy and a company of United States troops were investigating the reported conspiracy. Certainly the presidential expedition was enveloped in an atmosphere of high romance![221]

It is said that camping trips have always been ideal testers of friendship. Camp life is an excellent form of association because it is bound to disclose every character trait. Each virtue is surely tried, and every vice is certain to show itself. Wit, cheerfulness, patience, and industry were in demand, and their opposites greatly discounted. Some knowledge of cooking, washing, caring for animals, and tying the diamond hitch was essential. Good hunters and fishermen were popular in these camps. Skill in constructing fir-bough lean-tos against storms and couches for sleeping came in handy. Last of all, the gift of storytelling and song made its possessor the head of the nightly campfire circle. Were these the people the poet envisioned?

Keep not standing fix't and rooted,

Briskly venture, briskly roam;

Head and hand, where'er thou foot it,

And stout heart are still at home.

In each land the sun does visit

We are gay, whate'er betide:

To give room for wandering is it

That the world was made so wide.[222]

Pack outfit owners were a lusty sort. Some of them divided their time between acting as guides and slaughtering game for both meat and hides. A few were wholly unscrupulous, both in their exploitation of the tourists and the Park.[223] Still others were high-type frontiersmen. A description has been left of one Texas Jack, named John Omohondro, originally from Virginia:

> He is tall, powerfully built, and as he rode carelessly along, with his long rifle crossed in front of him, he was a picture. He was dressed in a complete suit of buckskin, and wore a flaming red neckerchief, a broad sombrero fastened up on one side with a large eagle feather, and a pair of beautifully beaded moccasins. The costume of the man, his self-confident pose, and the quick, penetrating glance of his keen black eye, would give the impression that he was no ordinary mountaineer.[224]

Still, Texas Jack was quite typical of most mountain scouts, being a man of life and blood and fire, blazing with suppressed excitement in a land of high adventure.

Although the stagecoach took over most of the tourist business after 1880 a few reliable pack masters remained in business. Among these was the firm of Grant, Brogan and Lycan of Bozeman, which conducted a seven-day tour for thirty dollars per person. Jordan and Howell of Cody had a fourteen-day schedule, while Howard Eaton, in his day, personally guided more than a hundred parties around the Park on a twenty-day tour.[225] In 1923 the trail he used was improved, named, and dedicated to his memory. The Howard Eaton Trail parallels the Grand Loop highway. It is maintained by the government and is one of the most scenic bridle paths in America. It was hoped that many people would take advantage of this facility, but its public use is meager.

Travel by stage in Yellowstone was started in 1878 and concluded in 1917. Since a generation of Americans saw the Park in that manner, a description of the procedure would be appropriate. The stagecoach itself was a remarkable vehicle. It was substantially built, quite commodious, and reasonably comfortable. Concord coaches were used; they varied in capacity from seven to as many as thirty-three seats and were drawn by four or six horses, according to size. Great leather springs, called thorough braces, produced a swaying motion which absorbed all but the most violent shocks. The driver's seat was perched above the body of the coach and underneath was a compartment for mail sacks and express packages. There was a strong platform in the rear of the coach upon which trunks and suitcases were loaded. Harness and other gear were always of the best grade and condition.

Several hundred thousand passengers were taken through Yellowstone by stagecoaches during the thirty-eight years of their operation. The drivers, therefore, were necessarily men of experience and resourcefulness. Indeed, they were a sovereign group and the cynosure of eyes as they cracked their whips and moved three span of horses away at a half-gallop, half-trot, trained, showy style. They were held in high esteem, as well they might be, for each held a position requiring judgment and skill. Several expert drivers who "tooled" Yellowstone coaches were William Woolsey, Hub Counter, and Oscar Scoda. They were firm in resolution, yet polite in manner, and obliging toward passengers. Generally:

> ... they were good entertainers, capable of making what would otherwise be a long, tedious night ride seem entirely too short to the passenger, who was fortunate enough to have a seat on the box beside him, and hear him relate his experiences with Indian and stage robber.[226]

The driver's sole duty consisted of handling the stage while on the line; others attended to the feeding and harnessing of the horses, but the teams knew their drivers and responded amazingly to their wills. A driver could flick a fly off the back of his team leaders and bring back his lash without tangling it in the harness or wagon wheels. Day and night these "kings of the whip" flung and pulled the "silk" to those fleet creatures of nature, and over their strength and fears they were ever masters. "Clear the road! Get out of the way thar with your draft teams!" was their good-natured salutation as they swung into view, only to disappear at high speed around a curve or through the lodgepole-lined road. Unrelaxed, they were ever watchful for gullies, boulders, and road agents. As they approached a station they forced their horses into full gallop and brought their coaches up with a grand flourish before the ever-expectant crowd on hand, waiting for friends or the mail. One driver boasted that he could drive his outfit down Beehive Geyser and come out of Old Faithful without losing a hair!

The advantages of travel by stage included interesting acquaintances and fresh views into human nature. Close quarters in the wilderness have always been a touchstone, even thus lightly approached. The regular trip lasted five days and always seemed too short. One tourist regretfully observed, "Nothing can be done well at a speed of forty miles a day."[227] As the stage prepared to pull out some would climb up the sides of the coaches and squeeze into the open seats on the roof. There, each obtained an unobstructed view of the landscape and a good sunburn. Others, less agile or venturesome, would remain in the interior, satisfied with less elevation, wind, and sun, and nearly as much advantage in sight-seeing.

There they sat, side by side, hour after hour, old and young, full of hope and fun and care. Some watched the scenery; others, the horses. All asked questions—some of them intelligent and well-conceived, some naïve, and still others ludicrous. They were usually addressed to the driver, as though skill in handling horses and familiarity with the area gave authority. Unfortunately, few drivers understood what they daily saw; still, as a defense against frustration, many acquired a knowing air. Great guesses were made, and occasionally the tourists were deliberately misled. Generally the driver's observations were offered in a spirit of fun to keep the folks from drooping. A few examples have been recorded. Driving among the Hot Springs on the Mammoth Terraces, one guide shouted, "Them as likes their bath hot goes in on the left, and them as likes it cold goes in on the right, and them as likes it middlin' goes in the middle."[228]

At Norris Geyser Basin the following conversation was heard: One tourist speaking to another, "If we're too late to see the Monarch Geyser erupt tonight, we'll go over and see him before breakfast." To which the driver replied, "No you can't, the Monarch Geyser is a monarch up here in the Park. You can't go see him when you get ready; you've got to go when he's ready."[229]

One Münchausen-minded guide informed his passengers that any geyser water, when bottled, retained a strange sympathy with its water nymph, so that when the geyser erupted the water became violently agitated; in one instance a bottle was shattered incident to a particularly powerful eruption! Many such stories were told by "Buckskin Charley," "Yankee Jim," "Billy" Hofer, and their compatriots. Rudyard Kipling left this description of Yankee Jim:

> Yankee Jim was a picturesque old man with a talent for yarns that Ananias might have envied.... Yankee Jim saw every one of my tales and went fifty better on the spot. He dealt in bears and Indians—never less than twenty each.[230]

Courtesy Northern Pacific Ry.
"Yankee Jim"—James George

James George, better known as "Yankee Jim," was a pioneer hunter and trapper who staked his claim in Yankee Jim Canyon of Yellowstone River, north of Cinnabar and Gardiner. He shrewdly built twenty-seven miles of toll road through the only available pass. Yankee Jim delighted in joshing the lady members of early parties concerning the prospects of bestowing a bit of affection upon him in lieu of the tolls. Little is known concerning his success in that direction, but he dealt effectively with the Northern Pacific Railroad in the matter of a right of way through his canyon.

As time passed, many people who were beyond the "gape-and-run" variety complained about the lack of a dependable source of information. The quips of guides who did not know a marmot from a cony actually displeased them. However, there were occasions when even these talkative fellows had the good taste to be silent.

> They will talk of the Canyon at the hotel and on the drive, but once there they simply lead you to the points of lookout and leave you with your own thoughts, or answer your questions in monosyllables.[231]

After a long trip on a warm day, through clouds of Yellowstone dust, the passengers presented an amusing spectacle. Men in yellow dusters, women in gray ones, topped off by Shaker bonnets. Hungry, weary, and dejected, they would alight on limbs half-paralyzed from inactivity. It was then that a person needed a friend, and that detail was not overlooked by the hotel management.

Perhaps Larry Matthews was more unique than typical, but a description of him will convey the idea of nineteenth-century Park hospitality. For several seasons Larry was chargé d'affaires at the Norris lunch station. Later he was advanced to the management of an inn at Old Faithful. When coaches pulled up to Larry's he would address each passenger in his genial Irish brogue. Every man received a title of dignity, while he referred to himself as the "Mad Irishman" or "Larry Geeser." Here is a picture of Larry in action:

> Step right up, Judge, eat all you can, break the company, it's all right with me. Fine spring lamb (spring of '72). Eggs, fresh eggs! Just laid this morning (on the table).

Thus he kept up a constant rattle that was very funny. As the coaches rolled away one could hear the tourists remark, "The jolliest man I ever saw ... such hypnotic ways, such spontaneous wit; surely no such mortal ever lived before."[232]

This growing business of transportation and accommodations was characterized by vigorous competition. Probably the first conveyance to enter the Park was a stagecoach owned by J. W. Marshall and his partner, named Goff. It left Virginia City, Montana, on October 1, 1880. Sixteen hours were required in traversing the ninety-five miles to Marshall's National Park House, a two-story, log-hewed structure located in the Lower Geyser Basin, near the junction of Firehole and Nez Percé Creek. These men also built mail stations at Riverside, four miles east of the West Entrance, and at Norris Geyser Basin.

Frank Jay Haynes, a youthful photographer from St. Paul, started a stage and photo business in 1881. His efforts have produced eminent success, and the end is not yet. The photography side of the business descended from father, Frank Jay, to son, Jack Ellis. The Haynes Studio still enjoys a flourishing trade, and its beautiful products are known all over the world.

The Northern Pacific Railroad extended its terminal to Cinnabar in 1883, where it remained until 1902, when Gardiner was reached. The next year an impressive ceremony was held at the North Gate when the Triumphal Arch was dedicated by President Theodore Roosevelt.

In 1883 the Yellowstone Park Improvement Company organized regular tourist travel. The usual routine consisted of alternating sojourns, whether in Concord stagecoaches, surreys, formation or spring wagons, and canvas "hotels." A trip around the Park cost twenty-five dollars, or a saddle horse could be secured for two-fifty per day. The following year (1884) George W. Wakefield put a line of coaches into operation from Cinnabar through the Park. W. Hoffman was also engaged in the stage business. These firms were rivals among themselves, and with other less formidable competitors, for the Northern Pacific's business. However, in 1886, the railroad effected a gentlemen's agreement with the new and energetic Yellowstone Park Association. Unless the purchaser of a railroad ticket objected he found a coupon attached to his ticket that delivered him into the care of the Yellowstone Park Stage Line and its associated hotels. Coupon holders paid nine dollars a day while in the Park. Five dollars were assigned to staging and four dollars to hotel and meals. Upon alighting from the train, each person was accosted from several quarters, much as by hackmen in cities, "Are you a coupon, sir?" "No." "Would you like my team then?"[233] Thus, each would press the bewildered tourist for his business. In 1892 the Huntley, Child, and Bach interests organized the Yellowstone Park Transportation Company. They soon dominated the North Entrance business, and other operators were bought out in 1903. Four years later this firm was prepared to receive one hundred and fifty passengers daily at the North Gate. An inventory of its rolling stock included four six-horse Concord coaches, of thirty-three seats capacity; ninety four-horse Concords, of eleven and seven seats; and one hundred two Glens Falls two-horse surreys, of five and three seat models. It was undoubtedly one of the best-equipped organizations of the kind in history.[234]

Passengers entering the Park by way of the West Entrance came north from Ogden, Utah, on the Utah Northern (later the Union Pacific) to Spencer, Idaho, or Monida on the Montana-Idaho border. There they were met by F. J. Haynes' Monida and Yellowstone Stage Line or the Bassett Brothers Company. During the season of 1915 the Haynes firm transported 20,151 tourists through the Park.

In 1903, when the East Gate road was opened, the Holm Transportation Company secured a permit to operate a stage line. The arrival of the Burlington Route to Cody, Wyoming, in 1912, gave great impetus to that business. The West Entrance had benefited by a railroad to its gate since 1907, when the Union Pacific extended the line to West Yellowstone. A branch line was also built to Victor, Idaho, which made Jackson Hole and the South Entrance much more accessible. A table of operators and charges, as of 1914, would represent the stage business in the heyday of its power.[235]

The evolution of permanent camps and hotels was complementary to the development of travel. The first permanent house built was in Clematis Gulch, on the north side of Mammoth Terraces. It was erected in 1871 by James C. McCartney. This "hotel" and C. J. Baronett's bridge and cabin at the forks of the Yellowstone River were the only improvements made before the Dedicatory Act was passed. These gentlemen managed to collect the sum of $9000 for their foresight and property, although they had to wait until March 1, 1899 to get it.

P. W. Norris' Annual Report of 1880 lists the following facilities then in operation: Mammoth, McCartney's house and Matthew McGuirck's baths; Norris, a rude cabin and barn; Riverside, a cabin and barn; Firehole River, near the forks, "a fine shingle roofed mail station and hotel." The latter three stations were built by Marshall and Goff. In the Upper Geyser Basin a small cabin was built by Superintendent Norris in 1879; at the Lake a cabin and boat were operated by Captain E. S. Topping.

Ernest Thompson Seton
"Uncle" John F. Yancey.

Two years later John Yancey secured a mail contract and established a station in Pleasant Valley at the base of Crescent Hill. Here he was familiarly known as "Uncle John." He was an old Kentucky frontiersman stranded in the Park by the flood tide of civilization. He chafed constantly at the uneventful days of the eighties and told his guests thrilling tales of the forties. A pen portrait has been preserved of him:

> Yancey is an odd character, whose looks encourage a belief in reincarnation, so forcibly does he remind us of the prehistoric. His hotel, too, belongs to the primeval; its walls are of logs; its partitions and ceilings of cheese cloth.... Uncle John's housekeeper, who performs the duties of cook and chambermaid, confidentially informed one of our party that it was hard to find time to wash so many bedclothes every day.[236]

The meals were most generous, which was a custom closely observed in those days. This type of accommodation was very repulsive to some people. Judge Lambert Tree, an ex-United States Minister to Belgium, characterized the management in general as outrageous. A report was current that three married couples and two young women were thrust into a small room to pass the night. The next camp was twenty miles away, and the only transportation belonged to the company. In addition, this same party was advised to walk up Mary Mountain because it was such a hard pull for the horses. Someone was evidently justified in making the statement, "As it is today [1884.], I do not think it too strong to say that at certain points on the route travellers are treated more like cattle than civilized people."[237]

These reports reached the Secretary of the Interior, and a number of new leases were promptly granted for the erection of hotels and the necessary outbuildings.[238] About this time Superintendent Wear was accused of persuading Graham and Klamer, owners of the Firehole Hotel, to sell out. In any case, a new hotel was built in the Lower Geyser Basin in 1884 by C. T. Hobart. He and Robert E. Carpenter also erected a frame building the next year on the present site of Old Faithful Inn. At the same time the Cottage Hotel was erected in Mammoth by Walter L. Henderson.[239] The Yellowstone Park Association also built hotels in Mammoth and Norris in 1885, Lake in 1887, Canyon in 1890, and the following year they completed the peerless Fountain Hotel. It was located on a hill in a strategic position in the Lower Geyser Basin. From its lofty veranda the Fountain Geyser could be observed playing. The Fountain House was an imposing structure. It was modern in every way, having electricity and steam heat. Two hundred guests could be entertained, and when they went to dinner a head waiter in evening dress greeted them. In 1887 the Norris Hotel burned down, and in 1894 the one at Old Faithful did likewise.[240]

During the season of 1894 the pressure of criticism was brought to bear upon the entire Yellowstone transportation and accommodation setup. The country was in the throes of a depression, and the rates seemed exorbitant. It appears that the Yellowstone Park Transportation Company had been very reluctant in allowing stopover privileges. It collected just as much by holding strictly to schedule; whereas, the hotels made more on holdovers. This diversity of interest suggested the idea that it might be expedient to have the management of both industries in the same hands.

It was William W. Wylie, of Bozeman, who conceived a plan which met the demand. Since 1883 he had operated a ten-day tour, using portable tents. He would organize a stage line and cater to the masses by establishing a string of permanent camps, with eating halls and sleeping quarters. By using canvas, his investment would be small, and he could cut the cost of a trip through the Park in half. Therefore, in 1896, he secured a franchise, and the "Wylie Way" went into operation.

Of course, the more conservative competitors resented this invasion from "the other side of the tracks." Captain George S. Anderson was also opposed to a string of "shanty towns." The matter was given a public hearing by Forest and Stream in its issue of February 5, 1898, entitled "Nuisances in Yellowstone Park." Mr. Wylie, known in Yellowstone as "the Professor," wrote a vigorous rebuttal for the following issue. Other publications entered into the controversy, as did many of Wylie's most satisfied customers. The question involved was whether the American people, in the enjoyment of their own pleasure ground, should be limited to one set of accommodations, which only the wealthy could afford.[241] The verdict of the public, from which there is no appeal, was definitely with "the Professor." The business flourished and won an acceptable position in the more complete system that evolved.

In the meantime an actual nuisance was committed by several hotel operators. They attempted to assemble and maintain wild life menageries. The government necessarily allowed stables and pastures for horses and cows, but that was all. Nevertheless, several managers also tried to raise pigs, although extreme precautions were essential to save them from bears. Colonel E. C. Waters had a "veritable stockade-pen of heavy logs bolted all around."[242] Perhaps the most flagrant offender in this respect was the Yellowstone Boat Company. As an inducement to take a boat ride, this firm confined buffalo, elk, and bighorn in corrals on Dot Island. This untoward act, together with the prices charged for boat rides, brought many complaints, and upon official request the animals were promptly released.[243]

Mosquitoes were an ever-present nuisance, sometimes assuming the proportion of a plague. Accustomed to the pursuit of fleet four-footed prey, they assailed slow moving Homo sapiens with particular gusto. Gleeful appreciation seemed discernible in their song. By day and night, unless the wind was blowing, the tourists were kept busy swatting those vexatious, glory-minded, musical-winged, bold denizens of the forest.

Perhaps the most persistent annoyance, next to mosquitoes, was the prevalence of dust. One traveler laconically observed that he rode "from geyser to canyon, to waterfall, in a chaos of dust, until he returned on the fifth day a wiser and dustier man."[244]

But an elderly man, probably afflicted with asthma, entered the Fountain Hotel, singled out the manager, and shaking his finger in his face, dramatically shouted, "A man who would permit women and children to enter the Park, with the roads in their present condition, is an old scoundrel!"[245] How did cyclists ever manage to get around? Incredible though it appears they went through right along after 1882. To be sure, their voices were added to the chorus calling for better roads. These protests resulted in the adoption of a sprinkling system that will be described subsequently.

The most revolutionary proposal for a change in travel facilities, coming in 1894, was a demand for railroads. There were propositions wholly independent of the Montana segregation case. Many people sincerely favored the entrance of trains on their own merits. The issue was discussed in the House of Representatives on December 17, by the Hon. Henry H. Coffeen of Wyoming. Speaking of the operators, he said:

> ... they are holding on to a theory of sacred maintenance of the stage coach and broncho riding method of reaching this great Wonderland at a time when the superior advantages of railroad travel ought to be granted to the people.... These journeys going round the Park, so to say, and coming in at the back door by tedious night and day stage rides are so expensive, the time and inconveniences so great and the season so short (three months) that the great bulk of our population must forever stay out and remain in ignorance of the scenes of the Park. Not one hundredth part of one per cent of our people per year could possibly visit the Park by these methods.[246]

While this argument did not produce a change of policy it did give an impetus to road building. A brief review of that important development would be appropriate.

Reference has already been made to the rude trails hacked out by government expeditions and early tourists and also to the trace improvised by C. J. Baronett and his associates, which led from Mammoth to his bridge at the forks of the Yellowstone and along the east branch to the mines at Cooke, Montana. In 1877 General Howard's captain, W. F. Spurgin, made a faint apology for a road in bringing his wagons from Mary Mountain to Tower Falls. It was the next year when the first wagons managed a round trip from Mammoth, and also the West

Entrance, to the Upper Geyser Basin. In building a road across the base of Obsidian Cliff, Colonel Norris employed a unique tactic in road making. Great bonfires were burned over the black glass, which made it expand; then cold water was dashed upon it, shattering the material so that it could be chopped out.

Golden Gate drive

In the early eighties the matter of road making was taken over by the army engineers. Until 1895 actual control was in the hands of non-resident officers, which proved unsatisfactory. After that the Acting Superintendent exercised supervision. Captain Anderson had a soldier's and a surveyor's eye for feasible routes. He favored the construction of twenty miles of good dirt road with fair grades to one mile of macadam and the resulting delay in opening the Park to the public.[24/] The principal supervisors were Captain D. C. Kingman and Major Hiram M. Chittenden. Through their combined efforts the Grand Loop was planned and patiently constructed. In 1892 the road from Old Faithful to West Thumb was started. It took five years to get through to Jackson Lake. At the same time work progressed on the long section from Thumb to Fishing Bridge and thence to the East Entrance. That project was finished and accessible from Cody in 1903. Two years later the difficult Dunraven Pass and the scenic Chittenden Road to the summit of Mt. Washburn were ready. These were the last links in the

Grand Loop. Of course, there have been continuous changes and refinements. In general the trend has been away from the plateaus to the more scenic river routes. Stretches through the Golden Gate, under Overhanging Cliff, and through the Gibbon and Firehole canyons are both interesting and costly.

In 1902 an experiment was made with the view of solving the dusty road problem. Several wide-tired sprinklers were tried out. The following year the number was increased, and more than thirty filling tanks were installed along the way. Most of them were filled by gravity and rams. In this way over a hundred miles of highway was moistened daily. Still, there were times when the dust was too thick for any effective treatment that man could devise.[248] Of course, nature had an adequate remedy, which it occasionally employed. Superintendent Albright related an instance:

> Once I had a large congressional party in Yellowstone. It was in charge of the late James W. Good. Yellowstone's roads were terribly dusty and the water sprinkling was of little value. We wanted Congress to adopt an oiling program but every night while the Committee was in the Park it rained and the roads were perfect. Nevertheless every day I told of the dust menace and urged the improvement, but the congressmen only laughed and some member would say "Albright's going to tell his old dusty road story again."[249]

Continuing the narrative, Superintendent Albright told this story:

> "Another year, I met a sub-committee of the House Appropriations Committee at the Grand Canyon National Park. Congressman, now United States Senator, Carl Hayden, was with the party when they reached the park. Here again we had a problem of terrible roads. The committee had not had much sleep the night before arrival due to changing trains, and when I took them over the worst road in the park they went to sleep on me. I bounced them into every rut and hole I could find, but even then I had to shake them to wake them up. For a long time they contended that the road was a boulevard, but finally authorized the improvement desired. On the same trip, Congressman Cramton of Michigan, for years the stalwart champion of national parks, saw a camper stop his car near the Grand Canyon Park office. He went over to him seeking information about the conduct of the

park. The tourist gave him a vigorous denunciation of the roads in the park, and Mr. Cramton always claimed that I planted the camper there to trap him."

The suggestion frequently came to the Superintendent that he should sprinkle the roads with water from Alum Creek. That would shorten the distance and simplify the task!

In 1917 the National Park Service assumed control over all road construction and maintenance. Since then a comprehensive policy of scientific road making has been followed; grades have been modified, while at the same time great cuts and fills have been avoided so far as possible; turns have been eased and widened; and in recent years all the roads have been paved with oil mix. An appropriation of $3,369,450 in 1933, under the National Recovery Act, became the basis of the marvelous improvements made in recent years. In 1937 a remarkably scenic highway was completed from Red Lodge, Montana, to the Northeast Gate. After 1928, Cecil A. Lord directed the engineering activities of the Park until his death in 1943, whereupon Park Engineer Philip H. Wohlbrandt assumed that important responsibility.

The year 1915 was indeed a banner one in Yellowstone transportation history. It was the first year automobiles were admitted, and consequently heralded the end of the stagecoach. Actually, staging lingered through another season, but the race was over as the poet said:

Here's to you, old stage driver,

We'll hear your shout no more,

Your stage with rust is eaten,

Beside the old Inn's door;

The auto-bus and steam car

Have cut your time in two;

Throw up your hands, old "stage hoss,"

They've got the drop on you![250]

Few people expressed any regret, because of the hardships incident to travel by stagecoach. Still, it is the opinion of many that advantages exceeded inconvenience. The West, as now seen from the window of a train or motor car, is not the country introduced by stagecoach. With all the additional comfort, there is a loss of an indefinable something, subtle, yet well understood by those who have driven at a six-mile-an-hour pace through the almost unbroken solitude of another era. In contrast, regularly scheduled airplane flights over the Park have been available from time to time since 1937. There are no airports in the Park, but they are to be found nearby at West Yellowstone and Gardiner, Montana.

It should also be remembered that during the previous forty years innumerable private parties made leisurely visits and camped where they pleased. The Park must have been an idyllic place in those "horse and buggy" days, a hunting and fishing Elysium, especially until 1894. Since then fishermen may take a generous catch of trout without any license except a bona fide presence in the Park.

Although admitted under the most onerous terms the automobile revolutionized the travel there as elsewhere. Always well-filled with regulations, official bulletins now fairly bristled with instructions to motorists. Fees were $7.50 for a single trip or $10.00 for the season; all cars were required to enter the gates between 6:45 and 7:15 A.M. A printed schedule specified the time of arrival at, and departure from, the control stations.[251] Fines were imposed for arrival at any point before the approved lapse of time at the rate of $0.50 per minute for each of the first five minutes, $1.00 per minute for each of the next twenty minutes, $25.00 fine or ejection from the Park, or both, at the discretion of the Acting Superintendent, for being more than twenty-five minutes early. The following regulations and restrictions were strictly enforced: Speed, twelve miles per hour ascending steep grades; ten miles per hour descending steep grades; eight miles per hour approaching sharp curves and passing other vehicles. The maximum speed limit in 1922 was twenty-five miles per hour. Teams had the right of way and also the inside of the roadway in passing. Motorists were required to sound horns at all curves where the road was not in view at least two hundred yards ahead. Surely the motorists were in a defensive position, but they came anyway. A total of 3,513 auto passengers toured the Park in the abbreviated season after August 1, 1915. The grand total for the year was 51,895 in all conveyances.

The advent of motor vehicles speeded up every phase of Park administration. However, World War I provided a respite for making adjustments. In fact, a thorough reorganization of the entire concession system was effected in 1917. The main feature involved was the consolidation of transportation under the management of the Yellowstone Park Transportation Company. The purpose of this franchise was to eliminate the pressure of rivals upon the passengers, facilitate supervision, and promote economy.[252] The Yellowstone Park Company proceeded to make a large capital investment by motorizing all transportation. Thereupon, the familiar yellow bus superseded the ancient stagecoach. It is an interesting thing to observe a caravan of twenty buses winding its way along a river drive or parked before a museum while a ranger-naturalist gives the passengers a quick orientation in the area.

It would be fair to inquire if the bus driver (gear jammer) showed any improvement over the stagecoach driver in the matter of instructing the public. Not if the 1921 edition of Truthful Lies correctly represents the situation, because that little booklet was a congeries of unadulterated nonsense reduced to a system.[253] However, a gradual improvement has been made, and in recent years all of the new drivers have gone around the "Loop" with a naturalist. From him they received helpful suggestions relative to natural interpretation. A few days after one of these induction tours the following conversation was reported to have taken place when passing a beaver dam: "Now, there is a beaver dam, but where are the dam beavers?" The driver straightened up and replied, "I'll be damned if I know."

At this point it should be remembered that, although the great concourse visit Yellowstone in cars, many tourists come in buses, motorcycles, and bicycles. It should also be noted that travel by horseback has always persisted. Until the advent of the automobile this method was in general use. Indeed, firms were organized to provide grand tours of several weeks' duration. The Howard Eaton Trail and various adjuncts are still used by horseback parties each summer. In fact, several trail-riding associations sponsor these trips under competent leadership. In this manner an excellent Park tradition is being sustained for the benefit and enjoyment of a chosen few possessed of the necessary time and hardihood.

In 1936 the long-expected union of transportation and accommodations took place. The Yellowstone Park Transportation Company acquired all of the housing facilities and deleted the word Transportation from its title.[254] In analyzing the business of previous years, President William M. Nichols and his associates noticed a definite trend away from commercial transportation and first class American plan hotel accommodations. Therefore, they rapidly expanded the lower-priced cabins, together with cafeterias and coffee shops. They are now pursuing a carefully worked out program of improvement. Practical pre-fabricated cabins are to be established in well-arranged units in every station.[255] In 1956 the company had available some 3,150 rooms or units of lodging, with an aggregate capacity for housing 8,500 people. These accommodations consist of hotels, lodges, and housekeeping cabins. The services of twenty-seven hundred employees were required to operate these facilities. The annual Park population census taken on August 9, 12, and 14, 1955, disclosed an average population of 14,912 for the three days. Of this number 11,183 were visitors while 3,729 were employees. The grand total for the 1955 season was 1,368,515 visitors.

Tourists require many things besides food and shelter. Yellowstone's policy has favored making these wants attainable. In this field regulations have also modified certain practices common to general business conditions. Franchises have been kept at a minimum, and competition does not exist within a particular camp. However, Park merchants are required to keep their prices in line with the index of the market area.

Motion pictures and other forms of indoor recreation are conspicuously absent, although the lodges sponsor two hours of entertainment and dancing for their guests and the public at large. These also function to keep the employees contented.

A general statement having been made, a brief sketch of Yellowstone's business enterprises would be in order. Frank Jay Haynes, the pioneer photographer, built his first picture shop at Mammoth in 1884. Since that time a Haynes Studio has been a familiar institution in Yellowstone camps. Another Mammoth Hot Springs store was opened in 1889 by Ole Anderson. For a time he was allowed to sell bottles of highly colored Park sand and also specimens coated with calcium carbonate. This store was purchased by Anna K. Pryor and Elizabeth Trischman in 1908. They soon reorganized it into the Park Curio and Coffee

Shop. Later they acquired the Mammoth general store and a grocery store near Canyon Junction. The latter had been established by a released Park soldier, George Whittaker.

The first store in the Upper Geyser Basin was built by Henry E. Klamer in 1897. A ten-year franchise for a geyser water swimming pool was granted Henry J. Brothers in 1914. The following year Charles A. Hamilton acquired control of these interests and laid the foundation for a thriving business there. Hamilton also has general stores at Thumb, Lake, and Fishing Bridge, and in 1953 acquired the Pryor interests in the Park.

The Yellowstone Park Service Stations are owned jointly by Hamilton Stores, Inc. and the Yellowstone Park Company. Gasoline, oil, and supplies are available at the lone multi-pump service station assigned to each camp.[256] The public garage business is in the hands of the Yellowstone Park Company. Thus, it is obvious that all of the Park's mercantile business is the concern of three operators, Haynes, Hamilton, and the Yellowstone Park Company. Each operates under the terms of a government franchise and is subject to National Park Service regulation and supervision at all times.

The essential public utilities are provided by the National Park Service. They consist of public camp grounds with cement cooking units, toilet facilities, telephones, water, lights, and sewage disposal. These substantial projects have been developed through the years with a capital expenditure that runs in excess of a million dollars.[257]

In 1912 a general hospital was built in Mammoth. It is closely affiliated with a similar institution in Livingston, Montana. Medical doctors and trained nurses are on duty at the principal stations throughout the Park. This arrangement assures the public of medical attention in case of accidents or illness.

In 1913 the government built a Community Chapel at Mammoth. During the summer months services are usually conducted there and at the lodges or amphitheaters by the Catholic, Protestant, and Latter-day Saint (Mormon) faiths.

The postal service in Yellowstone has had a colorful evolution. The mail has always come through, either by scout, stage driver, bus, or "star route" mail car. In 1937 a fine post office was erected in Mammoth. It does business there the year around; while postal stations at Old Faithful, West Thumb, Lake, Fishing

Bridge, Canyon, and Tower Falls are open only during the summer season.

Thus does a cross-section of America meet by canyon, geyser, lake, and waterfall. They also foregather around counters, tables, lobbies, and evening camp fires. It would be difficult to find a more representative assembly of American society. Many people consider this interesting human equation one of the most enjoyable experiences in the Park.

CHAPTER XIII
"THE YELLOWSTONE IDEA"

It has already been disclosed that Yellowstone Park has served the nation as an experimental unit in certain fields of conservation. While this is true, it would not be correct to regard the Park as the single place of origin for such a complex and salutary movement. Today the conservation of natural resources is one of America's most popular and cherished causes, but it was not always so. A brief review of the conservation issue will provide a background for a correct appraisal of the position of the National Park System in relation to the nation's over-all conservation program.

When the first colonies were established along the Atlantic seaboard America was a land of trees. This profusion of flora constituted an obstacle counted more serious than hostile Indians.[258] The natives had already fully cleared limited areas from the ravages of ancient fires, but the great forest stood almost limitless, and it was dense. Ambitious farmers yearned for the sight of bare ground; all trees irritated their eyes and caused them to reach for their axes. They wanted soil as rich as a barnyard, level as a floor, stone free, cleared clean of trees, without cost.[259] Except for the absence of trees, these amazing requirements were largely possible of fulfillment because never before had "heaven and earth agreed better to frame a place for man's habitation."[260] Here, indeed, was another Eden once it was redeemed from the leafy wilderness.

Colonials rallied to the challenge of a conquest over nature. They "drove" whole groves by partially felling each in a series and then touching off a chain reaction with the downfall of a ponderous giant. Thus did settlers cleave their way into the forests, rejecting in nature all that was not of immediate practical value. A little poem published in 1692 depicts their philosophy:

In such a wilderness ...

When we began to clear the land ...

Then with ax, with Might and Strength,

The trees so thick and strong ...

[These] we with Fire, most furiously

To ashes did confound.[261]

Next to the destruction of trees in clearing operations came the use of wood for fuel. A river steamboat or railroad locomotive required from twenty to thirty cords per day. "Woodhawks" literally denuded whole forests to supply these needs. Houses were largely built of wood, and it was liberally used in all domestic operations. In winter the family kept warm, not by securing "sich uppish notions" as blankets, but by throwing more wood on the fire, "nobody needn't suffer with a great fire to sleep by."[262] Rails were used in building fences at the rate of twenty-six thousand per section. The increase of population and acceleration of industrial activity in the early nineteenth century took a heavy toll from the forests. Fires were started by sparks from steam engines and by careless hunters, with the result that the precious blotter of humus, millenniums in building, was often destroyed in a flash. For two centuries America had advanced westward in a wood age, and trees were always in the way.

However, there were wise men who had always deplored tree waste. William Penn insisted that one acre of forest remain for each five cleared. Benjamin Franklin invented a stove to save fuel. George Washington and Peter Kalm warned of dangers ahead from floods and erosion through wanton clearing of land.[263] In 1813, Thomas Jefferson sagely wrote:

> The spontaneous energies of the earth are a gift of nature, but they require the labor of man to direct their operation. And the question is so to husband this labor as to turn the greatest quantity of this useful action of the earth to his benefit.[264]

It will be noted that the foregoing suggestions were made by practical men upon sound considerations. However, there came an occasional complaint upon the philosophic and aesthetic level. Jonathan Edwards, André Michaux, George Catlin, and William Cullen Bryant were among those who visualized nature as a dynamic organization of living creatures worthy of existence in their own right and for the joy they gave. Their appreciation is illustrated by this verse:

To see a World in a Grain of Sand

And Heaven in a Wild Flower,

Hold Infinity in the palm of his hand,

And Eternity in an hour.

To be sure, little resulted from this approach; the time was not ripe. But these slender stirrings of thought and twitchings of conscience in high places were bound to be fruitful in results later on.

By the middle of the nineteenth century the springs and streams which had previously provided a murmuring labyrinth of dependable forest hospitality and protection had become irregular, undependable, and sometimes downright vicious. The lifeblood of the land, which, under nature's balance, had throbbed daily and monthly almost as evenly as the sea, was now given to torrential rages in early June which were reduced to feeble trickles in July. Restless farmers found their plantings delayed until after the spring floods abated, and although the willing seed germinated quickly the tender plants were desiccated by midsummer heat. These conditions made it increasingly apparent that Americans would soon be compelled to approach nature as a friend rather than as an adversary. Any other course was suicidal.

By 1850 a new and more persuasive corps of conservationists was emerging. They affirmed that a nation desiring nature's rewards must first learn her laws and then obey them implicitly.[265] They defined conservation as the protection and development of the full usefulness of natural resources, including forests, waters, minerals, scenery, and the land itself. Among these far-seeing men were Henry Thoreau, Ralph Waldo Emerson, and John Muir. Through a persuasive campaign of lecturing and writing they established the plain fact that Americans, as a people, had never learned to love the land and regard it as an enduring resource. Rather had they viewed it as a field for exploitation and a source of immediate financial return.

Although the effect of these declarations was quite negligible, still Congress did appoint several timber agents in 1850. This was the first glimmering of a systematic approach to the inspection and policing of federal timber resources. But what have these humble beginnings in conservation to do with the Yellowstone National Park idea? Only this, a child cannot take a second step until it takes the first. Americans have never been particularly inclined toward sentimentality. A national pleasuring ground, such as Yellowstone Park, designed to serve "as a great breathing place for the national lung, as a place to which every American citizen can resort," could not have come into being without considerable intellectual preparation.[266]

Congress could hardly be expected to enact protective legislation to stem this traditional exploitation until the idea of conservation became reasonably articulate and popular. Remember, that even at mid-century the thinkers were still groping for a program. Perhaps the first American possessed of both the appreciation and imagination to forecast what later evolved into the National Park program was George Catlin. When traveling up the Missouri River in 1832 he was so impressed as to write, "The realms might in future be seen preserved in their pristine beauty and wildness, in a magnificent park ... containing man and beast, in all the wild and freshness of their nature's beauty."[267]

In 1844 Ralph Waldo Emerson generalized upon the public need for recreational areas. "The interminable forests," said he, "should become graceful parks for use and delight." Henry Thoreau was even more penetrating when he wrote:

> Why should not we ... have our national preserves ... in which the bear and panther, and some even of the hunter race, may still exist, and not be "civilized" off the face of the earth ... for inspiration and our true re-creation? Or should we, like villains, grub them all up for poaching on our own national domains?[268]

Perhaps these men reached these conclusions more by inspiration than logic, but in George P. Marsh, conservation had a sound advocate. He spoke and wrote with authority upon the principle of "conserving unique areas for their greatest values," whether utility or scenery. In his book, Man and Nature, published in 1864, he argued persuasively for balanced economy and pointed to the fact of man's ultimate dependence upon elemental things. These wise views concerning forest influences upon precipitation, springs, sand storms, floods, and man's own property made a deep impression upon many people.[269] Since then the good work has been continued by other scientists. In 1948, Our Plundered Planet, written by Fairfield Osborn, reviewed the nation's unpalatable record of negligence and waste. He characterized the Americans as energetic, destructive, violent, and unthinking. Considering the element of time, the

United States has received more reckless treatment than any other segment of the world. As a result, vast resources are gone beyond hope of redemption, but others are renewable through the application of scientific principles.

The tide of the world's population is rising; the reservoir of the earth's resources is falling. Since World War II, America seems to be in the middle position of strain. In these circumstances, will it be possible to maintain and enlarge the standard of living as in the past eras? Fairfield Osborn insists that our attitude toward conservation holds the key to the problem. Success in this endeavor will require supreme cooperation among government, industry, labor, scientific research, and the public at large. Should this grand partnership eventuate, Mr. Osborn has promised that "no end is visible or even conceivable to this kingdom of adventure."

Interest in these great truths is well established now and will not be permitted to decline, because America has many scientists at work in the field of soil conservation. This work is furthered by the specialists of the U. S. Soil Conservation Service. The soil experts constantly remind the farmers, and others, that America possessed an average top "black" soil depth of nine inches when settlement was first started. They now estimate the average to be between six and seven inches. Soil conservationists hasten to point out that rocks disintegrate slowly, and that ages, not centuries, are required for the growth and decay of plants needed in the production of rich humus soil. Soil scientists do not simply call attention to dangers. They have developed dependable and salutary cultivating practices such as contour plowing of tillable soil and terracing of range land. They advise plowing stubble and cover crops under to add fertility and cohesion to the soil.

Experimentation has been fruitful from the standpoint of discovering grass and legume adaptability to the different soil conditions. One phase of national security is contingent upon the effectiveness with which these practices are applied by all who work with farm, range, and forest resources. The record will prove that nearly 300,000,000 acres of land have been practically destroyed by erosion in the United States. Twice that acreage is rapidly deteriorating under the same forces.

Remember, that it was only a century ago when Americans received their first rudimentary lessons in exercising a little common sense in the exploitation of resources, whether for crops, lumber, mineral, livestock, or recreational opportunities.

Referring again to the status of conservation and natural philosophy in the middle nineteenth century, it should be noted that several California citizens first beheld the beauty of Yosemite in 1851. Inspired and overwhelmed by the sheer grandeur of these high Sierra marvels, they returned to commune again and again. Artists, photographers, and authors joined the growing procession, and most of them concurred in the opinion that it was "the greatest marvel on the continent." Increasing appreciation and popularity developed into a movement for segregation under state ownership and operation. In 1864 an application was made for a federal land grant with that end in view. A strong committee, headed by Israel Ward Raymond, drafted the resolution and passed it along to U.S. Senator John Conness. He presented a bill which was passed and signed by President Lincoln on June 29, 1864. The grant was given "upon the express conditions that the premises shall be held for public use, resort and recreation shall be held inalienable for all time."[270]

The federal government was gradually warming toward the reservation idea in areas of little economic resistance from private interests. Even so, there was no thought of a national park program, but a tract of federal land had actually been made available to the general public for a strictly non-utilitarian purpose. The general direction was visible, but the course was not clearly charted.

Reflective visitors to Yosemite, such as Samuel Bowles, pondered a wider application of the land grant and reservation principle. It was in 1865, after Bowles viewed the glories of Yosemite, that he made this statement:

> The wise cession and dedication [of Yosemite] by Congress and proposed improvement by California ... furnishes an admirable example for other objects of natural curiosity and popular interest all over the Union. New York should preserve for popular use both Niagara Falls and its neighborhood, and a generous section of the famous Adirondacks, and Maine, one of her lakes and its surrounding woods.[271]

Surely Bowles' statement disclosed a profound appreciation of a growing need. He had found, as Dr. Hans Huth aptly says, "a formula not just for the protection of this or that area of interest to some group or other, but for a systematic approach to an overall system of protection of specific features of nature throughout the nation."[272] However, one tremendously important element was still missing from the formula. It was simply a repetition of George Catlin's proposal of 1832, in clearer terms to be sure, but still the all-important factor of bringing the program under the aegis of the federal government was lacking. This element was supplied by the Washburn-Langford-Doane party in their memorable campfire discussion at the junction of the Firehole and Gibbon rivers on September 19, 1870, when it was specifically proposed that the federal government should be induced to establish a National Park. Within less than two years the native virtue of the idea, backed by the rugged energy of its originators and others, resulted in the passage of the Yellowstone Park Act. Yellowstone, therefore, was the first federal venture in the field of protection. Hence, technically speaking, it may stand as the birthplace of the National Park Idea.[273] True, the issue of protection and conservation had a long history, but one doesn't actually name a baby until it is born. In this light, the Yellowstone experience is the matrix in which the National Park Idea achieved existence as a new American institution.

Such is the partial record of many influences that culminated in the "Dedicatory Act" of March 1, 1872. In this chain of progress people associated with Yellowstone played a small but significant role. They helped translate a growing conservation movement into a fruitful channel. A fortuitous combination of time and place reduced opposition to a minimum. The next question would logically be: what contribution, if any, has Yellowstone National Park made toward the development of the present conservation program?

The creation of Yosemite and Yellowstone parks set a precedent for democratic control of natural curiosities, including scenic forests, but that was all. No action was then contemplated by Congress in respect to conserving commercial timber stands. However, Congress was plagued by petitions, and a few forward-looking legislators were endeavoring to formulate a basis for a forest policy. The American Association for the Advancement of Science advocated a program of tree planting, taxes to discourage hasty timber cutting, a forestry course for farmers, and the establishment of forest reserves. In 1873, under the guiding hand of Franklin B. Hough, the association memorialized Congress and the state legislatures regarding the cultivation of timber and the preservation of forests.[274]

That same year Congress appropriated two thousand dollars for a study of American forest and timber production. Mr. Hough directed the work and issued a series of reports. Secretary of the Interior Carl Schurz was sufficiently impressed by this survey to create the Department of Forestry within his department.[275] In addition, he appointed a forestry agent and sent him to Europe to study forest methods.

Such Fabian tactics suggest that the conservationists were not strong enough to really come to grips with the problem. But the leaders were alert, and in 1891 they made a notable gain by a devious maneuver. A conference committee of the two houses was adjusting differences in a bill that revised the general land laws. Advocates of conservation through their leader, John W. Noble, Secretary of the Interior, dominated the committee. It was he who suggested the inclusion of a new section, although that was a violation of procedure, which provided that:

> The president of the U. S. may, from time to time, set apart and reserve, in any state or territory having public land bearing forests, any part ... whether of commercial value or not, as public reservations, and the president shall, by public proclamation, declare the establishment of such reservations.[276]

In that way Congress stumbled onto a plan which worked because, by granting reserve creating power to the president, the timber lobby was circumvented. This measure provided a definite wedge against the compact, aggressive forces of exploitation. President Benjamin Harrison acted promptly by creating, in 1891, the Yellowstone Timber Reserve in Wyoming. He, thereby, created the first National Forest, and before his term expired he set aside a total of thirteen million acres, all in the Far West.

Another side of conservation was inaugurated in 1872 when J. Sterling Morton of Lincoln, Nebraska, introduced a resolution for a state-wide Arbor Day. By 1885 the idea had gained enough popular support to warrant the establishment of Arbor Day as a legal holiday, and since then more than half of the states have followed Nebraska's example.

However, it was a Pennsylvanian who became the most effective conservationist of all; Gifford Pinchot was well educated, energetic, and interested in the cause. As manager of the Vanderbilt forest interests in North Carolina he evolved a policy of perpetual timber yield. The indefatigable Mr. Pinchot was prepared to make a contribution to the conservation movement on a national level, and Theodore Roosevelt's accession to the presidency in 1901 gave him that opportunity. President Roosevelt, also, brought much field experience to the conservation problem. His interest was one of conviction as well as good sense, sentiment, and politics. He viewed the presidency as a stewardship for the nation's resources. More than anyone before or since he dramatized this issue. As head of the forest bureau, Mr. Pinchot became the President's strong right arm, and together they made America acquainted with her conservation needs. A survey of national resources disclosed the fact that of the original 800,000,000 acres of virgin forest, less than 200,000,000 remained. Furthermore, four-fifths of this acreage was in private hands. Mineral resources, also, had been exploited as if inexhaustible. By propaganda, lobbies, public meetings, and conferences, Roosevelt and Pinchot focused attention upon abuses and neglect. Their watchword was that America's natural resources must be administered in the interest of "the greatest good to the greatest number—and that for the longest time."[277]

The general response to the President's Governors' Conference at the White House in 1907, and to other conferences, was most gratifying. Conservation agencies sprang into action on all sides. Even the National Lumber Manufacturers' Association established new standards and specifications for the wood-using industries. The dynamic leadership of Theodore Roosevelt and his associates enabled the people to comprehend the basic relationship of conservation and national welfare. Almost everyone united in the view that a new frontier had been formed and its conquest was to be made upon the principles and forces of conservation.

Congress had led the way toward legislative regulation, beginning with the Yosemite Act in 1864, followed by the Yellowstone "Dedicatory Act" of 1872. Since then one legislative pearl after another has been collected and strung upon the fabric of the National Forest and Park systems.

Today there are thirteen federal agencies charged with the administration of the federal conservation laws. Consolidation of these bureaus would undoubtedly enhance the effectiveness of the over-all service. Besides that, there are forty-eight state agencies and, in addition, one hundred and twenty-four organizations of either national, state, or local character specifically dedicated to conservation.[278] From the origin herein described, the National Forest Service has developed until there are now 180,000,000 acres within the confines of one hundred and fifty National Forests. The administration of these far-flung areas is co-ordinated by twelve regional offices and other adjunctive agencies, such as experiment stations and laboratories.

The guiding philosophy of National Forest management is known as "multiple use." This term describes a broad program involving the inter-relationship of wild life protection, livestock grazing, logging, mining, irrigation watersheds, wood chopping, recreation, summer home areas, and hunting and fishing activities. Railroads and other roads are built in National Forests according to plan and under supervision. How much of this esteemable policy and program has been derived from the National Park experience? The two services have developed simultaneously; as the boundaries of parks and forests often impinge, so have their policies. Both services have many ends in common; each learns from the other.[279] The essential differentiation of service lies in the difference between "conserving an area for its greatest value" and "utilization of resources in multiple purpose." It is a matter of degrees of conservation according to circumstances. For example, public hunting is prohibited in all 23,899,030 acres of the 181 areas under the supervision of the National Park Service. However, the service itself may adopt a policy of fauna diminution.

Having sketched the history of forest and land conservation, it would be appropriate to similarly narrate the movement to conserve wild life. Until a half century ago the American attitude toward wild life was almost wholly one of indifference. The frontiersman killed a deer per meal and gave little thought for the morrow. Only the Indians were preservers of game, as the saying, "No Indians not much game; heap Sioux, plenty of buffalo, elk and deer," so aptly attests.[280] It has already been explained how this difference in racial behavior eventuated in almost perpetual strife between white and red men. There were occasional exceptions, as in the case of Daniel Boone. In 1775 he proposed a measure for the protection of game in Kentucky because it was already necessary for him to travel a score of miles from home to find buffalo.

The pristine American wild life heritage was on a par with the endowment of forest and land. The toothsome white-tailed deer was omnipresent in the East and much of the Middle West. Other species of deer, elk, moose, bison, and antelope were in great abundance. Reports from Lewis and Clark, Zebulon Pike, J. J. Audubon, B. L. Bonneville and others prove that no pioneer ever pushed so far, or entered regions so difficult or remote, that he did not find a host of birds and beasts awaiting his pleasure and profit.[281] Man has always had a predatory disposition toward wild life, but this was not so serious in the ages of club, stone ax, and bow and arrow. American animal abundance was contemporaneous with these times.

Wild life conservation became an imperative issue only after the invention of flintlock, breechloaders, repeaters, automatics, and fixed ammunition. These weapons in the hands of commercial hunters, unscrupulous sportsmen, and "game hogs" threatened extinction of many species of life. Most devastating of all threats was the impact of the market hunter; no bird, mammal, or reptile species can long withstand such exploitation. Professional gunners who pursue creatures for money are invariably skillful, diligent, and persistent.[282] Often the sportsman is equally skillful and efficient in slaughter. The Earl of Dunraven left this description of a chase in the vicinity of Fort Laramie:

> We killed elk, white-tail and black-tail deer, antelope, swans, immense geese, ducks and small game without count. This elk running is perfectly magnificent. We ride among the wild sand hills till we find a herd, and then gallop after them like maniacs, cutting them off, till we get in the midst of them, when we shoot all that we can. Our chief hunter is a very famous man out West, one Buffalo Bill. To see his face flush, and his eyes shoot out courage is a sight to see, and he cheers us on till he makes us as mad as himself.[283]

Concerning the high sport of the Earl's party, Mary Kingsley made the witty observation that "In the course of these wanderings they shot ... every kind of living thing ... on the Western Continent ... with the solitary exception of their fellowmen."[284] America has handled its wild life in such a careless, greedy fashion that several species of animal and fowl became extinct, and many others were brought within the range of annihilation. The danger point varies with each species, but there is an area for each wherein the survivors are too few to cope with circumstances, and recovery is impossible. This fact became quite clear to certain conservationists around 1900.

Outstanding leadership was provided by Madison Grant, John F. Lacey, Henry Fairfield Osborn and Willard Dutcher.[285] These men so wrote and spoke as to arouse the public and sting the true sportsmen into action. People who did not shoot were impelled to call a halt on those who did, particularly upon the lawless element. The public was assured that much could be done to save a wonderful inheritance. In order to finance the conservation campaign aggregate bequests in excess of one-half million dollars were made by Albert Wilcox, Mrs. Russell Sage, Charles W. Ward, and Mary Dutcher. President Theodore Roosevelt nourished the movement in every way within his power. He gave the vanishing species the benefit of every doubt. Under his direction five national parks, three bison herds, fifty-three bird refuges, and four game preserves were established.

Warnings and appeals directed toward conservation went through all channels, legislative, educational, practical, and sentimental. The farmers were assured that the rejuvenated bison, deer, and elk herds would not be allowed to roam at will over their valuable land. Rather there were millions of acres of brushy, rocky, and semi-forest lands, wholly unsuited for agriculture, in which the conservation work could be done. Sportsmen were promised opportunities for shooting plentiful game in open seasons as soon as the proper balance of wild life had been restored. Their response to this program has become increasingly impressive. They have effected almost innumerable associations designed to achieve these ends. Much thought and effort have been given to the cause, and they have contributed liberally, besides paying license fees. Revenue from all sportsmen sources must approximate a billion dollars a year. Hence, it is correct to say that combined sportsmen organizations represent one of the most effective agencies of conservation.

By 1912 the movement had achieved general acceptance. The Department of Agriculture issued annual "progress reports." Every state had either a State Game Commission or a State Game Warden. Montana had established two state preserves. Several states were successfully experimenting with the introduction of new species of game birds, such as Chinese ring-necked, golden, and silver pheasants. The federal government had created fifty-eight bird refuges and five great game preserves. It had taken steps to protect bison herds in four national ranges, besides protecting the fur seal and providing hay for starving Yellowstone Park elk and others in the Jackson Hole area.

The efforts of government agencies were effectively buttressed by a number of private organizations such as the New York Zoological Society, National Association of Audubon Societies, Campfire Club of America, Boone and Crockett Club, and the American Game Protective and Propagation Association. Since 1912 gratifying progress has been made, although there are still many problems remaining. Yellowstone's Park Biologist, Walter H. Kittams, and many other specialists are applying the best modern techniques of range management and wildlife management to effect a solution to these problems consistent with National Park Service ideals.

It has already been noted that Yellowstone National Park has served as an area of experimentation in the field of wild life management. When the reservation was established in 1872 a proposal was made to outlaw hunting. The suggestion was not heeded by Congress, and as a result trappers and hunters plied their trades early and late, seven days a week, month after month.

A representative description of wild life exploitation in the Yellowstone Wonderland may be found in the Earl of Dunraven's book, Hunting in the Yellowstone. This is an account of his trip through the Park in 1874. While camped at Mammoth Hot Springs he wrote: "Some of us went out hunting and brought in a good store of fat antelope ..."[286] If that entry strikes a note of discord because of present practice, observe the significance of the Earl's record in describing the following Yellowstone camp:

> In the afternoon we passed quite a patriarchal camp [near Sheepeater's Cliff], composed of two men, with their Indian wives and several children; half a dozen powerful savage looking dogs and about fifty horses completed the party. They had been grazing their stock, hunting and trapping, leading a nomad, vagabond, and delicious life—a sort of mixed existence, half hunter, half herdsman, and had

collected a great pile of deer hides and beaver skins. They were then on their way to settlements to dispose of their peltries, and to get stores and provisions; for they, too, were proceeding down the river or up the canon.[287]

Within the decade it became obvious to Park officials that the fauna would not long survive this savage onslaught from squaw men, professional gunners, fierce dogs, and expert scouts and guides vying for tourist patronage. Along with this realization came another discovery; soldiers in remote stations had formed enjoyable companionships with wilderness creatures. These lonely men were delighted by the universally charming wild life trait of responding with confidence and alacrity to friendly human advances. It became increasingly apparent to the officials that Yellowstone birds and mammals would quickly recognize overtures of friendship and protection. The idea was advanced that nearly every species in the Park might become as tame as range cattle if given an opportunity to move safely within rifle-shot for several years. Recommendations to that effect forwarded to the Secretary of the Interior by Superintendent Norris in 1879 were passed on to Congress, and they played an important part in the passage of legislation on March 3, 1883, under which the killing of game was first suppressed. In subsequent years the laws were strengthened and administration improved. This was the beginning of wild life conservation practice by the federal government. Since then the various species of native fauna have achieved a generally satisfactory balance. The Park's policy of protection can definitely be credited with saving the grizzly bear from extinction, and the trumpeter swan is receiving his chance to survive. It may be too late in this case.

Today the alert tourist may reap the reward of that wise and fruitful policy in observing mountain sheep, antelope, mule deer, elk, moose, coyotes, marmot, and squirrels as they roam around in the Park. Indeed, the quiet but energetic visitor who ventures upon the forest trails may even see the rare sand-hill crane and trumpeter swan. Besides, he will frequently hear the passing whisper of the honker's wing. Actually, he may "shoot" both birds and mammals with the camera and take home trophies of everlasting enjoyment.

The wildlife policy of the National Park Service has evolved gradually, and is based upon long experience in preserving areas of outstanding significance. It has been determined that animals shall not be encouraged to become dependent upon man, and their presentation to the public shall be wholly natural. Every species shall be left to carry on its struggle for existence unaided, unless it becomes endangered, and no management measure or interference with biotic relationships shall be undertaken prior to a properly conducted investigation. Numbers of animals must not be permitted to exceed the carrying capacity of the range available to them. Predator species will be given the same protection as all other animals, except in special instances where a prey species is in danger of extermination. These principles, and others, control the actions taken with respect to wildlife, and assure the continued existence of native wildlife in our National Parks.

CHAPTER XIV
GENERAL ADMINISTRATION

Nathaniel P. Langford was appointed Superintendent of Yellowstone National Park on May 10, 1872. No salary was allowed, but nothing daunted, on July 4 he arranged to join the Snake River detachment of Dr. F. V. Hayden's second expedition. This party employed as guide one Richard Leigh, better known as "Beaver Dick." This picturesque squaw man and his wife, Jenny, with her brood, not only acted as scout but also as friend and entertainer. "Beaver Dick" knew the Tetons and south Yellowstone country like a book, and he regaled the company with many tales of hair-raising experiences in the wilds. They were respectful in the presence of one of the last genuine frontiersmen of the West.

The new superintendent was characteristically indefatigable in his reconnaissance during this journey. Making personal side trips, he climbed the Grand Teton, called on Gilman Sawtelle at Henrys Lake, and joined Hayden in the Upper Geyser Basin by mid-August.[288] On this expedition the reports of much petrifaction along the East Fork of Yellowstone River (now called Lamar) were confirmed. Many trees were found that were filled with beautiful crystals of amethyst. Several species of trees that do not now grow in the Park were also found in a petrified state. Among these were magnolias, sycamores, aralias, oaks, and ferns in abundance. This, and subsequent investigations, disclosed an interesting story of climatic change. Obviously Tertiary flora was of a Southern type, and Yellowstone's climate in that time was comparable to southern California's today.[289]

Photo by W. H. Jackson
"Beaver Dick" (Richard Leigh) and family, 1871

Members of this same expedition also visited the Heart Lake and Norris Geyser-basins.[290] Hayden and Langford were more than pleased with the results. Wonderland's charms were still a potent draught to the thirst of these great nature lovers. Their enthusiasm never flagged, although there were many discouragements. Several accidents must have induced considerable reflection, if not doubt, about the realization of their hopes. One horse went to its doom in quagmire; another broke its neck in a somersault. Horses sensed the inexperience and uncertainty of their riders in this environment, and there were several stampedes.[291] This time Langford viewed Yellowstone in the light of what the public would require, and the task ahead must have appeared insurmountable. Still, his good judgment told him that the Park would surely become a favorite resort for future tourists. Plans were conceived for trails, roads, and accommodations, and in the spring of 1873 he appointed David E. Folsom as assistant superintendent, also without pay.

Langford's annual report of 1873 showed that five hundred people visited the Park that season. A request was made for an appropriation of $10,000 for improvements, but no funds were provided for any purpose. As time passed, the general situation became increasingly untenable. The frontiersman's indifference to schedules and comforts caused much inconvenience and dissatisfaction to the travelers. A program of development and a system of concessions was imperative. Of course, these things would require time, planning, and money, but this fact was little recognized by newcomers. Langford was roundly criticized in the press for conditions over which he had no authority or means to control. However, during the winter he faithfully devoted his spare time to making plans, and his full time in summer was given to their execution. For five long years he gave the best that was in him, without funds or support, never losing his faith in the future of Yellowstone, and because of his enthusiasm his friends called him "National Park" Langford.[292]

In 1877 a new superintendent succeeded Langford. Philetus W. Norris, of Michigan, received the appointment, with pay, and the following year a $10,000 appropriation was made available "to protect, preserve, and improve Yellowstone Park." Norris, although a rather quaint man, proved to be extremely zealous and energetic. On foot and horseback he eventually toured all of the Park and its immediate environs, considering a thorough personal exploration of Wonderland essential to a wise administration of his office. In 1878 he discovered Monument Geyser Basin, and later in the season an attempt was made to explore the Hoodoo area on the upper Lamar River drainage, but the Crow Indians challenged his right, and "Miller, Rowland, and myself, narrowly escaped."[293] However, he persisted, and in due time the world learned about

Superintendent Philetus W. Norris

... that mysterious Hoodoo region, where all the devils now employed in the geysers, live and kill the wandering bear and elk, so that the sacred hunter finds in Death Gulch piled high carcasses of the dead whom no man has smitten.[294]

There is obvious exaggeration in Kipling's description of wild life destruction by natural gases. However, evidence confirming the lethal power of Yellowstone's natural carbon dioxide gas may be secured without going into the remote Hoodoo region. Birds die almost daily from inhaling the fumes that arise from springs on Orange Mound in the Mammoth Hot Springs. Park naturalists are in a quandary as to the procedure of warning birds concerning the danger.

Norris wrote voluminously and accomplished much, leaving his mark and name upon various sections of the Park. He caused trails, roads, bridges, and crude campgrounds to be made, in so far as the limited funds would allow. A policy of wild life protection was also adopted. In 1880 Harry Yount was given the assignment as gamekeeper. Yount was a typical leatherstocking frontiersman. He was rough, tough, and intelligent. In the role of game protector he spent the winter of 1880 in the Park. He thereby became one of the first white men of record to spend the entire year in Yellowstone.[295] Harry initiated many of the practices of resourcefulness and traditions of good will that characterize the ranger service, and he may be considered as its father.

The need of a game protection program was apparent from the outset. Indian, trapper, and miner visitations had taken a heavy toll of elk, deer, antelope, and buffalo. After 1872 tourist parties were largely made up of, or guided by, mountain men who undertook to provide game for the campers. Thus, a trip through Yellowstone was, in effect, a hunting and fishing expedition, actuated by the slogan "slay and eat."

In 1876 William Ludlow, a government surveyor, was moved to write an effective appeal for game protection to George Bird Grinnell, editor of Forest and Stream. His argument was buttressed by many observations of the slaughter "of the largest and finest game animals in the country."[296] In 1879 Superintendent Norris made a similar observation in his annual report. He stated that, with the rapid influx of tourists and the demand for such food, the policy could not long continue without serious results. He, thereupon, issued an order for the protection of the bison as the herd was not in excess of six hundred. However, this commendable move proved ineffective, and the hunters went merrily about their avocation.

About this time Norris left the Park service, but before doing so he had completed and occupied a unique structure on Capitol Hill, called Fort Yellowstone. It was a blockhouse of hewn timber with a balcony and three wings, surmounted by a gun turret. He wanted to be prepared for the next Indian attack, while the problems actually confronting the Park officials were of quite a different character. Yellowstone was still a wilderness, and many visitors would not endure restraints. In 1883 Secretary of the Interior Hoke Smith caught two hundred trout in one day, and the next year Secretary of War Dan Lamont only caught fifty-three![297]

Old Fort Yellowstone.

In 1882 Patrick A. Conger, of Iowa, succeeded Norris as superintendent. His administration was weak and vacillating in practically every respect. Scarcely anything was improved, but all difficulties were aggravated. Vandalism, forest fires, and general mismanagement were added to the problem of vanishing wild life. John S. Crosby, Governor of Montana, wrote a scathing denunciation of the Park officials to the Secretary of the Interior, Henry M. Teller.[298] This official contemplated the leasing of considerable portions of the Park to responsible persons in the hope that they would, through self-interest, give the protection which the government had failed to provide.[299] While Montana's governor complained and the Secretary hesitated Wyoming territorial officials took action. The Wyoming legislature intervened by providing stringent measures for the protection of timber, game, fish, and natural curiosities of the Park. A jail was erected, and the territorial officials got ready for business. Cowboy type-cast officers had a lively time enforcing regulations and levying fines for personal emolument upon strangers toward whom they felt a natural suspicion.[300] Vexatious arrests, made under the sweeping provisions of the act, defeated the purpose of the Park "as a pleasuring ground for the people." Citizens questioned the right of a territory to exercise criminal jurisdiction and judicial powers in a federal reservation. The act was repealed in 1886, but the effect was to leave the Park in a worse plight than ever before. As it became generally known that the superintendent had no support beyond the rules of the department and their own personal force,

> the rules and regulations were ignored, while outlaws and vagabonds from the surrounding region made the nation's pleasure ground a place of refuge. The hotels were frequented by gamblers and adventurers, who preyed upon the unwary tourist, while forest fires, originating mysteriously in remote and inaccessible places, raged unchecked.[301]

Robert E. Carpenter took office as Park Superintendent in August, 1884. In his view the Park presented an opportunity for personal and corporate exploitation. He was in full accord with a conspiracy to obtain private ownership of strategic locations. This scheme was advanced by an organization known as The Improvement Company which went directly before Congress with its proposition. In this effort, the nadir of private greed and administrative indifference was reached. However, the bad cause was lost, the superintendent removed, and a new and better administration came into being.[302] The influence of General Phil Sheridan was a constant factor in promoting the welfare of the Park. Beginning in 1881, he made a series of annual tours of the region. After each inspection he earnestly appealed to public sentiment, in behalf of proper government, for the area. Whereupon, Congress passed the Sundry Civil Bill of March, 1883 which forbade the granting of leases in excess of ten acres to a single party and provided for the employment of ten assistant superintendents. This measure also authorized the Secretary of the Interior to call upon the Secretary of War for troops to patrol the Park.

In May, 1885 David W. Wear of Missouri brought intelligent and vigorous effort to the problem. At the close of the season he wrote a comprehensive report that carried a tone of real interest and purpose: "The discipline of the force was bad; no head to anything.... The game had been shot with impunity and marketed at the hotels."[303] He secured the services of a trusty mountaineer, and together they rounded up the worst of the "skin hunters" and punished them to the full extent of the law. Of course, that was simply arrest and expulsion from the Park, together with the forfeiture of equipment used in the violation.

During the season of 1885 a committee of congressmen visited the Park for the purpose of ascertaining how wisely the recent appropriation of $40,000 was being used and inquiring into the administration of laws.[304] The report of this and other investigating groups seemed to be that, although Superintendent Wear was performing his duty efficiently and fearlessly, the whole situation was honeycombed with error, corruption, confusion, and suspicion. The Park was in need of redemption; something had to be done. The high purposes of the Dedicatory Act were being frustrated. An avalanche of petitions, representing opinion from thirty-one states, reached the Department of the Interior and could not be ignored.

Therefore, the Department of the Interior called upon the United States Army to effect a new birth. This action was taken under the authority of the act of March 3, 1883, wherein the Secretary of War, upon the request of the Secretary of the Interior, was directed to provide:

> Details of troops to prevent trespassers or intruders from entering the Park for the purpose of destroying the game or objects of curiosity therein, or for any other purpose prohibited by law, and to remove such persons from the Park if found therein.[305]

Accordingly, on August 20, 1886, Captain Moses Harris with a troop of the first cavalry took charge. Detachments of soldiers were soon stationed at Norris, Lower and Upper Geyser basins, Canyon, Riverside, and Soda Butte. Old frontiersmen were notified to desist from their poaching activities; prowling Indians were ordered to stay away; forest fires were checked; and the tone of all departments of service and accommodation improved. The Hayes and Lacey acts granted the necessary authority in respect to leases, protection, and punishment. Captain Harris proved to be a forthright administrator. He established a system of patrols stemming out from the permanent stations. The patrolmen were instructed to not only follow the regular roads and trails but to occasionally visit unfrequented places.[306] The patrolmen were ordered to keep a sharp lookout for bear trappers, poachers, and forest fires. Persons traveling in the Park between October 1 and June 1 were to be viewed with suspicion: in fact, they were to be questioned closely and watched as they journeyed from station to station.

There were many frontiersmen who continued to ignore the Captain's warnings about poaching. This challenge was accepted, and on August 19, 1888 a scouting party apprehended a trapper near the southern border. He gave his name as Andrew S. Page but later admitted he had been arrested the previous year as John Andrews. His horse and outfit were confiscated, and he was expelled from the Park.[307] In September of the same year Thomas Garfield was caught in the act of trapping beaver in Willow Creek. He was given the same treatment. Garfield made ominous threats to get even, and a few days later a forest fire was started by someone near Norris. In spite of occasional arrests the practice of poaching persisted. Trapping habits were deep-seated and penalties, too mild.

In the years that followed the cases of Tom Newcomb, June Buzzel, Jay Whitman, James Courtney, A. G. Vance, E. Sheffeld, Pendleton, and Van Dych were tried with various degrees of success.[308]

The most notorious case was that of Ed Howell of Cooke, Montana. Early in March, 1894, a party was organized to visit the winter range of the buffalo. Members were Captain George L. Scott, Lieutenant William W. Forsyth, Scout Felix Burgess, A. E. Burns, Frank Jay Haynes, Sergeant Troike, and two other noncommissioned officers. They traveled on skis, and when they reached the Canyon, Emerson Hough and Billy Hofer joined them. About twelve miles up Pelican Creek they discovered the cache of a poacher. Six bison heads were suspended in a tree. Several shots were heard, but as it was snowing the direction was difficult to determine. However, Scout Burgess was able to approach the poacher without being seen or heard, even by the dog. He got the drop on Howell, which was a good thing in view of the character of the man.[309] He had driven a half-dozen other bison in the deep snow and killed them.

The culprit was taken to Mammoth where the presence of the writer Emerson Hough and a representative of Forest and Stream gave national publicity to the case. Howell was quite a robust personality, and he responded to the limelight. "How does a poacher operate to avoid two troops of soldiers?" "It is the simplest thing in the world," said Howell, "just wait for a snowstorm, enter the desired area, make a wide detour to check tracks of pursuers, if any, and go to work." "Why did you do it?" "Well, bison heads are worth from $100 to $400 apiece."[310]

The articles in Forest and Stream apprised the nation of the fact that there were less than one hundred head of bison left in the Park and that the government's failure to provide real protection was threatening the extinction of all the larger animals. One side of the reaction was critical of the army administration. Said one observer, "I would rather have three good, intelligent, honorable men, inured to the life of prospector and hunter, in these mountains to watch the Park, than all the soldiers now there....."[311]

However, a constructive remedy was provided by legislation in the passage of the act of May 7, 1894. This measure positively prohibited hunting and trapping in every form, under heavy penalties. A clear-cut basis of jurisdiction was provided by the Vest Bill. A United States Commissioner was appointed, "who shall reside in the Park," to issue processes and hear cases. An appeal from his decisions might be made before the Federal District Court for the District of Wyoming. Hon. John W. Meldrum was the first man to receive this assignment. He held the position until 1935 when he was succeeded by T. Paul Wilcox.Within a year after the passage of the Protective Act, Captain George S. Anderson was able to report that a healthy effect was evident. That was not the end of poaching because it has existed in a slight and subtle manner to this very day. However, around the turn of the century, the poacher gave way to the road agent as the Park's most exciting criminal.

W. S. Chapman
Poacher caught in the act.

In Captain Harris' report of 1888 there is reference to a stage robbery of July 4, 1887. Subsequently, William James and a man named Higgenbottom were convicted and fined $1000 each and given a year's sentence in the Montana State Penitentiary. Again, on August 14, 1897, two masked men held up and robbed six Yellowstone Park Transportation coaches and one spring wagon. The place of the robbery was between Canyon and Norris, the amount of the "haul" being over $500. These offenders were apprehended and identified as Charles Reebe, alias "Morphine Charley," and Charles Switzer. They were also convicted, fined, and imprisoned.[312]

On August 24, 1908, on Spring Creek, one masked man successfully held up nine coaches carrying a total of one hundred and fifteen people. The booty collected totaled $1,363.95 in cash and $730.25 in watches and jewelry. The entire cavalcade consisted of thirty-two coaches, escorted by one trooper. The road agent did not show himself until the soldier and eight of the coaches had passed. Thereafter, each one was held up and ordered on its way before the next one arrived. The victims of this outrage held a meeting in the Lake Hotel and drafted a set of resolutions reviewing all of the facts. They complained because they were deprived of personal firearms and denied sufficient protection to life and property. They also petitioned for redress. These resolutions, together with the names of the victims, were printed in a souvenir edition and widely distributed.[313]

Perhaps the most daring robbery in Yellowstone history was executed near Shoshone Point, on July 29, 1915. It was there that Edward B. Trafton, alias Ed Harrington, an outlaw from Teton Basin, duplicated the feat of the 1908 season; the amount taken was about $2200. However, Trafton was apprehended and convicted of the latter crime on December 15, 1915. His sentence was a five-year term in Fort Leavenworth, Kansas.

Robberies of a less dramatic character still occur. In 1941 two rangers fished several purses out of Cauliflower Geyser. They had been snatched from parked cars, rifled, and cast away, but the geyser threw them up, and they were used as evidence in effecting a conviction. Times and methods change, but crime goes on forever.

Another problem that has constantly confronted every administration is vandalism. A vandal is any person who takes flowers or specimens and writes on or defaces natural objects, and his name is legion. The more cunningly contrived a work of nature becomes, the greater the temptation to remove it to one's own premises. This urge reduces even dignified people to the most amazing behavior. They will pry and chop in such a way as to destroy an ornament for all time. Again, there is the untoward desire to throw tokens, small coins, bottles, poles, and detritus into pools and geysers "just to see what will happen."

Not even Old Faithful is exempt from this wantonness. It is a matter of record that one party, wishing to experiment, filled its orifice "with at least a thousand pounds of stones, trees, and stumps" and then sat down to await further developments. Another group wrote this shameless account: "We abused that spring [geyser] with everything in our power. We threw sticks into it and stones, but it was no use; nothing would rile it."[314] Name writing in pools and geysers is particularly alluring to a certain class as nature fixes the insult indelibly so that in after years all men may read, in letters as large as a neon sign, that "Sadie, Mamie, and Jack" visited the Park. Many a ranger, attempting to eradicate such legends with his wire brush, has heartily agreed with the following statement "... and when the man from Oshkosh writes his name with a blue pencil on her sacred face, let him spend six months where the scenery is circumscribed and entirely artificial."[315] Will the public never learn that, although it owns the Park, ownership may be expressed in much more appropriate ways?

The offense of "soaping" geysers is said to have originated in 1885 when a Chinaman encompassed a small spring with his tent and started a laundry. When the spring became impregnated with soap there was an eruption, and up went tent, washing, and Chinaman! It is a fact that soap produces viscosity which retains heat, and as steam rises it may aid explosive action. Hence, if some visitors could have their way, the beautiful sapphire springs and geysers would be "in the suds" constantly throughout the season.[316] Such activity is strictly prohibited by the government.

In recent years Park officials have been greatly distressed by another type of violation. Large numbers of people are disposed to cast tax tokens and pennies into the otherwise beautiful hot springs and geysers. Familiar with wishing wells in commercial resorts, they fall short in adjusting to national park standards of conduct. As one ranger said, "They forget what kind of animal throws a (s)cent!"

Many lovers of Yellowstone would like to see the rangers crack down upon rule violators with a vengeance. They argue that a full 10 per cent of the human race will lie, steal, and destroy flora, fauna, and features whenever and wherever they find a chance to do so. Of course, the rangers are quick in recognizing varying degrees of moral and social responsibility. Their policy to date is one of energetic education and moderate restraint by authority.

The problem of forest fires causes much concern during July and August. Fires may start from natural causes, as from lightning, and friction caused by trees rubbing together during violent windstorms, but about 50 per cent of them are caused by the carelessness of man. Of course, nature manages to extinguish forest fires eventually, but man has learned to cooperate.

The officials have developed efficiency in organization and methods of fighting fires. Major lookouts are established upon Mt. Washburn, Mt. Holmes, Mt. Sheridan, Purple Mountain, and Pelican Cone. Lookouts also stand guard in other strategic positions. Fireguards are employed to clear trails and be available on a moment's notice. District rangers train and direct employees within their jurisdictions and take daily "fire weather" readings. Tools, equipment, and provisions are always packed and ready for action. When a fire breaks out a base camp is set up at a road terminal; from there the flow of men and supplies is governed through radio communication. Fire camps are established in safe places, by the water supply nearest the burning area. Tools, sleeping bags, and food reach the fire camp on the backs of mules, by reason of the skill of expert packers. However, airplanes are sometimes used in parachuting fighters and supplies to the spot in a hurry.

Accepted principles of procedure consist of: speed in the first instance before the fire "blows up"; striking hard at daybreak after it has calmed down and before the wind fans it; cutting a line with saw and ax; trenching it in with shovel and Pulaski; using pumps where possible; and always praying for rain. Fighting fire is an arduous, dirty business.

Yellowstone forests are predominantly of lodgepole pine. This species is thin-skinned and non-resistant to fire, but it takes pains to store its seeds up in tightly closed cones. These hold the seed fertile for several years. Thus, although raging fire may devour the forest, the scorched cones open, and the hoarded seed shoots new growth triumphantly out of the ashes.[317]

It has been observed that lodgepole forests are not very valuable for lumber; neither do they present the most attractive appearance. Still, the trees grow profusely, and in so doing they provide an excellent agency for water conservation. Let fire destroy the forests upon the sources of the Snake and Yellowstone rivers, and many of the present garden spots of the West would be added to her barren wastes. Therefore, in the mature opinion of many experts, the forests of this area are more valuable in the conservation of soil and water than they would be for grazing and lumbering. The present policy will keep the mountains at home, prevent floods, and assure a more constant water supply.[318]

Perhaps the most tantalizing problem has arisen from the half-century application of the Protective Act of 1894, wherein:

> The killing, wounding, or capturing, at any time, of any bird or wild animal, except dangerous animals, when it is necessary to prevent them from destroying life or inflicting an injury, is prohibited within the limits of the Park.[319]

Wild and dangerous despite appearances.

People possessing firearms must have them sealed upon entering the Park. Thus, the animal inhabitants virtually enjoy a natural life expectancy so far as man is concerned.[320] It is an anomalous situation, without a parallel since the Garden of Eden. On the whole, the animals have lost their fear of man, and still very few of them show any disposition to injure him except in self-defense. Deer, black bear, marmot, squirrels, and many species of birds are very responsive to opportunities of human association. Several other types exhibit good-natured indulgence toward human curiosity, but a few species are so elusive as to be almost inaccessible. In fact, there are some creatures that possess such a decided allergy to the presence of man that their survival is jeopardized by human proximity. Moose, grizzlies, bighorn, antelope, beaver, and swan conform to this type. They require an environment of varying specifications from swamp to rocky crag, but possessing the element of seclusion as a common denominator. Park officials recognize these factors and endeavor to meet the requirements for the health of their denizens. Furthermore, they are willing to allow the so-called predators the use of the Park as a sanctuary, or refuge, even though their instincts seem to be of a wholly destructive character. The latch key is out for wolverine, coyote, and cougar.

It should be emphasized that in the case of black bear human contacts are fraught with dire consequences for all concerned. Approximately a hundred tourists sustain bear bites or scratches each season, and many bears are killed for these offenses. Park officials frequently doubt the possibility of reconciling the presence of black bear and people. If the latter were governed by the principle of intelligence, it would be an easy matter. But they simply refuse to believe that the bears are wild. As a result, they take privileges with a mother and cubs which no one would ever think of trying with a neighbor's hound.

It is admitted by all that black bear cubs are among nature's most interesting creatures. They are the "Happy Hooligans" and "Katzenjammer Kids" of the Park. What a spectacle they provide, standing Jesse James-like along the highway, tumbling over each other in fun, or scampering up a tree in fright! "Do you mean to tell me those cute creatures will harm anyone?" says a lady, "Why they smile and wiggle their tails in the most cunning manner!" "Yes, lady," replies the ranger, "but you must not believe either end of a bear."

When a serious injury or a death occurs strong resentment is expressed against the administration. It is advised to decide either to turn the Park over to the bears or to the people. Then a party of tourists expresses great disappointment over not having been "held up" by a bear. What will be the outcome of this tug-of-war? It is to be hoped that the public will eventually learn to obey the regulation, "Do Not Feed or Molest the Bears."[321]

Grizzly, king of the Rockies.

The American bison was probably saved from extinction in Yellowstone. Although native to the region, the joint ravages of poachers and septicemia finally reduced the herd to a mere remnant. In 1895 a hay harvesting project was started in Hayden Valley. This enterprise was subsequently moved to the Lamar Valley where a buffalo ranch, now called the Lamar Unit, was established. Feeding these animals in the coldest months during winters of exceptional severity has proved salutary. Another precaution was taken in 1902 when twenty-one head were purchased from the Goodnight and Allard herds in Texas and Montana, respectively. Since then the herd has flourished and is now stabilized at eight hundred head. The increase is reduced periodically and distributed among near by Indian agencies.

A reduction policy has also been adopted to control the northern elk herd. Summer is lavish in its gifts to Park elk. Lush grasses, shady dells, and cool weather make an ideal condition for them. Fall finds them fat and sleek, with bulls bugling in every glen. Perhaps the summer range is adequate for thousands of them, but then winter comes, with its weakening cold and deepening snows, and they are forced by storms into restricted areas where hunger stalks them on every side. It is evident, therefore, that the maximum must be limited by the winter range capacity. In view of these conditions the officials of the Park and the state of Montana have worked out a satisfactory policy of diminution. A number of elk-hunting permits are issued to citizens who foregather along the northern boundary to participate in a bombardment that is swift and effective. In this manner the Park herd is kept in balance, and surplus elk do not migrate to the valleys to bother the ranchers. Of course an advantage accrues to these hunters because each one is very sure of getting his elk. This program should preclude a repetition of the agitation aroused during World War I when proposals were pressed upon the Food Administrator to allow hunting parties a free reign in securing Park elk and buffalo.[322]

More serious attempts to invade the Park's wilderness area came in the form of several irrigation projects, a railroad, and the northern boundary segregation issue. Each of these propositions, which threatened to modify the natural character and unity of the reservation, was strenuously resisted by Park administrations and the public generally.

In 1919 an irrigation project was sponsored by Idaho interests. It was a comprehensive plan that contemplated a dam on Yellowstone River, thereby raising the level of Yellowstone Lake. The water from this mighty reservoir would then be tapped by a tunnel through the Continental Divide, which would deliver the water into the Snake River. Other dams were designed to impound water along Fall and Bechler rivers. When bills S3925 and H.R.10469 reached their respective floors they were subjected to strong denunciation and defeated.[323] The next year, 1920, Senator Walsh, of Montana, also introduced a bill for the purpose of building a dam across the Yellowstone River at the lake outlet. This project also contemplated the generation of electricity. Extensive hearings before the Senate Committee on Irrigation resulted in the bill's death at that stage.

The movement for the extension of the Northern Pacific Railroad from Cinnabar to Cooke City, Montana, was not so easily arrested. From the first discovery of gold on Clarks Fork, in 1870, there had been a campaign for a railroad, as the early prospects were promising. However, little progress was made, and when the railroad bill of 1894 was defeated certain mining interests in Montana became alarmingly hostile. Frustrated in the extension of a line through the only accessible route, because of National Park sentiment, these interests came out for segregation. On March 1, 1894, the Helena Independent declared:

> Congress should make the Yellowstone River [Lamar] and Soda Butte Creek the northern boundary of the Park and charter a railroad to Cooke City on the north of these Streams....[324]

The Livingston Post struck a more ominous note in its issue of November 30 of the same year:

> Everybody concedes that the destruction of the Park by fire would be a public, a national calamity, and about the only way to avert such an impending danger is for Congress to grant the reasonable request of the people of the West by passing the segregation bill.[325]

In his report of 1895 Captain George S. Anderson, Acting Superintendent, quietly exulted, "It is a pleasure to note that the various bills for the segregation of the Park were killed in the last Congress."[326] This official was anything but popular in Montana at that time. Thus, it would appear that Yellowstone, like nearly every national institution, has been at the crossroads of conflicting interests, and its present status has not been achieved without vigilance.

Throughout the years the reports of the army superintendents conformed to a regular pattern about travel, roads, concessions, wild animals, fish, protection of natural phenomena, accommodations, fires, sanitation, violations, and recommendations. Whether captains, majors, colonels, or generals, these army men performed commendable service. Still, it was an army regime dealing with a civilian situation. Hence, there were some incongruities and many deficiencies.

What were the facts relative to the army administration in Yellowstone? Did conditions warrant a change? The circumstances responsible for the assignment in 1884 have been given. Two troops of cavalry comprised the normal complement. A main base, called Camp Sheridan, was established in Mammoth, and a series of stations were located at the principal points of interest. At these posts detachments of soldiers acted as guardians of their respective domains. From each station daily mounted patrols started toward other posts on either flank until they met.[327] In that manner, two hundred miles of forest road were observed between each dawn and dusk as the soldiers made their tours from "Slough Creek to Bison Peak, Grizzly Lake to Hellroaring Creek, and Canyon to Wedded Trees" ... almost ad infinitum.

Each soldier carried a bucket and shovel as defense against fire and a little book of Rules, Regulations and Instructions, called the "bible," to prepare him for any contingency. Among his routine instructions these orders appear: "... kill mountain lions, coyotes and timber wolves ... permit no cats and dogs ... keep pack trains off the road when vehicles are passing ... allow no one to approach within one hundred yards of bears...."

Each patrolman was required to record his daily activities in a journal and turn it over to his commanding officer. A perusal of these journal records is, on the whole, rather dull. The reading is not equal to the performance because spelling and diction were not among the soldiers' qualifications for duty. Still, there are occasions when, although "the letter killeth, the spirit giveth life." Incidents dealing with clues leading to the arrest of poachers and road agents, seizure of vandals, searches for lost persons, rescues of people treed by grizzlies and moose, or breakdowns, tip-overs, and runaways fairly shine with the excitement of the time.[328]

The soldiers had the finest western horses:

> Our horses are good all-around animals, good jumpers, runners and drillers. Each horse understands the trumpet calls.... If the army mules are with the herd, the horses feel safe, for as soon as a bear or deer appears, they make a dash for them, and when the game sees those mules, with ears laid back, coming on a dead run, it always makes tracks for the woods.[329]

The soldier's uniform consisted of a dark blue blouse and light blue trousers, unstrapped and cut spoonshape over the boot, cartridge belt, revolver, peaked cap, and worsted gloves with black buttons. These boys, like soldiers generally, were partial to their uniforms and dress parade assignments. Fire fighting and trail clearing were onerous indeed, and while "a little road making on service is not a bad thing, continuous navying is enough to knock the heart out of any army."[330]

The army's public relations seemed to have been very satisfactory. The soldiers were uniformly friendly and helpful toward the tourists. John Muir considered it a "pleasing contrast to the ever changing management of blundering, plundering politicians.... The soldiers do their duty so quietly that the traveler is scarce aware of their presence."[331] Tourists called the soldiers "Swatties"; an English term in popular use at that time.One Charles D. Warner, of New York City, was also led to rejoice that there was at least one spot in the United States where law was promptly enforced. He considered the military administration an object lesson for the whole nation in point of efficiency and impartiality.[332] Opposite reactions came from nearly all who ran afoul the law.Perhaps the greatest weakness in the army regime was in the educational inadequacy of its personnel. About 1910 a difference in tourist interests was obvious. People, generally, began to inquire into the causes and effects of the natural phenomena. It became increasingly apparent that an effective public stewardship required knowledge of chemistry, botany, geology, zoology, and history. The reign of the "cock and bull" type of story was drawing to an end. The era of greater natural history interpretation and appreciation was dawning. Unless something could be done to educate the Park's guardians a considerable educational opportunity would be lost, not to mention the loss of scientific solution of forest problems in general.

W. S. Chapman
Cavalry Troops in Park Patrol

This need is clearly reflected in Captain Anderson's report concerning geysers:

> I find there is a general belief in the minds of the tourists that there is some measure of regularity in the period of eruptions of most if not all of the geysers. At various times during the last three years I have had records made by the guards of the observed eruptions. Of course, these do not include all of the geysers, nor have all of the eruptions of any one of them been noted. I enclose for publication as an appendix to this report, a table made of observation upon them during the past three years. A casual inspection of it reveals the fact that none but Old Faithful has the slightest pretense to regularity.[333]

A rhythmic regularity was there all right, but, strangely enough, it required the careful observation of the casual scientist to discover a fact which entirely escaped the more permanent, but less observant, soldiers. In 1926 the Geophysical Laboratory of the Carnegie Institution directed Dr. Eugene T. Allen and Dr. Arthur L. Day to make an exhaustive study of Yellowstone's thermal features. After seven seasons of research, in cooperation with the National Park Service, they were able to publish a monumental treatise on this subject.[334] Later observations by such naturalists as George Marler, W. Verde Watson, and Herbert Lystrup not only confirmed the principle of rhythmic recurrence in many cases but discovered behavior patterns that enabled rangers to forecast a given eruption with uncanny accuracy.

Factors of this character were in the mind of Secretary of the Interior Franklin K. Lane in 1915 when he appointed Stephen T. Mather as his assistant. Mr. Mather's portfolio particularly related to the formulation of an integrated National Park policy.

CHAPTER XV
THE NATIONAL PARK SERVICE

Although there were thirteen national parks in 1912, each received a separate appropriation and had separate management. The business of these playgrounds was scattered among three departments, and nowhere in Washington was there a single official or desk wholly devoted to their interest.[335] To this problem Stephen Tyng Mather brought high intelligence, sound philosophy, and supreme endeavor. By 1915 he had achieved administrative experience that ripened into wisdom equal to undertake the preservation of America's scenic and recreational heritage.

With this general proposition in mind, Mr. Mather made two visits to Yellowstone during the season of 1915. There he carefully analyzed the administrative policies and personnel. While it is only fair to state that other federal officials were also planning a new national park organization and procedure it was largely Mr. Mather's Yellowstone report that provided the needed impetus. From then on he supplied the energy, foresight, and devotion to effect a transition.

On August 25, 1916 the National Park Service Bill received President Wilson's signature. This measure placed the control and general supervision of the entire national park activity squarely into the hands of a Director of National Parks. The bill was sponsored by Senator Reed Smoot of Utah and Representative William Kent of California.

Thereafter, on October 1, 1916, the troops of U.S. Cavalry left Fort Yellowstone for duty along the Mexican border. With C. A. Lindsley as Acting Superintendent a fine ranger corps was organized of mountain scouts and released soldiers. Shortly afterwards Congress reversed its action and voted to deny the use of Department of the Interior funds for protective purposes. This forced the return of the soldiers, and the army resumed control on June 30, 1917.

During the next six months National Park Service officials, aided by the army officers, gathered data which proved the inadvisability of continuing the use of troops. It should be noted that the attitude of the officers throughout was cogently expressed by Captain Harris:

> And it is believed that to the extent in which the present method of government and protection is an improvement upon former methods it is due to the visible power and force of the National Government as represented by the military garrison in the Park.
>
> It is not to be inferred that the claim is made that a military government is the only one practicable for the Park, or even that it is the best adapted or most suitable. It is believed, however, that no efficient protection can be given to the Park without the support of a well-organized and disciplined police force of some description.[336]

In this spirit, the cost of a military garrison and its lack of opportunities to drill were reviewed. It was clearly demonstrated that a ranger force of a chief ranger, four assistants, twenty-five permanent Park rangers of the first class, and twenty-five seasonal rangers would constitute a "well-organized and disciplined police force" and something else besides. It was also pointed out that the cost would be considerably less. This effort resulted in a second withdrawal of the troops in 1918. At the same time another ranger force was effected with substantially the same personnel as developed in 1916.[337] In due time the members of this new corps acquired a modest attitude of confidence in their own capacity which still abides.

Mr. Mather assumed office as the first National Park Director on May 16, 1917. In a short time the fruits of his vision were disclosed. Under his inspiring leadership the National Park program was steadily expanded. Peace was made with, and a degree of cooperation obtained from, the natural antagonists of the National Park Service. Several wealthy citizens who had acquired vast private estates were induced to donate portions thereof for the general public. Sportsmen who had observed the diminution in numbers of wild creatures were converted to the idea of refuges through self-interest. The positions of the lumber, grazing, irrigation, and water-power interests were less yielding on this all-out conservation issue. They would evidently favor a compromise. The general public gradually responded to the suggestion that the country beautiful was even more alluring than beautiful cities.[338]

In Secretary Lane's third annual report in 1919 the National Park Service policy was announced under three broad principles:

> First, that the National Parks must be maintained in absolutely unimpaired form for the use of future generations as well as those of our own time; Second, that they are set apart for the use, observation, health, and pleasure of the people; and Third, that the national interest must dictate all decisions affecting public or private enterprise in the Parks.[339]

Since then the program has made steady progress. Its purposes and policies have been enlarged and clarified. The acceptable qualities of parkhood were defined. Such an area must be supremely significant, having a national appeal whether scenic, archaeological, scientific, or historical. Only such features of natural architecture were to be included as would represent the highest accomplishment within its class. For example, Grand Canyon of the Colorado exemplifies the most extraordinary achievement of stream erosion, whereas Yellowstone is most unique in the realm of thermal activity.[340]

The National Park represents the apex of the conservation program, wherein the principle of optimum use is the dominating force. The twin purposes of enjoyment plus conservation always remain uppermost. Commercialization beyond actual requirements is not to be tolerated, and to this end close supervision is maintained.

Natural species of animals and plants were to abide in normal relationships, free from man's interference, except under urgent circumstances such as were described in the discussion of wild life control. The primitive appearance of Yellowstone forests is distasteful to some people. It was a carping German traveler who said, "Look at your dead trees and burned stumps in the woods ... and your streams are full of driftwood. It is not cared for."[341] In that sense Yellowstone is not a park but a wilderness full of the beauty of natural disorder. All things remain as nature leaves them. No man disturbs landslide, log jam, or wind-swept lodgepole avalanche.

The appearance of the trails, roads, bridges, buildings, and facilities of all kinds is gradually being brought into harmony with the natural environment. Under the guidance of landscape artists, structural design and location are made conformable to maximum scenic advantages while at the same time, being inconspicuous themselves. A few examples will illustrate this trend toward artificial recession. In 1889 Captain Boutelle complained against the statute which prescribed that no hotel shall be erected within four hundred and forty yards of any object of interest. He urged a reduction of one-half the distance.[342] Now, all the accommodations in the immediate Grand Canyon area are being moved a modest distance away, where they will still provide the services which visitors need, but not intrude upon the natural scene. Another case is afforded by the bear shows. Formerly they were provided in several places; then modified to a less artificial presentation on Otter Creek. In 1942 they were discontinued. It is truly exciting for thousands of people to observe thirty or forty grizzlies jostle and cuff each other around a "combination salad" platform. Still, the circumstance is highly artificial, a sort of Roman holiday affair, and therefore inappropriate. It is hoped that the Lord of all American wild life may be allowed to go his way undisturbed, otherwise grizzlies may become "holdup bears and bums." Such an eventuality, on a nocturnal basis of operation, is by no means improbable. That development would consign this magnificent animal to a precipitous disappearance from the earth.

Yellowstone's educational opportunities were early recognized and utilized by the scientists. The passing of time has widened this field-study interest. Supervised groups now come from all parts of America, with individual scientists hailing from both home and abroad. In fact, more than a hundred specialists have spent from a few weeks to several years in the Park. The results of these efforts have run up the volume of scientific titles to approximately five hundred.

By 1920 naturalist activity was in the course of development, the outcome of an avowed purpose to facilitate the real enjoyment of the people. To this work Director Mather brought especial perception, skill, and even personal funds. In fact, he may be considered as the father of the movement. It was in 1918, when visiting Lake Tahoe, that Mather observed the activities of a young man named Harold Bryant, whom the management had employed to interpret nature to their guests. Dr. Bryant's work so impressed the Director that he took him to Yosemite where his success with the public was immediate. Ranger-naturalists were appointed in other parks, and later Dr. H. C. Bryant was placed in charge of the educational branch of the service. Two notable institutions quickly caught the vision and cooperated. In

1925 the Yosemite School of Natural History was founded as a non-profit scientific organization. Courses in botany, zoology, and geology were given. Emphasis was placed on field work, and the final trip lasted two weeks. The instructional staff was composed largely of University of California professors, while the twenty trainees were chosen from a hundred candidates.[343] In 1935 Yale University furthered the naturalist incentive by providing a fellowship. Since 1937 two have been granted. Yellowstone Park has taken advantage of these services.

After a decade of experimentation in field trips, fireside lectures, and exhibits a Research and Education branch was created within the National Park Service. This bureau outlined a policy of portraying certain phases of the American scene in a correlated story. Laboratories were developed in Berkeley, California; Fort Hunt, Virginia; and Washington, D. C. The leading men in this program were H. C. Bryant, F. W. Miller, W. W. Atwood, F. R. Oastler, A. F. Hall, H. C. Bumpus, and C. P. Russell.

In 1920, Superintendent Horace M. Albright, assisted by J. E. Haynes, organized the naturalist program in Yellowstone. M. P. Skinner was the first Park Naturalist. He was succeeded by Edmund J. Sawyer in 1924. Four years later Dorr G. Yeager assumed the office; in 1932 Dr. C. Max Bauer became Park Naturalist and served until 1946, when David de L. Condon was advanced to the position.[344] All of these men have been nature-wise and public-minded. As time passed two assistants to the Chief Naturalist and thirty-five seasonal Park ranger-naturalists completed this organization. Robert N. McIntyre became Chief Park Naturalist in 1959.

W. S. Chapman
Park Ranger-Naturalist and tourist group.

Today Yellowstone's Naturalist Division stands as the symbol of America's love for the great out-of-doors. Its philosophy is wise and comprehensive. Its scientists have delved deeply for the facts. Still, there is a spirit of self-abnegation among the personnel. They serve all and sundry in every possible way, and yet they are pledged to the preservation of the natural treasures. Their contribution to protection of park values is shared with that of the ranger staff. The number of public contacts runs into the hundreds of thousands annually. Wise, indeed, is the tourist who avails himself of this free guide service.

The principal points of interest are visited over footpath or by auto caravan. Daily schedules of these activities are posted, and an illustrated lecture is held in an amphitheater each night. Many citizens have expressed their satisfaction with this naturalist service:

> He unravelled before our city-wearied eyes the skein of beauty nature has hidden in this great preserve. With skillful phrase he repictured for us the aeons during which the mountains were wrinkling and the cobalt lakes were born. His keen eyes found us mountain sheep ... his wide knowledge compassed the flowers and birds along the way. He knew when and where to take us to see the beaver at work, and where the water ouzel bubbled forth its cascade of song. He answered all our questions with calm courtesy. Around the

nightly campfire he brought to us in song and story the romance and exuberance of the west....

The fire of his enthusiasm welded us to the National Park idea and out-of-doors as nothing had ever done. We returned to the east inspired by a new understanding of the greatness of America and the magnificence of its beauty.[345]

In 1928 the Laura Spelman Rockefeller Foundation made a donation to be used by the American Association of Museums in the Park. Under the direction of Dr. Hermon C. Bumpus museums were erected at Old Faithful, Madison, Norris and Fishing Bridge. The main museum at Mammoth was improved and a number of roadside exhibits were established.[346]

Mission 66 was begun by the National Park Service in 1956. It is a conservation program to assure full protection of irreplaceable scenic, scientific and historic treasures and to develop and staff the Parks to permit their wisest possible use for your enjoyment. Completion is scheduled for 1966, the 50th anniversary of the establishment of the National Park Service, hence Mission 66.

Under this program, new roads, bridges, campgrounds and other facilities are being built. A fine new visitor center was opened in 1958 at Canyon Village and a large number of attractive new roadside exhibits and signs interpret the human and natural history of the great natural museum that is Yellowstone. During the score of years required to develop the naturalist branch, the protective division was not marking time. In 1920 James McBride became the first Chief Ranger. Since then Samuel Tilden Woodring, George F. Baggley, Francis D. LaNoue, Maynard Barrows, Curtis K. Skinner and Otto M. Brown have served. Nelson Murdock became Chief Ranger in 1960. Under their supervision the character of the personnel has been gradually changed. Originally a mountain scout and ex-soldier organization, it is now composed of college graduates. These men divide their time and effort between applying the principles of forest and wild life management with those of public relations. Physically robust, mentally alert, sociable and understanding, they properly exemplify the traditional informality and hospitality of the West. Of course there have always been a few political appointees present among the seasonal Park rangers. This makes the group quite varied, somewhat in keeping with the universality of the tourists themselves. Many a city lad has had the time of his life in his fleeting role as a "ninety-day wonder." Still there has always been a restraining influence reaching out from the chief ranger's office. A young man is not allowed to become too self-conscious over his uniform or badge of authority. The Superintendent presides over the protective and naturalist divisions and all other units of the National Park Service in Yellowstone. Only four men have held this position since the army withdrew in 1918. C. A. Lindsley was succeeded by Horace M. Albright in 1919. Mr. Albright served for ten years, after which Roger W. Toll took office. Edmund B. Rogers was appointed May 25, 1936, and served until November 1, 1956, when Superintendent Lemuel A. Garrison succeeded him. The superintendent's office is the nerve center of the Park. From there all activities are co-ordinated. This official is also the liaison man with the National Park Service; he makes all estimates and recommendations; he contends for assistance from cooperating agencies, such as the Civilian Conservation Corps, Emergency Relief Administration, and Public Works Administration.[347] The Public Health Service, the Geological Survey, and the Fish and Wildlife Service each lend cooperation in their special fields. It is also his function to consider many letters of introduction and requests for special favors. He is expected, personally, to welcome numerous delegations and important national and foreign personages. Information and courtesies flow from his presence continuously. He must determine the bounds of concessionaires, hear major complaints, oppose all invasions by mercenary interests, and, if necessary, labor to expand the Park's boundaries.

Madison Junction Historical Museum.

Beginning early in the twentieth century there were advocates of an extension southward. Many people wanted to have the cathedral-like Tetons incorporated in the Park. A campaign for a Greater Yellowstone was launched, and in 1918 Representative Mondell introduced a measure (H.R. 11661) providing for their incorporation.[348] However, the matter was delayed, and the passing of time resulted in the establishment of the Grand Teton National Park. A national park may only be created by an act of Congress; whereas an executive order is sufficient for the creation of a national monument or a moderate extension of a park boundary. Through a proclamation issued by President Hoover on October 20, 1932, Yellowstone National Park acquired a triangular strip of 7,600 acres of land, now called the Stevens Creek area. It is located northwest of Gardiner townsite, and it was enlarged to the extent of nearly a thousand acres the next year. In affairs of this character the National Park Service and the Superintendent work in close cooperation with the Secretary of the Interior. Indeed, the superintendency of Yellowstone is one of the ranking positions of its kind in the National Park Service. His final obligation is to be sure that the original objective "for the benefit and enjoyment of the people" is still the chief and ever-constant purpose.

It has been pointed out that the fulfillment of this objective is rather difficult, because various interests and groups have their own ideas concerning the purposes and methods of administering national parks. For example, in Idaho, there are some organizations that seek an Idaho entrance to the Park on Fall River. They point to the fact that distance and time would be appreciably reduced in reaching Old Faithful via this route. Besides, they aver, such an entrance would traverse a beautiful scenic area. These contentions are both valid and understandable. So is the demand for landing strips and airport facilities within the reservation boundaries.

The latter project, it is held, is identical to the position raised by motorists in 1915. National Park officials have met these issues squarely. Director Conrad L. Wirth and his Yellowstone representatives have vetoed both proposals. "Surely," they reason, "the Park is for the people, but if it is multisected by highways and airways, what will become of the primitive areas?" Sizeable regions are essential for the propagation and preservation of wild life. In addition, they point to the fact that as of this date most people conceive of the parks as havens of relative quiet and rest.

During the travel season of 1959, Yellowstone was host to 1,489,112 visitors. This multitude exceeded the total of all persons entering the Park in the first half century of its existence. Facilitating their enjoyment and at the same time preserving the domain as a pleasuring ground for their descendants requires a good measure of understanding on the part of the public, together with a high degree of understanding and training upon the part of the officials.

Earth tremors are common in the Yellowstone region. The Hayden Survey reported feeling severe shocks near Steamboat Point on Yellowstone Lake in 1871. They named the site "Earthquake Camp." Other quakes have been reported, mostly of a minor nature. At 11:38 p.m. on August 17, 1959, an earthquake of magnitude 7.1 on the Richter Scale struck the Yellowstone area. The epicenter of the quake was along the western boundary of the Park in the vicinity of Grayling Creek.

The greatest earthquake damage took place in the Madison Canyon about 7 miles below Hebgen Dam and outside Yellowstone. A massive slide of about 80 million tons of earth and rock blocked the canyon and entombed a number of campers along a half-mile stretch of the Madison River. This natural dam has created Earthquake Lake, a feature that will attract attention for years to come.

In Yellowstone National Park dangerous rock slides covered Park roads at several points along the Madison, Firehole, and Gibbon rivers, and at Golden Gate. Tall chimneys toppled from Old Faithful Inn and other Park buildings, and there was structural damage to many roads and buildings.

The hot springs showed a greater change in this one night than had been observed in the entire history of the Park. Close study of the thermal features revealed that most springs had discharged water copiously during the quake and aftershocks, and then ebbed below normal levels. Investigation revealed that at least 298 springs and geysers had erupted the night of the quake, and 160 of these were springs with no previous record of eruption. Other changes occurred slowly. The Fountain Paint Pot did not manifest unusual activity until several days after the quake, but then encroached upon walks and parking areas. Most of the hot springs became turbid, and even cold springs that fed the mountain streams on the west side of the Park discharged an opaque mud which discolored the creeks and rivers.

Equilibrium was gradually restored in the geyser basins. Some of the earthquake changes were permanent, others transitory. All of them make this chapter in the living geology of Yellowstone an intensely interesting one for Park visitors to learn about.

Upon receiving reports about earthquake effects throughout the Park, Superintendent Lon Garrison exclaimed, "The Lord had his arms around us. We had 18,000 people inside Yellowstone that night, and not one person was killed or badly hurt. Think what would have happened if the quake had come during daylight—at Old Faithful Inn, for example, where the chimney fell into the dining room."

Thus, out of Yellowstone's development under scouts, soldiers, and rangers, has come invaluable experience for the good of the whole nation. From its humble origin a service has evolved that now administers more than one hundred and seventy-five national park service areas. Perhaps the value of this program toward the enrichment of American life cannot be assessed. However, something of its breadth has been caught and cast in the bronze plaque at the Madison Junction Museum:

Stephen Tyng Mather
July 4, 1867 Jan. 22, 1930

> He laid the foundation of the National Park Service. Defining and establishing the policy under which its areas shall be developed and conserved unimpaired for future generations. There will never come an end to the good that he has done.

Yellowstone is one of these irreducible frontiers which should never vanish, but to find a frontier one must first have the spirit of a frontiersman. Therefore within its confines are vast wilderness zones into which people may still go who cherish the elemental conditions of earth and its denizens. Here there may always be a pristine land, reminiscent of the primitive environment of mankind. Here is a temporary refuge for people distraught by the strain and turmoil of modern life. It is becoming increasingly clear that the nation which leads the world in feverish business activity requires playgrounds as well as workshops. If America would maintain its industrial supremacy let her plan not only the conservation of materials but of men.[349] Therefore, let them come to Yellowstone and other national parks and achieve physical, mental, and especially spiritual regeneration for all time to come. In Yellowstone, the National Park Service will be on hand to so direct the experience of the visitors to the end that even from afar and after many years their memories will return again. And, as the deepening twilight seems to bring the earth and the sky together, they may reflect upon a land where white-robed columns of steam ascend from the fissures of geysers long dead, like ghosts revisiting the scenes of their activity.[350]

Such is the desire of all large and generous minds. They are in full agreement with the glowing tribute of the Earl of Dunraven:

> All honor then to the United States for having bequeathed as a free gift to man the beauties and curiosities of Wonderland. It is an act worthy of a great nation, and she will have her reward in the praise of the present army of tourists no less than in the thanks of the generations to come.[351]

And so, here is Yellowstone—The Gem of the Mountains. Is she not worthy of the fullest measure of preservation, appreciation, and defense? Surely, the Park is an incomparable heritage in the divine legacy that is America. May her fountains never fail but go dancing eternally along, shedding joy and inspiration upon the hearts of all who seek a certain treasure.

W. S. Chapman
Park Ranger.

APPENDIX I
YOUNG MEN CAMPING IN YELLOWSTONE WILDERNESS

An adaptation of Rudyard Kipling's
"The Feet of the Young Men"
By Merrill D. Beal

When Yellowstone Park is opened then the smokes of council rise,

Pleasant smokes 'ere yet twixt trail and trail they choose.

Then the ropes and girths are tested while they pack their last supplies,

Now the young men head for camps beyond the Tetons!

Faith will lead them to those altars, hope will light them to that shrine,

Pilot knobs will safely guide them to their goal.

They must go, go, go, away from home!

On the summit of the world they're overdue.

Away! The trail is clear before you,

When the old spring fret comes o'er you

And the Red Gods call for you!

They will see the beaver falling and hear the white swan calling,

They'll behold the fishhawk fumble as bald eagle takes a tumble to rob him of his haul.

They will lie alone to hear the wild geese cry.

They may watch the blacktail mating as they work the chosen waters where the mackinaw are waiting

And the cutthroats jumping crazy for the fly!

They must go, go, go, away from here!

On the summit of the world they're overdue.

Begone! The way is clear before you

When the old spring fret comes o'er you,

And the Red Gods call for you!

They will see the lakeside lilies where the bull moose meets the cow,

Or maybe silver grizzlies nurse the sow.

They must climb the blue-roofed Rockies and observe that windy rift

Where the baffling mountain eddies chop and change.

They will learn the long day's patience, belly down on talus drift,

And hear the thud of bison on the range.

It is there that they are going where the bighorn and the ewes lie,

To a trusty, nimble ranger that they know;

They have sworn an oath to keep it on the brink of Mitsiadazi

For the Red Gods call them out and they must go.

Let them go, go, go, away from home!

On the summit of the world they're overdue.

Be off! The trail is clear before you

When the old spring fret comes o'er you,

And the Red Gods make their medicine again.

"So it's onward ponies, sally, this is not the place to dally!"

For the young men's thoughts are turning to a camp of special yearning,

Hidden in a hanging valley.

They must find that blackened timber, they must head that racing stream,

With its raw, right-angled log jam at the end,

And a bar of sun-warmed gravel where a lad can bask and dream

To the click of shod canoe poles 'round the bend.

It is there that they are going with their rods and reels and traces,

With a silent, smoky packer that they know;

To their beds of fleecy fir-mat with the star light on their faces,

All are ready now to hold the evening show.

So they go, go, go, away from here!

On the summit of the world they're overdue.

So long! The trail is clear before you,

When the old spring fret comes o'er you,

And the Red Gods call you forth and you must go!

In the afterglow of twilight, tales of wonder find their voice,

Trapping, fighting, robbing, poaching yield a choice:

There's John Colter's mighty run and Jim Bridger's towering fun,

There's Everts' five-week fast and Ed Trafton's crimson past.

There's George Cowan's rugged vim; there's Buckskin Charley,

Beaver Dick and Yankee Jim!

Nez Percé Joseph's flight and capture will fill each soul with rapture

In this camp of keen desire and pure delight.

Let them go, go, go, away from home!

On the summit of the world they're overdue.

Away! The trail is clear before you

When the old spring fret comes o'er you,

And the Red Gods mix their medicine again.

Photo by Jack Young
Young men camping in Yellowstone

When the mountain yarns cease flowing and the night is in the glowing, conversation wanes.

Then a sudden clap of thunder makes them huddle up the number to fend against the rains.

When the fleeting squalls are over and the clouds ride high and fair,

They will hear the lodgepole crackle and inhale the pine-sap air.

Then bacon scent and wood smoke will attract an eager bear,

He will grunt and sniff and gurgle as he wends nocturnal rounds.

As darkness dims youth's vision, so sleep crowds out all sounds,

But the eerie detonation of the bull elk's morning call

Will waken them from slumber by a singing water fall.

Hence, they go, go, go, away from here!

On the summit of the world they're overdue.

Carry on! The trail is clear before you

When the old spring fret comes o'er you,

And the Red Gods call for you!

Unto each the voice and vision, unto each his hunch and sign,

Lonely geyser in a basin, misty sweat bath 'neath a pine.

Unto each a lad who knows his naked soul!

Unto each a rainbow arching through a window in the sky,

While the blazoned, bird-winged butterflies flap by.

It is there that they are going to a region that they know,

Where the sign betrays the badger and the shaggy buffalo.

Where the trail runs out in breccia midst rock forests row on row.

It is there life glides serenely without conduct that's unseemly,

In a land where thoughts and feelings overflow.

Quick! Ah, heave the camp kit over!

For the Red Gods call them forth and they must go.

Let them go, go, go, away from home!

On the summit of the world they're overdue.

Farewell! The trail is clear before you

When the old spring fret comes o'er you,

And the Red Gods mix their medicine once more.

APPENDIX II
THE PROBLEM OF "COLTER'S ROUTE IN 1807"

It may seem unfruitful at this time to attempt a solution of the problem of John Colter's 1807 route of discovery in Yellowstone. Many people require no proof of anything cited in the records of such great scouts as Jedediah S. Smith, Kit Carson, and John Colter. Their integrity need not be questioned. Still, it is within the province of the historian to sift and test all of the evidence until the truth falls into place as elements in a jigsaw puzzle. Even myths and legends should be examined for any implications and bearing they might have upon a fact. It is in this light that the following discussion of the Colter discovery problem is presented. This case is entirely hypothetical, since no specific reference to his route has been found anywhere among source material, except as it is approximated upon the Map of 1814.

Beyond the known facts of Colter's journey in 1807, the Map of 1814, and the "Colter's Hell" legend, there is a complete hiatus, or vacuum. However, the Map of 1814 is certainly a tangible thing; let it tell its own story: It is known that William Clark had a friend in Philadelphia named Nicholas Biddle who arranged for the publication of The Lewis and Clark Journals. In order to properly depict the journey, Mr. Biddle secured the services of a prominent Philadelphia cartographer named Samuel Lewis. Twice in 1810 Clark sent sheets of map material to Mr. Biddle.[352] John Colter reached St. Louis in May, 1810. It is certain that he called upon Clark and gave him information, if not sheets, depicting his famous journey of 1807. This data was undoubtedly sent on to Mr. Biddle, either as Colter drew it or as it was accurately redrawn by Clark. At least one of Colter's sheets was incorporated in the final Map of 1814.[353] The first, or eastern prairie, side of the Colter plat traced his journey up Pryors Fork, about fifty miles west of Fort Manuel, through Pryors Gap. Then he crossed over to Clarks Fork, which he ascended, probably to Dead Indian Creek. From this creek Colter crossed over a divide to the North Fork Shoshone River where he first smelled sulphur. This he called Stinking Water

River, most probably referring to the present De Maris Mineral Springs near Cody, Wyoming.

On Stinking Water River he encountered the "Yep-pe Band of Snake Indians 1000 souls." This was evidently a clan of the Crow tribe. From these Yep-pe Indians, denizens of both prairie and mountain, he undoubtedly learned of the Yellowstone geysers and other marvels. This accounts for his side trip which brought him back to the Yep-pe camp. It is likely that some of these Indians directed Colter along another route in returning to Manuel's Fort. Obviously they went down the North Fork Shoshone, or Colter's Stinking Water River, to its junction with Shoshone River. This, he followed to Gap Creek (now Sage Creek) which he ascended to Pryors Gap.[354] By this alternate route Colter again reached Pryors Fork where he crossed over to return to Fort Manuel.

From this examination it is obvious that the western boundary of Colter's first map lies east of 110° longitude, and up to that point no difficulty whatever is encountered with either the route or the map. This line undoubtedly defines the west border of Colter's first sheet. It became a part of the Map of 1814 without change. Hence, it is a correct representation of the "Buffalo Bill country" around Cody, Wyoming. Published in 1814, it could only have been the work of John Colter, because no other white man had visited that area. Because of the accuracy of Colter's first plat, or east portion of the map, his course to the Yep-pe Indian camp can be followed like tracks in the snow. Just so, the return route east of 110° can be identified as coming down Sunlight Creek and back up Dead Indian Creek to the Yep-pe Indian camp. From there he followed a shorter route, in returning to the eastern edge of the map sheet, that is to say, the head of Pryors Fork.

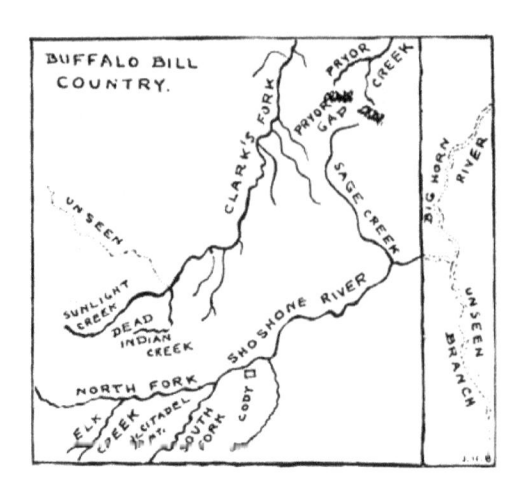

M. D. Beal
Yellowstone section of Colter's route.

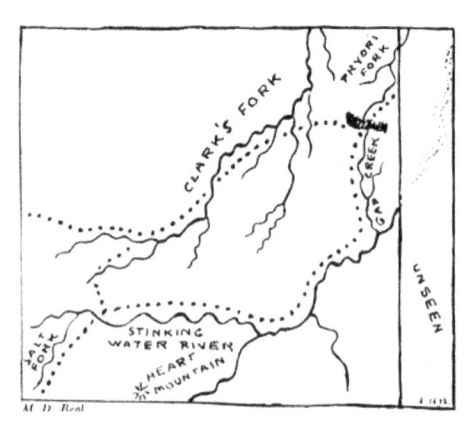

Logic and a reasonable sense of procedure would support this route as the trail of Colter's Yellowstone Discovery. Conclusive proof is lacking.

Thus, it is evident that the eastern courses of Colter's journey, both going and coming, are accurately depicted on the Map of 1814. East of 110° it is an accurate and authentic mapping of the area, just such a one as an intelligent trapper would make. Whatever is depicted corresponds to actual geography. It is factual, tangible, verifiable, and indisputable.

This part of the map proves that Colter did take an extended journey in a southwesterly direction, but it does not prove that he discovered Yellowstone Park. The dependable part of the map simply accounts for the eastern part of the figure eight which is essential to describe the complete journey.[355] The reliable part leads him only to the southeastern border of Yellowstone Park and brings him back from farther north along its eastern boundary.

The western portion of the dotted line on the Map of 1814 is purely fictitious and encompasses an area far beyond that occupied by Yellowstone Park. Indeed, this part of Colter's route winds among a labyrinth of geographical unreality.[356] Therefore, Colter's route, as represented by the western loop of the dotted line, is likewise invalid. Here, then, is the problem of Colter's discovery: How could the map of his exploration, which necessarily described a figure eight, be at once so authentic in the east and so fictitious in the west? The Yellowstone area of the Map of 1814 is certainly one of organized confusion, but it does not follow that Colter drew that portion of the map as it appears.

Actual geography and common sense prove that a trapper on foot could not possibly have seen both the Arkansas and Platte rivers. Just as surely, geography and common sense attest that in traveling a normal western loop of the figure eight he would have seen precisely what the map does not depict, namely: Upper Yellowstone River, Snake River, Yellowstone Lake, and the thermal areas at Thumb of Lake and near Hayden Valley.

Thus, by elimination, an obvious conclusion evolves, namely that the western loop is not as Colter drew it. Instead of actuality, there is fiction; nothing in this part of the map conforms to reality. That geography only exists upon the Map of 1814. John Colter died in 1813 so he never even saw the route as depicted, to say nothing of traveling along it.

J. N. Barry
Western section of Colter's route.

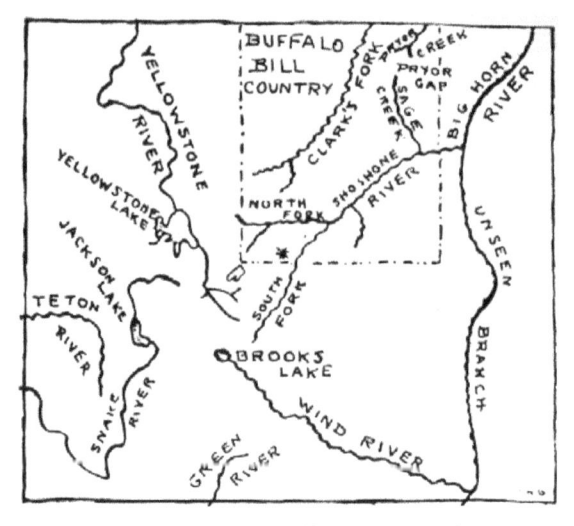

A true sketch of the Yellowstone Park area.

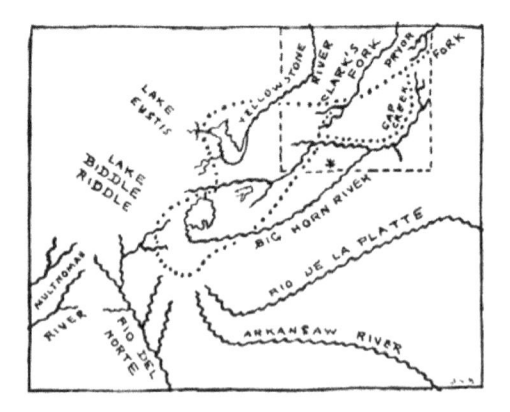

Fictitious geography depicted on the map of 1814. Note the complete incongruity between the real map and the guess map.

The failure of writers to recognize the fictitious character of this portion of the Map of 1814 has led to a comical performance. They have assigned to Colter the role of a human helicopter who hopped over mountains and valleys visiting the drainage basins of all the river systems within a radius of five hundred miles of the Yep-pe Indian village. First they trail him on Teton River, Big Sandy, Gros Ventre, and Greybull. Then they track him over South Pass, Teton Pass, and Union and Twogwotee passes. These authors have never trudged the wilds of which they write nor even measured them on a real map. Where, then, did Colter travel? The answer to that problem largely depends upon a rational interpretation of that fantastic map sheet. Perhaps an investigation of the process by which the map was produced will offer a clue.

As stated before, Clark sent map materials to Biddle, who in turn passed them on to Samuel Lewis, a professional cartographer, to be worked into a map of the Trans-Mississippi West. This was a very difficult assignment because the sheets were of various scales, which necessitated overlapping, crowding, and uncertainty as to latitudes and longitudes.[357] The manner in which Lewis fitted them into a mosaic represents a remarkable work of art. Deficiencies are largely attributable to the inadequate data received, but in the case of Colter's journey another element is involved.

In the course of compilation, between 1810 and 1814, Clark must have sent a redrawing of the route of Colter's journey.[358] By way of review, let it be remembered that Colter reached St. Louis in May of 1810. He called on Clark and evidently presented several sheets of trapper map to him. This was the material which depicted his journey of 1807, and it seemed to be highly appreciated by Clark. That it was given preference by Clark over the contemporary exploration of Zebulon M. Pike simply substantiates the belief that Colter's journey made a profound impression upon Clark at that time.[359] On December 20, 1810, Clark apparently sent the original Colter sheets, or properly redrawn copies of them, to Nicholas Biddle. Clark also inserted, or superimposed, two rivers upon the Colter drawing. They were Clarks Fork and Bighorn rivers.

It is important to remember that Clark had full confidence in Colter's representation of his journey at this time, that is, December, 1810. The following year Andrew Henry returned from his exploration of the Madison and Snake river regions. He had seen only ordinary country. This report seems to have destroyed Clark's belief in Colter's story of marvels. Not wishing to deceive anyone by the delusions of a deranged trapper's mind, Clark apparently directed Samuel Lewis to retain Colter's east plat, that is, the Buffalo Bill country, but suppress the western section, the Yellowstone Lake region. In lieu of Colter's depiction of the western loop of his figure eight Clark evidently sent the draft that now appears on the Map of 1814.

What possible reason can be assigned for this action? It is anybody's guess; no one can now determine what Clark thought, but following is a rational hypothesis: In the close of the year 1811, Andrew Henry and his men returned from their trapping venture in the Upper Snake River basin. They had skirted the western border of Wonderland along the line of the Madison and Gallatin rivers and explored the sources of Henrys Fork of the Snake River. Yet, Henry had not seen any hot springs, geysers, or great lakes. No doubt Henry had heard trappers joke about "Colter's Hell." Personally, he showed no confidence in it. Evidently both he and Clark considered that Henry's and Colter's journeys overlapped. Actually, the Gallatin Range intervened between them. It is reasonable, therefore, that Henry's report and attitude affected Clark's original belief in Colter's story. Where he first believed he now doubted. Perhaps Clark concluded that Colter's terrible experiences had deranged his mind. It is certain that Clark sent his new knowledge of the Henrys Fork country to Biddle in 1812 because it appears on the Map of 1814.[360] It was undoubtedly at this time that Clark sent in his redrawn, guesswork version of the western portion of Colter's map. No one knows exactly what changes Clark made, but the Map of 1814 proves conclusively that Clark did not depict the "Colter's Hell" country which contains the wonders of Yellowstone Park as it was originally presented to him.

It was a valid reaction for Clark to have become suspicious of Colter's reliability, and the substitution of his own geographical speculation for Colter's Yellowstone sketch was probably sincere. Clark was too honest to depict the delusions of an "insane" man. Also he was very anxious to have a reasonably complete and integrated map. The only alternatives were to allow the Colter marvel sheet to appear or else to mark a considerable area "unexplored." He was caught in the bonds of uncertainty and made a compromise. The result was a sheet of bogus geography which is entirely incongruous, not only with the facts, but with Clark's uniformly excellent map work.[361]

Clark's choice of alternatives only complicated the problem of his cartographer. Lewis no doubt recognized the vast discrepancies between Colter's genuine depiction and Clark's counterfeit so he evidently decided upon a compromise of his own. How this expert reconciled the conflicting data of the two map sheets into one pattern is at once a masterpiece in cartography and psychology. The technique he adopted might be called "double entry map making." He used the Yellowstone Lake part of Colter's sketch as an element for a concealed map; it appears as a mountain range. Such a grotesque range cannot be found in any of the surrounding territory, but when visualized as a lake it is amazing how it conforms to what a trapper traveling a logical route would have seen of Yellowstone Lake, namely, the South Arm and Thumb. Lewis shied away from any clear-cut representation of the geyser region. However, besides including the disguised lake portion of Colter's map, he did other things to "poke fun" at Clark's speculations. He drew Lake Eustis in the manner of a gargoyle. It must have been deliberately "satanized." Nothing with such a preposterous shape was ever known among men. Why didn't Clark revolt at this representation? Surely he never drew anything like that himself. That is not all of Lewis' "fun making." He drew still another lake and gave it the shape of a deformed piece of liver. Its appearance is ridiculous in the other extreme,[362] but, as if to add insult to injury, Mr. Lewis raised a question as to this lake's legitimacy. Clark named it Biddle in honor of his patron, Nicholas Biddle, whereas, upon the English version, the name appearing is Riddle! Lewis was able to "get away" with this performance because Clark did not see any proofs, only the published work.

J. N. Barry
"Double-entry" map of Yellowstone.

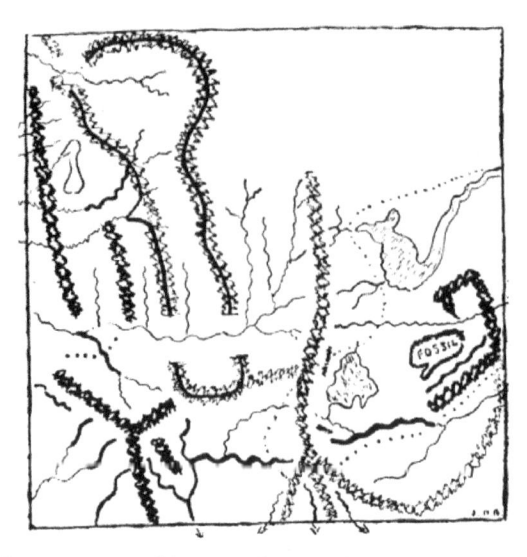

Samuel Lewis' "Double-entry" map. An attempt to reconcile Colter's draft of the Yellowstone country with Clark's obvious assumptions.

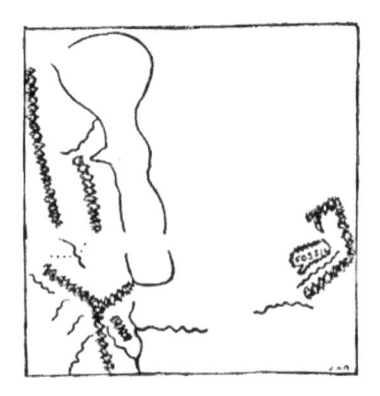

When segregated these "concealed" elements give a logical representation of what Colter undoubtedly saw, namely the southwest arm and thumb of Yellowstone Lake.

Remembering that Samuel Lewis was employed to reproduce a map conforming to data and specifications furnished by Clark, what more could he do to manifest his skepticism, if not displeasure, over the incorporation of fictitious geography upon this super-important map of the West? Remember, Lewis was a professional cartographer; he had seen, and had already drawn,

Colter's sheet of real country. On the original draft the southwest Arm and Thumb of Lake Yellowstone undoubtedly appeared. Now he was asked to redraw it into counterfeit geography. Disturbed by the substitution of Clark's sheet of "Gulliver's geography" for Colter's journey, he disguised a lake in a mountain range, drew a gargoylian lake (Eustis), and raised the enigma of Biddle-Riddle.[363] After all, cartography is simply a scientific refinement of pictography, or storytelling. The message of Samuel Lewis, as revealed in the Yellowstone segment of the Map of 1814, might reasonably be: "This portion of the map is bogus. I do not know what the true conditions are. Colter's data appears all right; Clark's later information says it isn't. It's all a Riddle; I leave a clue." Against this background, with the fiction cut away, it may now be possible to explore the problem of Colter's route through the Yellowstone country.

Did Colter make a western loop trip beyond the Yep-pe Indian camp? Of that there can be no doubt. Clark's representation does not impugn Colter's word in respect to the reality of the journey itself but only as to where he went and what he saw. If an approximation of his route can be reproduced, the question of what he saw will automatically fall into place like the pieces of a jigsaw puzzle. The problem, then, is to correctly reconstruct the west loop of the figure eight. This procedure has become possible by reason of the proposition that has been established in this discussion, particularly when it is remembered that Colter knew his way around and could be relied upon to make a proper orientation to the total environment. Now his course can be followed by segregating another feature from what has been referred to as "Lewis' Concealed Colter Map."

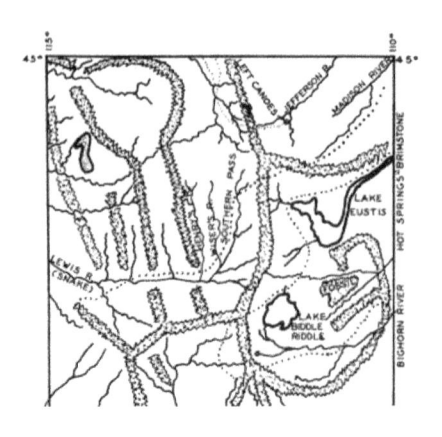

J. N. Barry
A section of fictitious geography.

A larger section of the Map of 1814 showing Samuel Lewis' ingenious combination of Colter's data, Clark's guesses and the Cartographer's own obvious design to pose a gumption test for students of Western geographic exploration.

West of longitude 110° it will be noted that two features stand out in bold relief, namely, a mitten-shaped mountain labeled FOSSIL (probably the Trident) and the crude outline of South Arm and Thumb of Yellowstone Lake. These two landmarks may be used as guide posts in following Colter's reconstructed loop through Yellowstone. Colter's authentic east loop journey, already described, brought him approximately to the 110° meridian. Colter's mitten-shaped landmark lies about seventy-five miles due west of the border on his second map sheet, but Clark's dotted line depicts Colter's route fifty miles south of the mountain shaped like a mitten and marked FOSSIL. It is valid to inquire how Colter could discern its shape or know of its fossils from that distance. His Indian friends knew nothing about fossils. The dotted line does not cross or even skirt this mountain. To reach the "Fossil Mountain" from Salt Fork, Colter could ascend by Elk-Wapiti or Fishhawk creeks. Each meets the requirements of direction and distance, and there is a good chance that somewhere along one of these routes a large petrified fish, or something like a fish, was seen then and may be eventually found. Such a discovery would remove all doubt about the direction in which he traveled.[364]

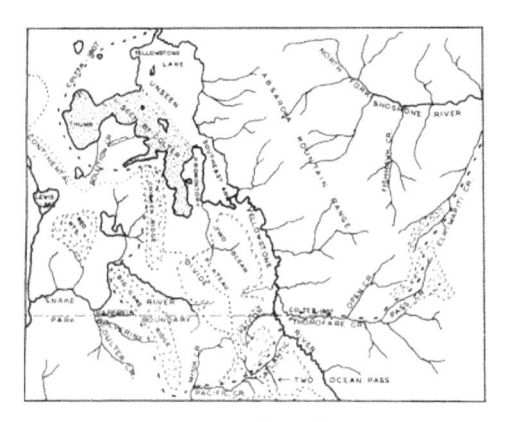

Western section of Coulter's route.

Logic and a reasonable sense of procedure would support this route as the trail of Coulter's Yellowstone discovery. Conclusive proof is lacking.

From the "Fossil Mountain" Colter probably descended Pass Creek to Thorofare Creek, which he followed to the Upper Yellowstone River. Then he might have ascended either Falcon, Lynx, or Atlantic creeks, preferably the latter, to Two Ocean Pass. Crossing the Continental Divide, he would then descend Pacific Creek, skirting Big Game Ridge, and cross the South Fork of Snake River, within the present confines of the Park. Thence he could go along Chicken Ridge, from where he would frequently view South Arm, headed toward Flat Mountain Arm. After crossing Solution Creek he would strike West Thumb.[365] The validity of this itinerary is wholly sustained by the genuine features of this area as they appear upon the Map of 1814. Indeed, the route seems obvious and indisputable in view of the actual conditions existing. On a crude map, where there are numerous, similar streams, various combinations are, of course, possible.

Leaving West Thumb, Colter would have circled the lake to its outlet and followed it to the Hayden Valley thermal area. Dragons Mouth and Mud Volcano were undoubtedly features that contributed to the vivid impression he carried away and transmitted to others. Even the "Hot Spring Brimstone" characterization on the Map of 1814 mildly suggests explosive thermal activity. The phrase also suggests that Colter mapped a geyser basin.[366]

Colter's return route from the area near the outlet of Yellowstone River supplies the final link in the figure eight. To reach the Yep-pe Indian camp he might have veered to the northeast, crossed Yellowstone River at the ford below Mud Volcano, and ascended Pelican Creek or one of the tributaries of the Lamar River. After crossing the Absarokas he evidently descended one of the creeks that empty into Clarks Fork. No one on earth can be certain about this part of his journey. There is no reference anywhere, and the Map of 1814 gives no clue. Still he did reach a tributary of Clarks Fork which he followed to its junction with Dead Indian Creek, thence to the Yep-pe band.

BIBLIOGRAPHICAL NOTE

In the preparation of the first four chapters the use of explorer and trapper journals was imperative. The Journals of Lewis and Clark, Patrick Gass's Journal, and Robert Stuart's Discovery of the Oregon Trail are basic.

Trapper activities and Indian life are effectively treated by Stallo Vinton in John Colter; Alexander Ross, The Fur Hunters of the Far West; Hiram Chittenden, The American Fur Trade; John Neihardt, The Splendid Wayfaring; J. Cecil Alter, Jim Bridger, Trapper, Frontiersman, Scout and Guide; Bernard De Voto, Across the Wide Missouri; and Robert Vaughn, Then and Now. A correct conception of original Indian life and character will reward the student of Rudolph Kurz's Journal and Washington Irving's two volumes: The Adventures of Captain Bonneville and Astoria. George Catlin's monumental treatise on North American Indians is also a classic on that subject.

Important in the field of writings dealing with the partial and final discovery of Yellowstone are Nathaniel P. Langford, Discovery of Yellowstone Park 1870, together with the shorter accounts of his companions as recorded in Louis C. Crampton's Early History of Yellowstone National Park and Its Relations to National Park Policies. The Yellowstone explorations of James Stuart and Walter W. DeLacy and others are found in Contributions to the Historical Society of Montana, volumes one to five inclusive.

John G. White's scholarly manuscript entitled "A Souvenir of Wyoming" contains much material of a provocative character. Nice points of detail are raised concerning John Colter's route and other trapper visitations.

The chapter on "Travel and Accommodations—New Businesses" was the result of a search through the standard magazines covering the half century from 1870 to 1920. The State College of Washington collection was found adequate for this survey.

It would be impossible to write the story of the Park's administration without a review of all the Annual Reports of the Acting Superintendents, and Superintendents of Yellowstone National Park. The Park Library has a complete file from 1872 to the present time. In addition, the Reports of the Secretary of the Interior and the Reports of the Director of National Parks, covering the same period, were essential cross references in this effort. A complete set of these reports is available at the State College of Washington. A perusal of the soldier (scout) diaries in the Park Library gave the substance for the discussion of that interesting phase.

Among guide books The Haynes Guide is in a class by itself. It is not only an invaluable hand book to the casual tourist, but it is an excellent encyclopedia for research.

The Earl of Dunraven's Hunting in the Yellowstone affords an excellent narrative from the standpoint of measuring the progress of all phases of Park activity.

Yellowstone Nature Notes is the best source for those sprightly experiences that make life so interesting and pleasant in the Park.

BIBLIOGRAPHY

MANUSCRIPT MATERIAL

Anderson, E. C. Diary 1909. Park Library, Mammoth, Wyoming.

Anderson, Henry. Diary 1910, 1911. Park Library.

Brown, Jesse R. Diary 1909, 1910. Park Library.

Burgess, Felix. Diary 1898, 1899. Park Library.

Cook, C. W. "Remarks of C. W. Cook, Last Survivor of the Original Explorers of the Yellowstone Park Region." Park Library.

Dorrity, Mrs. James. "Story of the Battle of Bear's Paw." M. D. Beal Collection, Idaho State College, Pocatello, Idaho.

Fitzgerald, S. M. Diary 1907. Park Library, Mammoth, Wyoming.

Graham, S. D. Diary 1906, 1907, 1908. Park Library.

Harlan, W. B. "The Fiasco at Fort Fizzle—1936." M. D. Beal Collection.

Holmes, W. H. Extracts from the Diary 1872, 1878. Park Library, Mammoth, Wyoming.

Langford, Nathaniel P. Diary, Second Trip to Yellowstone 1872. Park Library.

Little, Raymond G. Diary 1911, 1912. Park Library.

Louck, D. J. Journal in Manuscript. State Historian's Office, Laramie, Wyoming.

Martin, Louis. Diary 1900, 1901. Park Library, Mammoth, Wyoming.

Mason, John E. Diary 1909. Park Library.

Matlock, Jesse M. "Dictation." M. D. Beal Collection.

Morrison, James. Diary 1897, 1898, 1899. Park Library, Mammoth, Wyoming.

McBride, James. Diary 1908, 1909, 1910, 1911, 1912. Park Library.

Peale, A. C. Diary of Field Operations, U. S. Geological Survey 1872. (Three volumes.) Park Library.

Phillips, Ulrich B. "Lectures on Early America." (Notes taken by the author at the University of California in 1933.)

Rubin, Walter. Diary 1911. Park Library, Mammoth, Wyoming.

Shambow, Louie. "Story of the Battle of Bear's Paw." M. D. Beal Collection.

Titus, N. C. "Story of Colonel Miles' Attack on the Nez Percé Camp." M. D. Beal Collection.

Thompson, Captain. U. S. A. "Memorandum of a Trip from Fort Ellis, Montana Territory to Yellowstone Park." (Sept. 1882.) Park Library, Mammoth, Wyoming.

Trischman, Harry. Diary 1909, 1910, 1912. Park Library, Mammoth, Wyoming.

Wall, M. J. Diary. Park Library.

White, John G. "A Souvenir of Wyoming." (One of eight typed copies of a trip made in 1916.) Park Library.

White, Mable McClain. "Dictation." M. D. Beal Collection.

Wilson, Charley. Diary 1910. Park Library, Mammoth, Wyoming.

Wilson, James. Diary 1907, 1908. Park Library.

Whittaker, George. Diary 1897, 1898, 1899, 1900. Park Library.

PRINTED JOURNALS, DIARIES AND AUTOBIOGRAPHIES

Bradbury, John. Travels in the Interior Of America, 1809, 1810, and 1811. London: Sherwood Neeley, and Jones, 1819.

Carson, Kit. Autobiography. Chicago: Lakeside Press, 1935.

Contributions, Historical Society of Montana, I, II, III, IV, V. Helena, Montana: Rocky Mountain Publishing Co., 1876.

Dunraven, The Earl of. Hunting in the Yellowstone. New York: The Macmillan Co., 1925.

Egan, Howard. Pioneering the West. Egan Estate. Richmond, Utah.

Ferris, Warren A. Life in the Rocky Mountains, 1830-35. Salt Lake City: Rocky Mountain Book Shop, 1940.

Folsom, David E. The Folsom-Cook Exploration of the Upper Yellowstone. St. Paul: H. L. Collins Co., 1894.

Gass, Patrick. Journal. Edited by James K. Hosmer, Chicago: A. C. McClurg and Co., 1904.

Guie, Heister D. and McWhorter, L. V., editors. Adventures in Geyser Land by Frank D. Carpenter. Caldwell, Idaho: Caxton Printers, 1935.

Howard, General O. O. Chief Joseph, His Pursuit and Capture. Boston: Lee and Shephard, 1881.

Jackson, William H. Time Exposure. New York: G. P. Putnam's Sons, 1940.

Kurz, Rudolph. Journal. Washington, D. C.: United States Government Printing Office, 1937.

Langford, Nathaniel P. The Discovery of Yellowstone Park 1870. St. Paul: J. E. Haynes Publisher, 1923.

Larocque, Francis Antoine. Journal. Sources of Northwest History, No. 20, University of Montana, Missoula.

McWhorter, Lucullus V. Yellow Wolf: His Own Story. Caldwell, Idaho: Caxton Printers, 1940.

Norton, Harry J. Wonderland Illustrated, or Horse Back Rides. Virginia City, Montana: Harry J. Norton, 1873.

Osmond, Mabel C. Memories of a Trip Through Yellowstone National Park. St. Louis, 1874.

Raftery, John H. The Story of the Yellowstone. Butte, Montana: McKee Printing Co., 1912.

Ross, Alexander. The Fur Hunters of the Far West. London: Smith, Elder & Co., 1855.

Russell, Osborne. Journal of a Trapper, 1834-1843. Boise, Idaho: Syms-York Co., 1921.

Smith, Willard E. "An Excerpt from the Journal of Willard E. Smith, 1839-1840." Edited by J. Neilson Barry. Annals of Wyoming, Vol. XV, No. 3, July, 1943.

Spalding, Elizabeth. Memories of the West. Portland, Oregon: March Printing Co.

Stanley, Edwin J. Rambles in Wonderland. New York: D. Appleton & Co., 1878.

Stuart, Granville. Forty Years on the Frontier. Cleveland, Ohio: A. H. Clark, 1925.

Stuart, Robert. The Discovery of the Oregon Trail. New York: Charles Scribner's Sons, 1935.

Synge, Georgina. A Ride Through Wonderland. London: Sampson Low, Marston & Co., 1892.

Turrill, Gardner S. A Tale of the Yellowstone. Jefferson, Iowa: G. S. Turrill Publishing Co., 1901.

Vaughn, Robert. Then and Now. Minneapolis: Tribune Printing Co., 1900.

Wingate, George W. Through Yellowstone Park on Horseback. New York: O. Judd Co., 1886.

Wislizenus, F. A. A Journey to the Rocky Mountains in 1839. St. Louis, Mo.: Missouri Historical Society, 1912.

ARTICLES IN MAGAZINES AND PERIODICALS

Baker, Ray S. "A Place of Marvels," The Century Magazine, LXVI (August, 1903).

Bauer, C. Max. "Notes on Indian Occupancy," Yellowstone Nature Notes, Vol. XII, No. 6 (June, 1935).

Bryce, James. "National Parks the Need for the Future," The Outlook, CII (Dec. 14, 1912).

Cook, C. W. "Valley of the Upper Yellowstone," Western Monthly, IV (July, 1870).

Cook, C. W. and Folsom, D. E. "Cook-Folsom Expedition to the Yellowstone Region 1869," Haynes Bulletin, Jan., 1923.

Elmendorf, Dwight L. The Mentor, II (May 15, 1915).

Everts, Truman C. "Thirty Seven Days of Peril," Scribner's Monthly, III (Nov., 1871).

Freeman, L. R. "Protect the Game in Yellowstone Park," Recreation, XV (Dec. 1901).

Ghent, W. J. "A Sketch of John Colter," Wyoming Annals, Vol. X, No. 3 (July, 1938).

Gibbon, Colonel John. "The Battle of the Big Hole," Harper's Weekly (Dec. 21, 1895).

Hague, Arnold. "Soaping Geysers," Science, XIII (May 17, 1889).

Hague, Arnold. "The Yellowstone National Park," Scribner's, XXXV (May, 1904).

Hayden, F. V. "More About the Yellowstone," Scribner's Monthly, III (February, 1872).

Hayden, F. V. "The Yellowstone National Park," American Journal of Science, III (March, 1872; April, 1872).

Haynes, Jack Ellis. "The Expedition of President Chester A. Arthur to Yellowstone National Park in 1882," Annals of Wyoming (January 1942.).

Heffelfinger, C. H. "The Man Who Turned Back," The Washington Historical Quarterly, Vol. XXVI, No. 3 (July, 1935).

Hough, Emerson. "Forest and Stream's Yellowstone Park Game Exploration," Forest and Stream, XLIII (A series of thirteen articles in the issues during the spring and summer of 1894).

Jackson, W. Turrentine. "The Creation of Yellowstone National Park," The Mississippi Valley Historical Review, Vol. XXIX, No. 2 (September, 1942).

Jackson, W. Turrentine. "The Cook-Folsom Exploration of the Upper Yellowstone 1869," The Pacific Northwest Quarterly, XXXII, 1941.

Jagger, T. A. "Death Gulch, A Natural Bear Trap," Popular Science, LIV (February, 1899).

Joseph, Chief. "Own Story," North American Review (April, 1879).

Kearns, William E. "A Nez Percé Chief Revisits Yellowstone," Yellowstone Nature Notes, XII (July-August, 1935).

Knowlton, F. H. "The Tertiary Flowers of the Yellowstone National Park," American Journal of Science, No. 7 (July, 1896).

Knowlton, F. H. "The Standing Fossil Forests of the Yellowstone National Park," Plant World, I (January, 1898).

Koch, P. "Discovery of the Yellowstone National Park," Magazine of American History, II (June, 1884).

Langford, Nathaniel P. "The Ascent of Mount Hayden," Scribner's Monthly, III (June, 1873).

Lewis, Henry H. "Managing a National Park," The Outlook, LXXIV (August, 1903).

Lewis, Lucien M. "To the Old Stage Driver," Overland Monthly, LXIX (July, 1917).

Linton, Edwin "Overland Sounds in the Vicinity of Yellowstone Lake," Science, No. 561 (Nov. 3, 1893).

Muir, John. "The Yellowstone National Park," The Atlantic Monthly, LXXXI (January, 1898; April, 1898).

Phillips, Paul C., editor. "The Battle of the Big Hole," Sources of Northwest History, No. 8, University of Montana, Missoula.

Rollins, Alice W. "The Three Tetons," Harper's, LXXIV (May, 1887).

Russell, Carl P. "Rendezvous Period of American Fur Trade," Oregon Historical Quarterly, XLII (March, 1941).

Russell, Carl P. "Scientists and Scientific Investigations in Yellowstone National Park," Department of the Interior, 1933.

Sedgwick, Henry D. "On Horse Back Through Yellowstone," World's Work, VI (June, 1903).

Smith, George O. "The Nation's Playgrounds," Review of Reviews, XL (July, 1909).

Staffer, Alvin P. and Porter, Charles W. "The National Park Service Program of Conservation for Areas and Structures of National Historical Significance," The Mississippi Valley Historical Review, XXX, 1 (June, 1943).

Warner, Charles D. "The Yellowstone National Park," Harper's, XCIV (January, 1897).

GOVERNMENT REPORTS AND PUBLICATIONS

Barlow, J. W. and Heap, D. P. Report of Barlow and Heap 1871. Washington, D.C.: Government Printing Office, 1872.

Congressional Globe. 42 Congress, 2nd Session, 1871-72. Part I, Washington, D.C.: Government Printing Office, 1872.

Congressional Record. 43 Congress, Session I, Washington, D.C.: Government Printing Office, 1874.

Laws and Regulations relating to the Yellowstone National Park, Wyoming, by the Secretary of the Interior. Washington, D.C.: Government Printing Office, 1908.

Ludlow, William. Report to the War Department 1875. Washington, D.C., 1876.

Mather, Stephen T. "Report of the Director of the National Park Service," Report of the Department of Interior 1918. Washington, D.C.: Government Printing Office, 1918.

Norris, P. W. Annual Report of the Superintendent of Yellowstone National Park. Washington, D.C.: Government Printing Office, 1878, 1879, 1880, 1881.

Reports of the Acting Superintendent of the Yellowstone National Park. Washington, D.C.: Government Printing Office, 1885 to 1915.

Reports of the Secretary of the Interior. Washington, D.C.: Government Printing Office, 1872 to 1941.

Reports of the Superintendents of Yellowstone National Park. Washington, D.C.: Government Printing Office, 1917 to 1943.

Rules, Regulations and Instructions for the officers and enlisted men of the United States Army, and of the scouts doing duty in the Yellowstone National Park. Department of Interior, Washington, D.C.: Government Printing Office, 1907.

Sherman, W. T. and Sheridan, P. H. Reports of Inspection Made in the Summer of 1877. Washington, D.C.: Government Printing Office, 1878.

Yellowstone National Park Bulletins. Department of the Interior, Washington, D.C.: Government Printing Office, 1914, 1915, 1916, 1918, 1923, 1939, 1940, 1941.

SPECIAL BOOKS AND BULLETINS

Allen, Eugene T. and Day, Arthur L. Hot Springs of the Yellowstone National Park. Washington, D.C.: Carnegie Institution, 1935.

Alter, J. Cecil. James Bridger, Trapper, Frontiersman, Scout and Guide. Salt Lake City: Shepard Book Co., 1925.

Arnold, Ross R. Indian Wars in Idaho. Caldwell, Idaho: Caxton Printers, 1929.

Bennett, Hugh H. "Thomas Jefferson Soil Conservationist." U.S. Department of Agriculture, No. 548. Washington, D.C.: Government Printing Office, 1944.

Catlin, George. North American Indians, I, II. Philadelphia: Leary Stuart and Co., 1913.

Crampton, Louis C. Early History of Yellowstone National Park and Its Relations to National Park Policies. Washington, D.C.: United States Printing Office, 1923.

DeSmet, P. J. Oregon Missions and Travels Over the Rocky Mountains. New York: Edward Dreneger, 1847.

De Voto, Bernard. Across the Wide Missouri. Boston: Houghton Mifflin Co., 1947.

Drew, Benjamin. Souvenir List of Yellowstone Park Holdup Victims. Park Library, Mammoth, Wyoming.

Fee, Chester Anders. Chief Joseph, the Biography of a Great Indian. New York: Wilson-Erickson, 1936.

Freeman, Lewis R. Down the Yellowstone. New York: Dodd, Mead and Co., 1922.

Goad, Edgar F. "Bandelier, Scholar of the Mesas." Washington, D.C.: Department of Interior Information Service, 1940.

Haines, Francis. Red Eagles of the Northwest. Portland, Oregon: The Scholastic Press, 1939.

Harris, Burton. John Colter, His Years in the Rockies. New York: Charles Scribner's Sons, 1952.

Hebard, Grace R. and Brininstool, E. A. The Bozeman Trail. Cleveland, Ohio: Arthur H. Clark Co., 1922.

Hemishunmeres, Mourning Dove. Coyote Stories. Caldwell, Idaho: Caxton Printers, 1933.

Hornaday, William T. Our Vanishing Wild Life. New York: New York Zoological Society, 1913.

Huth, Hans. Yosemite, The Story of an Idea. Reprint from the Sierra Club Bulletin, March, 1948.

Kieley, James F. A Brief History of the National Park Service. Washington, D.C.: United States Department of Interior, 1940.

Lillard, Richard G. The Great Forest. New York: Alfred A. Knopf, 1948.

Linderman, Frank B. Blackfeet Indians. St. Paul: Brown, Bigelow, 1935.

Lowie, Robert H. The Crow Indians. New York: Farrar and Rinehart, 1935.

Mickey, Karl B. Man and Soil. Chicago: International Harvester Co., 1945.

Mulford, Walter. Forest Influences. New York: McGraw Hill Book Co., 1948.

Neihardt, John G. The Splendid Wayfaring. New York: Macmillan Co., 1920.

Norton, Harry J. Wonderland, or Horseback Rides Through Yellowstone National Park. Virginia City, Montana, 1873.

Rees, John E. Idaho, Its Meaning, Origin and Application. Portland, Oregon: Ivey Press, 1917.

Remington, Fredrick. Pony Tracks. New York: Harper and Bros., 1895.

Shields, G. O. Battle of the Big Hole. New York: Rand, McNally Co., 1889.

Story, Isabelle F. Glimpses of Our National Parks. Washington, D.C.: United States Printing Office, 1941.

Topping, E. S. Chronicles of the Yellowstone. St. Paul: Pioneer Press Co., 1888.

Van Tassell, Chas. Truthful Lies. Bozeman, Montana, 1921.

Victor, Frances Fuller. The River of the West. Hartford, Conn.: Columbian Book Co., 1871.

Vinton, Stallo. John Colter, Discoverer of Yellowstone Park. New York: Edward Eberstadt, 1926.

Wagner, Glendolin and Allen, William. Blankets and Moccasins. Caldwell, Idaho: Caxton Printers, 1933.

Wellman, Paul I. The Trampling Herd. New York: Carrick and Evans, Inc., 1939.

GENERAL SECONDARY REFERENCES

Adams, James Truslow. The Epic of America. Boston: Little Brown and Co., 1933.

Bancroft, H. H. History of Washington, Montana and Idaho. San Francisco: The History Company, 1896.

Beal, M. D. History of Southeastern Idaho. Caldwell, Idaho: Caxton Printers, 1942.

Brockett, L. P. Our Western Empire. San Francisco: William Garretson and Co., 1881.

Chittenden, Hiram M. The American Fur Trade. New York: Press of the Pioneers, 1935.

Chittenden, Hiram M. Yellowstone National Park. Palo Alto, California: Stanford University Press, 1933.

Clark, Dan Elbert. The West in American History. New York: Thomas Y. Crowell Co., 1937.

Driggs, Howard R. Westward America. New York: G. P. Putnam's Sons, 1942.

Gardiner, Dorothy. West of the River. New York: Thomas Y. Crowell Co., 1941.

Guptill, A. B. Practical Guide to Yellowstone National Park. St. Paul: F. Jay Haynes and Bro., 1890.

Hafen, LeRoy, and Rister, Carl C. Western America. New York: Prentice-Hall, 1941.

Haupt, Herman. The Yellowstone National Park. St. Paul: J. M. Stoddart, 1883.

Haynes, Jack Ellis. Haynes Guide. St. Paul: Haynes, Inc., 1943.

Hockett, Homer Co. Political and Social Growth of the United States 1492-1852. New York: The Macmillan Co., 1933.

Irving, Washington. Astoria. New York: G. P. Putnam's Sons.

Kipling, Rudyard. American Notes. Issued in several editions. One chapter contains an account of a trip through Yellowstone in 1889.

Nevins, Allen. Frémont: Pathmaker of the West. New York: D. Appleton Century Co., 1939.

Paxson, Frederick L. The Last American Frontier. New York: Macmillan Co., 1922.

Sanders, Helen F. History of Montana. Chicago: The Lewis Publishing Co., 1913.

Walgamott, C. S. Six Decades Back. Caldwell, Idaho: Caxton Printers, 1936.

Yellowstone Park Scrap Books I, II, III. Park Library, Mammoth, Wyoming.

FOOTNOTES

[1]The forests are composed principally of conifers. Of these the lodgepole pine predominates. It has a shallow root system, and as a result the area is conspicuous by the amount of fallen timber.

[2]A frontiersman's characterization of the climate in the Park. The statement is usually attributed to James Stuart.

[3]John E. Rees, Idaho Chronology, Nomenclature, Bibliography (Portland, Oregon: Ivey Press, 1917), p. 61.

[4]Teton and Snowy ranges, although partly integrated with Yellowstone, actually lie beyond the south and north borders respectively.

[5]The plateaus are Buffalo, Mirror, Two Ocean, Pitchstone, Madison, and Central. The ranges are Gallatin, Washburn, and Absaroka. The ridges include the Big Game, Chicken, Specimen, and Crowfoot. The Red Mountains form a unit by themselves in the south-central area.

[6]These are Electric, Pollux, Atkins, and Eagle peaks, and Schurz and Humphreys mountains.

[7]Warm River originates west of the Park, but Firehole is the best example of a really warm river. It does not freeze over in temperatures 50° below zero. There are literally thousands of hot springs in Yellowstone. Dr. A. C. Peale estimated three thousand, while Dr. Arnold Hague said the number probably exceeded twenty-five hundred.

[8]Reference to this stream is made again in relation to the "Overland Astorians" in Chapter II. See also, Dee Linford's "Wyoming Stream Names," Annals of Wyoming, XV, 2 (April, 1943), 165-70.

[9]These sources are the Firehole and Gibbon, respectively.

[10]This is the lowest temperature ever recorded on an official United States Weather Bureau thermometer in Continental United States.

[11]John E. Rees, op. cit., p. 61.

[12]Homer C. Hockett, Political and Social Growth of the United States 1492-1852 (New York: Macmillan Co., 1933), p. 368.

[13]Ibid., p. 369.

[14]Ibid., p. 371.

[15]Fridtjof Nansen, "The Norsemen in America," The Geographical Journal, XXXVIII, 6 (Dec. 1911), 558.

[16]Reuben G. Thwaites, Original Journals of the Lewis and Clark Expedition 1804-1806 (New York: Dodd Mead and Co., 1905), p. 262. Clark reached Yellowstone River on July 15, 1806.

[17]Francis Antoine Larocque, Journal (Sources of Northwest History No. 20, University of Montana), p. 20. Dee Linford says the name Yellowstone was used by David Thompson in 1798, but that Americans did not learn about the river until about 1805. See "Wyoming Stream Names," Annals of Wyoming, XV, 3 (July, 1943), 269.

[18]Patrick Gass, Journal (Chicago: A. C. McClurg, 1904), p. 253. In 1832 a steamboat named the "Yellowstone" arrived at Fort Union.

[19]P. Koch, "Discovery of Yellowstone National Park," Magazine of American History, II (June, 1884), 498.

[20]Just how far Coronado penetrated the Rockies is a disputed point. It is certain that Verendrye reached Pierre, South Dakota. Some contend that he came as far as the Little Bighorn River. It is probable that some of Henry's men were free trappers, which accounts for the fact that they split in groups when the fort was abandoned.

[21]Others to participate in this discovery were Milton Mangum, Clifford Mangum, John T. Elliott, Budge Elliott, William Thornock, and David Beal.

[22]Robert Stuart, The Discovery of the Oregon Trail (New York: Charles Scribner's Sons, 1935), p. CXXXVI. Etienne Provot and Thomas Fitzpatrick have both been credited with the discovery of South Pass. Certainly the latter's visit in 1824 marks the date of effective discovery.

[23]W. J. Ghent, "A Sketch of John Colter," Wyoming Annals, X, 3 (July, 1938).

[24]Stallo Vinton, John Colter, Discoverer of Yellowstone Park (New York: Edward Eberstadt, 1926), p. 27.

[25]W. J. Ghent, op. cit. The copious journals of Lewis, Clark and Sergeant Ordway make repeated mention of Colter, and Whitehouse names him six times. Floyd does not mention him by name nor does Gass, although the latter refers to him specifically.

[26]Reuben G. Thwaites, op. cit., V, 314.

[27]Stallo Vinton, op. cit., p. 24.

[28]Ibid., p. 43. Colter's strange behavior in turning back to the wilderness after three successive starts toward home, is analyzed by C. H. Heffelfinger in his article, "The Man Who Turned Back," The Washington Historical Quarterly, XXVI, 3 (July, 1935).

[29]Ibid., p. 45. Lisa had a son named "Remon" for whom the fort was named, but different documents bear the name Raymond, Manuel, and Lisa.

[30]Judge Henry M. Brackenridge (1786-1871) was educated in Missouri and Maryland. As a lawyer, he specialized in international affairs and served as a federal judge in New Orleans. In 1810 he made a trip up the Missouri in the company of Manuel Lisa. Six years later (1814) Brackenridge's account of this journey was published. On page 91, of Views of Louisiana, we find the first reference to Colter's wilderness journey. Obviously the source of this information was Manuel Lisa since he asked Colter to make the trip. That Colter started on such a journey is indisputable. Where he went, what he saw, and how he returned are matters of opinion. Brackenridge confuses Colter's return from this trip with that of another one.

[31]Ibid., p. 91.

[32]John Colter's discovery of Yellowstone has caught the imagination of many people. Probably a hundred authors have written about it. Each one disagrees with the other, until poor Colter has been turned into a human grasshopper, hopping around from place to place without either rhyme or reason.

[33]Stallo Vinton, op. cit., p. 195.

[34]Some writers tell that an early winter overtook him, and he was obliged to make snowshoes. This is probably an error. He undoubtedly secured a horse from the Yep-pe Indians.

[35]This particular story is verified by the fact that members of the Wilson Price Hunt Expedition called on Colter at his farm near St. Louis to get information upon this specific point. See Reuben G. Thwaites, "Bradbury's Travels in the Interior of America in the years 1809-1811," Early Western Travels, 1748-1840, V, xliv.

[36]The Map of 1814 does not disclose anything unusual. It merely designates "Boiling Spring" and "Hot Springs Brimstone," which were widespread and general.

[37]Washington Irving, The Adventures of Captain Bonneville (New York: G. P. Putnam's Sons, 1843), p. 252. The first edition was entitled, Rocky Mountain Scenes and Adventures.

[38]It is a remarkable thing that historical research has not more satisfactorily probed the Colter problem. Obviously his journey is so obscure as to warrant scientific investigation.

[39]Its legend reads: "A Map of Lewis and Clark's Track, Across the Western Portion of North America, From the Mississippi to the Pacific Ocean; By Order of the Executive of the United States in 1804, 5, 6. Copied by Samuel Lewis from the Original Drawing of Wm. Clark."

[40]There are two fictitious lakes on the Map of 1814 of such grotesque shape as to arouse one's skepticism. One of them has a shape that resembles a gargoyle.

[41]The date of this communication was December 20, 1810.

[42]Colter's first sheet is readily identifiable, and part of another sheet may be segregated with the use of imagination and understanding.

[43]Many writers have failed to identify Gap and Sage as the same creek. They also befuddle Wind and Shoshone rivers. There is no evidence that Colter ever heard the name Bighorn River.

[44]The figure eight results from the fact that he went to the Yep-pe camp, left it, came back, and left it again at the appropriate angles.

[45]In 1941, Paul J. Shamp, a U.S. forester, reported the discovery of numerous petrifications in the vicinity of Pass and Scatter creeks in the Thorofare country. This is the line of Colter's route.

[46]Colter did not see Southeast Arm of Yellowstone Lake. He probably supposed the Upper Yellowstone flowed into South Arm. Hence, his conception of Yellowstone River would have been ten miles farther west than it is. Neither could he have visualized the serpentine character of Snake River, since he knew it at only one place.

[47]Colter may have reached Chicken Ridge by Fishhawk, Mountain, or Lynx creeks or via Falcon, Mink, or Crooked streams. It must be remembered that this map sheet has been much messed up. It is impossible to know what has been erased; yet, enough of Colter's map remains to provide a logical basis for the above itinerary. It is relatively unimportant which creeks he negotiated to reach Chicken Ridge. The vitally important fact is that he drew a sketch of South Arm from that angle which added to the Thumb makes an accurate map of what a trapper would have seen of Yellowstone Lake.

[48]J. Neilson Barry has made the most intensive study of the Map of 1814. It is his opinion that Colter drew other map sheets besides the one of the Buffalo Bill country. He also has hope that these sheets may be discovered among the Lewis-Clark-Biddle papers.

[49]In E. Willard Smith's journal entry for December 20, 1839, there is an item that suggests a possible clue to mystery of Colter's petrified fish story: "There is a story told by an Arapahoe Chief of a petrified buffalo standing in the lake ... in a perfect state of preservation, and they worship it as a great medicine charm.... Nothing would induce this Indian to tell where this sacred buffalo is to be found. Great presents were offered him in vain." It is possible that Colter saw something he was not free to divulge. See "An Excerpt From the Journal of Willard E. Smith," Annals of Wyoming, XV, 3 (July, 1943), 287-97.

[50]John G. White, "A Souvenir of Wyoming," Vol. I, p. 56. This is a fine work of research in manuscript. It was written in 1916. There are five volumes in the Yellowstone Park library. The time of this Indian episode was in the autumn of 1808.

[51]Ibid.

[52]Upon the details of this episode, the three basic authorities on this period of Western adventure, are in agreement. They are Henry M. Brackenridge, Views of Louisiana; Thomas James, Three Years Among the Indians and Mexicans; and John Bradbury, Travels In the Interior of America.

[53]Concerning Colter's part in this battle, Henry M. Brackenridge wrote, "On his return a party of Indians in whose company he happened to be was attacked and he was lamed by a severe wound in his leg; Notwithstanding which he returned to the establishment entirely alone and without assistance." This incident is almost invariably associated with Colter's return from the discovery of Yellowstone Park. The error logically arises from the compressed character of the Brackenridge narrative. Perhaps the facts were not clear in his own mind. Actually he has confused two different experiences.

[54]P. Koch, "The Discovery of Yellowstone National Park," Magazine of American History, II (June, 1884), 499.

[55]Hiram M. Chittenden, Yellowstone National Park (Palo Alto: Stanford University Press, 1933), pp. 22-31.

[56]Frank Triplett, "Colter's Race for Life," Conquering the Wilderness, No. 16, Chapter 10, Washington State College Library; Pullman, Washington. This plant is also called "ground-apple." It is an edible root found in that region.

[57]W. J. Ghent, op. cit., p. 113.

[58]John G. White, "A Souvenir of Wyoming," I, 28. This fact is affirmed by James in his Three Years Among the Indians and Mexicans.

[59]W. J. Ghent, op. cit., p. 115.

[60]Stallo Vinton, op. cit., p. 110.

[61]W. J. Ghent, op. cit., p. 115. The evidence is not conclusive as to whether or not Colter gave his account to Bradbury and Brackenridge in person. It is certain that he had personal dealings with Thomas James, and it is certain that he spent a half day in conversation with members of Hunt's party on May 18, 1811. See "Robert Stuart's Narratives" in Philip Ashton Rollin's The Discovery of the Oregon Trail (New York: Charles Scribner's Sons, 1935), p. CV.

[62]Ibid., p. 66. It should be pointed out that Colter did not say "everywhere."

[63]Rudolph Kurz, Journal (Washington, D. C.: United States Government Printing Office, 1937), p. 37.

[64]Frank B. Linderman, Blackfeet Indians (St. Paul: Brown, Bigelow, 1935), p. 9.

[65]Ibid., p. 12.

[66]Elizabeth Spalding, Memories of The West (Portland, Oregon: March Printing Company), p. 78.

[67]Robert Vaughn, Then and Now (Minneapolis, Minnesota: Tribune Printing Co., 1900), p. 197.

[68]Mourning Dove, Coyote Stories (Caldwell, Idaho: Caxton Printers, 1933). p. 46.

[69]Rudolph Kurz, op. cit., p. 154.

[70]Ibid., p. 34.

[71]Alexander Ross, The Fur Hunters of The Far West (London: Smith, Elder & Co., 1855), p. 249.

[72]H. M. Chittenden, The American Fur Trade (New York: Press of the Pioneers, 1935), II, 877.

[73]P. Koch, "The Discovery of Yellowstone National Park," Magazine of American History, II (June, 1884), 497.

[74]Helen F. Sanders, History of Montana (Chicago: Lewis Publishing Co., 1913), I, 681.

[75]Contributions, Historical Society of Montana (Helena, Montana: Rocky Mountain Publishing Co., 1876), I, 168.

[76]Indian reservations nearest the Park are the Crow at Hardin, Montana; Shoshone, Fort Washakie, Wyoming; and Bannock, Fort Hall, Idaho. Other agencies are located at Fort Peck, Poplar, Tongue River, and Lame Deer, all in Montana. The Blackfeet and Flathead reservations are near Glacier Park.

[77]Alexander Ross, op. cit., p. 48.

[78]John G. Neihardt, The Splendid Wayfaring (New York: Macmillan Company, 1920), pp. 265-6.

[79]Alexander Ross, op. cit., pp. 228-9.

[80]Francis Fuller Victor, The River of the West (Hartford: Columbian Book Co., 1871), pp. 64-5.

[81]Cecil Alter, James Bridger, Trapper, Frontiersman, Scout and Guide (Salt Lake City: Shepard Book Co., 1925), p. 355.

[82]Helen F. Sanders, op. cit., p. 141.

[83]Earl of Dunraven, Hunting in the Yellowstone (New York: Macmillan Co., 1925), pp. 184-5.

[84]Frances Fuller Victor, op. cit., p. 238.

[85]F. A. Wislizenus, A Journey To The Rocky Mountains In 1839, (St. Louis: Missouri Historical Society, 1912), pp. 87-8.

[86]Alexander Ross, op. cit., II, 236.

[87]C. Max Bauer, "Notes on Indian Occupancy," Yellowstone Nature Notes. XII, 6 (June, 1935), 1.

[88]P. W. Norris, Annual Report 1879 (Washington D. C.: Government Printing Office, 1880), p. 10.

[89]P. W. Norris, Annual Report 1880, p. 605.

[90]Some of these places were specifically listed: Bunsen Peak, Willow Creek, Stinking Water Pass east of Yellowstone Lake, Barlow Fork of Snake River, Bridgers Lake, and, the best one of all, three miles below Mary Lake. See Fifth Annual Report 1881, p. 36.

[91]P. W. Norris, Fifth Annual Report 1881, pp. 32-8.

[92]Ibid., p. 38.

[93]P. W. Norris, Annual Report 1878, p. 982.

[94]Experienced rangers who have reported these finds to the author include David deL. Condon, Lee L. Coleman, John W. Jay, John Bauman, Rudolf L. Grimm, Wayne Replogle, Lowell G. Biddulph, George Marler, and William Sanborn.

[95]William E. Kearns, "A Nez Percé Chief Revisits Yellowstone," Yellowstone Nature Notes, XII (June-July, 1935), 41.

[96]Edwin Linton, Science, No. 561 (Nov. 3, 1893), pp. 244-5.

Mr. Linton and Prof. S. A. Forbes heard the sounds upon two occasions. Each gave a scientific presentation. Elwood Hofer, Dave Rhodes, and F. H. Bradley have written accounts of similar experiences.

[97]Report of the Secretary of the Interior (Washington: Government Printing Office, Nov. 30, 1880), p. 573.

[98]Frederick Bottler discovered a trapper's cabin at the head of Antelope Creek in 1878. The advanced decay of its timbers indicated that it was forty or fifty years old. See P. W. Norris, Annual Report 1880, p. 606.

[99]Niles Weekly Register, Third Series, IX, 6 (Oct. 6, 1827), p. 90. Also, Yellowstone Nature Notes, XXI, 5 (Sept.-Oct., 1947), p. 52. Sweet Lake is now known as Bear Lake, Idaho.

[100]P. W. Norris, Annual Report 1878, p. 987. Smith was killed by a band of Comanches in 1831, when leading a caravan across the Cimarron Desert toward Santa Fe.

[101]Meek's experience was published by Mrs. Frances Fuller Victor in The River of the West (Hartford, Conn.: Columbian Book Co., 1871), pp. 75-7.

[102]Warren A. Ferris, Life in the Rocky Mountains 1830-35 (Salt Lake City: Rocky Mountain Book Shop, 1940), pp. 204-6.

[103]Osborne Russell, Journal of a Trapper, 1834-1843 (Boise, Idaho: Syms-York Co., 1921), p. 32.

[104]Helen F. Sanders, op. cit., p. 657.

Mr. Ducharme, Joe Power, L'Humphrie, Louis Anderson, and Jim and John Baker were members of this group. Remains of horses have been found on this battleground.

[105]J. Cecil Alter, James Bridger, p. 107.

[106]Walter W. DeLacy, "A Trip Up the South Fork of Snake River," Contributions, Historical Society of Montana, I, 132.

[107]James Stuart, "The Yellowstone Expedition of 1863," Ibid., I, 191.

Montana mineral production vaulted to $18,000,000 by 1865. Thereafter a gradual decline began, but a strong revival came in the eighties when deep mining of silver and copper ore bodies proved profitable. The combined mineral output in 1889 was $41,000,000.

[108]P. Koch, "The Discovery of Yellowstone National Park," Magazine of American History, II, 511.

[109]E. S. Topping, Chronicles of the Yellowstone (St. Paul: Pioneer Press Co., 1888), p. 44.

[110]P. W. Norris, Annual Report 1880, p. 7. Miller Creek was named for Adam Miller's retreat in this instance.

[111]Grace R. Hebard and E. A. Brininstool, The Bozeman Trail (Cleveland: Arthur H. Clark Co., 1922), II, 229.

[112]Robert Vaughn, Then and Now, p. 165.

[113]Hebard and Brininstool, op. cit., II, 229.

[114]Ibid., p. 230.

[115]Ibid., p. 244.

[116]Anonymous. The quotations used in the Bridger stories represent the author's organization of existing folk lore. Some of these stories and others are given in H. M. Chittenden's Yellowstone National Park.

[117]John G. White, "Souvenir," I, 134.

[118]Hiram M. Chittenden, op. cit., pp. 39-40.

[119]Hebard and Brininstool, op. cit., II, p. 243.

[120]This information was obtained by the author from Jesse M. Matlock, formerly Mrs. William Peterson and Mabel M. White, an adopted daughter, in an interview at Salmon City, June 7, 1943. The latter remembers hearing Mr. Peterson express regret that the Folsom-Cook-Peterson Expedition was not given more recognition for its discovery. Mr. Peterson died in 1918.

[121]C. W. Cook and D. E. Folsom, "Cook-Folsom Expedition to the Yellowstone Region 1869," Haynes Bulletin (Jan. 1923).

[122]C. W. Cook, "Remarks of C. W. Cook, Last Survivor of the Original Explorers of the Yellowstone Park Region," Yellowstone Park Library, Mammoth, Wyoming. Two sons of Cornelius Hedges were present at the celebration which was sponsored by The National Editorial Association.

[123]W. T. Jackson, "The Cook-Folsom Exploration of the Upper Yellowstone 1869," The Pacific Northwest Quarterly, XXXII (1941), 320-21.

[124]Hiram M. Chittenden, Yellowstone National Park, p. 60.

[125]Nathaniel P. Langford, The Discovery of Yellowstone Park 1870 (St. Paul, Minn.: J. E. Haynes, 1923), p. 80.

[126]Louis C. Crampton, Early History of Yellowstone National Park and Its Relations to National Park Policies (Washington, D. C.: United States Government Printing Office, 1923), p. 14.

[127]Yellowstone Park Scrap Book, I, 33. Park Library, Mammoth, Wyoming.

[128]L. P. Brockett, Our Western Empire (San Francisco: William Garretson and Co., 1881), p. 1247.

[129]Ibid., p. 1243.

[130]Cornelius Hedges, "Yellowstone Lake," Crampton's Early History, p. 110.

[131]Truman C. Everts, "Thirty Seven Days of Peril," Scribner's Monthly, III (Nov. 1871), 1-17.

[132]Cornelius Hedges, "Journal," Contributions, Montana Historical Society, V, 387.

[133]Nathaniel P. Langford, op. cit., p. 158.

[134]Gustavus C. Doane, "Report Upon the Yellowstone Expedition," Crampton's Early History, p. 138.

[135]Henry D. Washburn, "The Yellowstone Expedition," Ibid., p. 96.

[136]Rudyard Kipling, American Notes, p. 159.

[137]L. P. Brockett, op. cit., p. 1254.

[138]F. V. Hayden, American Journal of Science, III (March, 1872), 174.

[139]Arnold Hague, "The Yellowstone National Park," Scribner's Magazine, XXXV (May, 1904), 519.

[140]W. Turrentine Jackson, "The Creation of Yellowstone Park," The Mississippi Valley Historical Review XXIX, 2 (September, 1942), 189-90.

[141]N. P. Langford, Preface to "The Folsom-Cook Exploration of the Upper Yellowstone in the Year 1869," Contributions, Historical Society of Montana, V (1904), 312.

[142]Truman C. Everts, op. cit., p. 16.

[143]H. M. Chittenden, Yellowstone National Park, p. 69.

[144]Ibid., p. 70.

[145]Louis C. Crampton, Early History of Yellowstone, p. 25.

[146]F. V. Hayden, "More About the Yellowstone," Scribner's Monthly, III, 4 (February, 1872), 389. This article contains a summary of the Hayden Expedition.

[147]H. M. Chittenden, op. cit., p. 71.

[148]In Dr. Hayden's "Brief Statement of the History of the National Park," which he forwarded to the Secretary of the Interior, Carl Schurz, on February 21, 1878, the following appeared: "I beg permission to state here, that so far as I know, I originated the idea of the park, prepared the maps, designating the boundaries, and in connection with the Hon. W. H. Claggett [sic], then Delegate from Montana Territory, wrote the law as it now stands.... It is now acknowledged all over the civilized world that the existence of the National Park, by law, is due solely to my exertions during the

sessions of 1871 and 1872." House Executive Documents, Forty-fifth Congress, Second Session, 1877-78, XVII, No. 75, 3. For this item credit is given by the author to W. Turrentine Jackson; see "The Creation of Yellowstone National Park," The Mississippi Valley Historical Review, University of Iowa, XXIX, 2 (Sept. 1942), 199.

[149]Congressional Globe, Forty-second Congress, Second Session, 1871-72, Part I, p. 520.

[150]Ibid., p. 697.

[151]W. T. Jackson, op. cit., p. 203.

[152]Ibid., pp. 204-5.

[153]Louis C. Crampton, op. cit., p. 31.

[154]Senator George G. Vest, a strong friend of Yellowstone, once referred to Mr. Dawes as the father of the Park, "for he drew the law of designation." If not the actual scribe, he was certainly the advocate of the principles involved. See L. C. Crampton, op. cit., p. 32.

[155]John Muir, The Atlantic Monthly, LXXXI (April, 1898), 509.

Dr. F. V. Hayden's tribute to Congress is equal to John Muir's. Hayden said, "That our legislators, at a time when public opinion is so strong against appropriating the public domain for any purpose, however laudable, should reserve for the benefit and instruction of the people a tract of 3,575 square miles, is an act that should cause universal satisfaction through the land. This noble deed may be regarded as a tribute from our legislators to science, and the gratitude of the nation, and of men of science in all parts of the world, is due them for this munificent donation." See "The Yellowstone National Park," American Journal, III (April, 1872), 295-96.

[156]Congressional Globe, p. 697.

[157]George Catlin, North American Indians (Philadelphia: 1913), II, 290.

[158]This refers to Chief Joseph's retreat which is described in Chapter XI.

[159]Alexander Ross, The Fur Hunters of the Far West, p. 257.

[160]Ulrich B. Phillips, "Lectures On Early America," a series of lectures given in Berkeley, Calif., 1932.

[161]Robert Vaughn, Then and Now, p. 156.

[162]Ibid., p. 295.

[163]James Stuart, Contributions, Montana Historical Society, I, 154.

[164]Edgar F. Goad, "Bandelier, Scholar of the Mesas" (Washington, D. C.: Department of Interior Information Service, 1940), p. 13.

[165]Alexander Ross, op. cit., p. 183.

[166]LeRoy R. Hafen and Carl C. Rister, Western America (New York: Prentice-Hall, 1941), p. 6.

[167]The most notorious foreigners to regale themselves among western American adventure scenes were Prince Maximilian of Wied-Neuwied, Sir George Gore of Ireland, and the Earl of Dunraven.

Maximilian spent the summer of 1833 on the upper Missouri. He was a shabby, toothless man, but of first-rate scientific ability. It is said that his accounts, together with

Bodmer's paintings, constitute an important record of the period.

Sir George Gore was a millionaire who spent two years in the West. He left a saga of ruthless slaughter and camp-life prodigality in his wake. His parting gesture was the destruction, by fire, of all the wagons, harness, saddles, and similar equipment. This was done to spite the Missouri Fur Company because of their exorbitant river transportation charges.

In 1871 the Grand Duke Alexis of Russia hunted bison on the Nebraska plains.

[168]Ibid., p. 572.

[169]Granville Stuart, Forty Years on the Frontier, edited by Paul C. Phillips (Cleveland: 1925), II, 104. This view was expressed by Representative James A. Garfield. See Congressional Record, Forty-third Congress, First Session, 1874, pp. 2107-9.

[170]Warren A. Ferris, op. cit., p. 244.

[171]Ibid., pp. 204-6.

[172]Dan E. Clark, The West in American History (New York: Thomas Y. Crowell Co., 1937), p. 573.

[173]Fredrick L. Paxson, Recent American History of the United States (Boston: Prentice-Hall Co., 1937), p. 28.

[174]LeRoy R. Hafen and Carl G. Rister, op. cit., p. 528.

[175]D. J. Louck, "Journal," State Historian's file, Laramie, Wyoming.

[176]Helen F. Sanders, op. cit., p. 313.

[177]Howard R. Briggs, Westward America (New York: G. P. Putnam's Sons, 1942), p. 276.

[178]Ibid., pp. 279-80. In 1862, Granville Stuart collected a herd and drove them to Bannock. Conrad Kohrs had a butcher shop there at that time.

[179]Dorothy Gardiner, West of the River (New York: Thomas Y. Crowell Co., 1941), p. 319.

Forts were located chiefly with an eye to the protection of travel. Some of the principal ones—Cook, on Judith River, Montana; Reno; Phil Kearney; C. F. Smith; and Casper in Wyoming—were built in 1866. D. A. Russell near Cheyenne, Fort Shaw on Sun River, and Fort Buford were established in 1867. Fort Laramie was built in 1849; Fort Bridger, in 1858; Fort Stambaugh at South Pass, 1869; Fort Steele on North Platte Crossing, 1868; and Fort Assiniboine near Havre, 1879.

[180]Granville Stuart, op. cit. Other prominent stockmen were C. D. Duncan, Robert Coburn, N. J. Dovenspeck, Amos Snyder, Adolf Baro, W. C. and G. P. Burnett, Pat Dunlevy, James Dempsey, Chas. Ranges, Edward Regan, N. W. McCaulley, and F. E. Lawrence.

[181]Dan E. Clark, op. cit., p. 596.

[182]Helen F. Sanders, op. cit., p. 316.

[183]Nathaniel P. Langford, The Discovery of Yellowstone Park, p. 181.

[184]Cornelius Hedges, Contributions, Montana Historical Society, V, 391.

[185]Dan E. Clark, op. cit., p. 625.

[186]Chief Joseph, "Chief Joseph's Own Story," as told by him on his trip to Washington, D. C., p. 3.

[187]Francis Haines, Red Eagles of the Northwest (Portland, Ore.: The Scholastic Press, 1939), p. 234.

[188]Ibid., p. 238.

[189]Chief Joseph, op. cit., p. 9.

[190]Helen A. Howard and Dan L. McGrath, War Chief Joseph (Caldwell, Idaho: The Caxton Printers, Ltd., 1941), p. 145.

[191]Chester Anders Fee, Chief Joseph, the Biography of a Great Indian (New York: Wilson-Erickson, 1936), p. 168.

[192]Francis Haines, op. cit., p. 262.

[193]Helen F. Sanders, op. cit., p. 268.

[194]Ibid., p. 282.

[195]W. T. Sherman, Reports of Inspection Made in the Summer of 1877 (Washington, D. C.: Government Printing Office, 1878), p. 34.

[196]Heister D. Guie and L. V. McWhorter, editors, Adventures in Geyser Land, by Frank D. Carpenter (Caldwell, Idaho: The Caxton Printers, Ltd., 1935), p. 279.

George F. Cowan was born in Ohio in 1842. He was with the first volunteers during the Civil War. He attained the rank of Sergeant. At this time he was one of Montana's leading attorneys.

[197]Chester A. Fee, op. cit., p. 218.

[198]Francis Haines, op. cit., p. 287.

[199]Heister Guie and L. V. McWhorter, op. cit., p. 223.

[200]Edwin J. Stanley, Rambles in Wonderland (New York: D. Appleton and Co., 1878), p. 166.

[201]Chester A. Fee, op. cit., p. 223.

[202]Heister D. Guie and L. V. McWhorter, op. cit., p. 225.

George F. Cowan's experiences were so peculiar that one is puzzled to know whether he was the most lucky or unlucky of men. A train of incidents followed his suffering in the Park. Near Fort Ellis the neck yoke broke, and the Cowan party was thrown out of the carriage. At Bozeman, when Mr. Arnold was dressing Cowan's wounds in the hotel room, the bedstead gave way and down went the injured man.

[203]Andrew J. Weikert, "Journal of a Tour Through Yellowstone National Park in August and September 1877," Contributions, Historical Society of Montana, IV (1900), 185-99.

[204]H. M. Chittenden, Yellowstone National Park, p. 142. Stewart was relieved of $260.00 and a watch.

[205]Ibid., p. 143.

[206]Heister D. Guie and L. V. McWhorter, op. cit., pp. 194-5.

Near the top of Mt. Everts, and toward its southern end, there is a cliff formed by an ancient flow of lava. Upon a flat space, at the foot of the cliff, one may find an inscription that reads, "Ben Stone 1877."

[207]Ibid., p. 145.

[208]O. O. Howard, Chief Joseph, His Pursuit and Capture (Boston: Lee and Shephard, 1881), p. 243.

[209]Helen A. Howard and Dan L. McGrath, op. cit., p. 258.

[210]Ibid., pp. 260-1.

[211]Chester A. Fee, op. cit., pp. 248-9.

[212]Helen A. Howard and Dan L. McGrath, op. cit., pp. 271-2.

[213]This was Joseph's understanding, as revealed in all subsequent statements.

[214]Chester A. Fee, op. cit., pp. 262-3.

[215]Ibid., p. 270.

[216]Ibid., p. 272.

[217]Helen A. Howard and Dan L. McGrath, op. cit., p. 183.

[218]Chester A. Fee, op. cit., p. 287.

[219]The Hayden and other government expeditions did quite a lot of trail work in an informal manner. That is to say, they had large parties and considerable baggage. In order to get through the forest quite a lot of trail building became necessary.

[220]Jack E. Haynes, "The Expedition of President Chester A. Arthur to Yellowstone National Park in 1883," Annals of Wyoming, January, 1942, p. 2.

[221]J. J. Leclercq, La Terre des Marveilles. An excerpt containing this story is in Mercer Cook's Portraits of Americans (New York: D. C. Heath and Co., 1939), pp. 47-8.

[222]John Muir, The Atlantic Monthly, LXXXI (Jan. 1898), 15.

Edwin J. Stanley's Rambles in Wonderland describes conditions as of that time.

[223]P. W. Norris, Annual Report 1880, p. 584. See also Elno's "The Lord of Hard Luck," Dillon Examiner, June 12, 1940.

[224]Heister D. Guie and L. V. McWhorter, Adventures in Geyser Land, p. 71.

Texas Jack served as a guide for the Earl of Dunraven in 1874.

[225]Jones Bros. and McGill of Cody and Hougan and Phillips of Salt Lake City, along with many others, conducted tours varying in duration and cost. The fee varied from five to ten dollars a day per person.

[226]C. S. Walgamott, Reminiscences (Twin Falls, Idaho, 1926), II, 78.

[227]John Muir, The Atlantic Monthly, LXXXI (April, 1898), 515.

[228]Alice W. Rollins, "The Three Tetons," Harper's, LXXIV (May, 1887), 876.

[229]Ibid.

[230]Rudyard Kipling, American Notes, p. 126. "Buckskin Charley" was Charles Marble; Yankee Jim's name was James George; Hofer's name was Thomas Elwood Hofer.

[231]Yellowstone Park Scrap Book, II, 52. There are three volumes of newspaper and magazine clippings in the Park Library at Mammoth, Wyoming.

[232]Ibid., pp. 60, 123. See also I, 33, and III, 33.

[233]Alice W. Rollins, op. cit., p. 74.

[234]Silas S. Huntley was the guiding mind of the organization from 1892 to 1901, when H. W. Child succeeded to the management, which he held until 1917. E. W. Bach was an active partner.

[235]The transportation setup as of 1914: Yellowstone Park Transportation Company, Gardiner, Round Trip $25.00; Yellowstone Western Stage Company, Yellowstone, Montana, $20.00; Holm Transportation Company, Cody, Wyoming, five days $25.00; Wylie Permanent Camping Company maintains permanent camps and operates a line from Gardiner, also West Yellowstone and Camp Cody (East Gate). The camps: Swan Lake Basin, Riverside, Upper Geyser Basin, Outlet of Lake, Grand Canyon, Camp Cody and Tower Falls. Lunch stations at Gibbon Geyser Basin and Thumb. Six day tour $40.00.

[236]Yellowstone Park Scrap Book, III, 20. Also Henry D. Sedgwick, Jr., "On Horse Back Through Yellowstone," World's Work, VI (June, 1903). Two of Yancey's buildings are still standing.

[237]Scrap Book, II, 4.

[238]Report of the Secretary of the Interior 1884, I, 73.

[239]A corrupt and incompetent concern called The Improvement Company started a hotel in Mammoth. In 1884 this firm attempted to secure private ownership of land in important localities through Congressional action. When the move failed the firm went under. Its interests were bought by the Yellowstone Park Association which was financed by the Northern Pacific Railway.

[240]The Norris Hotel was replaced by a camp hotel and eating house, which served until 1900, when a new one was completed. The hotel at Old Faithful had not been profitable and was not replaced until 1903, when Old Faithful Inn was built.

[241]J. E. Rickards, ex-Governor of Montana, to the editor of The Salt Lake Tribune, July 17, 1897.

[242]Scrap Book, II, 56.

[243]Report of the Department of the Interior 1907, p. 533. The Boat Company charged three dollars for a ride from Thumb to Lake Fishing Bridge.

[244]Henry D. Sedgwick, op. cit., p. 3572.

[245]Scrap Book, I, 61.

[246]Ibid., Captain George S. Anderson earnestly prophesied that there would not be a square mile of forest left standing in six months if railroads were permitted to enter.

[247]Charles D. Warner, "Yellowstone National Park," Harper's, XCIV (January, 1897), 323.

[248]Annual Report 1907. Several wells had to be dug between Norris and Canyon.

[249]Horace M. Albright, Park Service Bulletin, April 14, 1934, p. 46.

[250]Lucien M. Lewis, "To the Old Stage Driver," Overland Monthly, LXIX (July, 1917), 52.

[251]Yellowstone Park Automobile Regulations for the Season of 1916. Department of the Interior Bulletin. Here is an example of the procedure:

SCHEDULE A

Gardiner to Norris	Miles	Not earlier than	Not later than
Leave Gardiner Entrance	0	6:00 A.M.	6:30 A.M.
Arrive Mammoth Hot Springs	5	6:20	7:00
Leave Mammoth Hot Springs	0	6:45	7:15
Leave 8 Mile Post	8		8:00
Arrive Norris	20	8:30	9:00

Schedule B was for the P.M.

Bicyclists were also closely regulated. Upon meeting a team the rider was required to stop and stand between his cycle and the team. He could not pass a team from the rear without a signal.

People on horseback were expected to observe every precaution in passing teams of all sorts.

[252]Reports of the Department of the Interior 1917, p. 812.

[253]Chas. Van Tassell, Truthful Lies (Bozeman, Montana, 1921).

[254]Reports of the Secretary of the Interior 1936, p. 132. The firms combined in this consolidation were The Yellowstone Park Hotel Co., The Yellowstone Park Transportation Co., The Yellowstone Park Lodge and Camps Co., and The Yellowstone Park Boat Company.

[255]Ibid., 1939, p. 300.

[256]There are two service stations in Old Faithful Camp. Some people complain because they cannot get their favorite gasoline. However, it would be both unsightly and impractical to allow each company a half-dozen representatives. There are no pumps at all at Madison and Norris stations.

[257]Park Service Bulletin, Nov., 1936, p. 12.

[258]Richard G. Lillard, The Great Forest (New York: Alfred A. Knopf, 1948), p. 32.

[259]Ibid., p. 68.

[260]Ibid., p. 9.

[261]Hans Huth, Yosemite, the Story of an Idea. Reprint from the Sierra Club Bulletin, March 1948, p. 48.

[262]Richard G. Lillard, op. cit., p. 85.

[263]Richard G. Lillard, op. cit., p. 256.

[264]Hugh H. Bennett, "Thomas Jefferson Soil Conservationist," U. S. Department of Agriculture, No. 548 (1944).

[265]Karl B. Mickey, Man and Soil (Chicago: International Harvester Co., 1945), p. 17.

[266]Hans Huth, op. cit., p. 73.

[267]George Catlin, The Manners, Customs, and Conditions of the North American Indians (London, 1841), I, 262.

[268]Hans Huth, op. cit., p. 52.

[269]Walter Mulford, Forest Influences (New York: McGraw Hill Book Co., 1948), p. 15.

[270]Hans Huth, op. cit., p. 68.

[271]Ibid., p. 69.

[272]Ibid.

[273]Hans Huth said Frederick Law Olmstead admitted failure in his attempt to discover the origin of public parks in this country. He attributed it to "a spontaneous movement of that sort which we conveniently refer to as the genius of our civilization." Ibid., p. 60.

[274]Richard G. Lillard, op. cit., p. 260.

[275]This agency was later transferred to the Department of Agriculture.

[276]Richard G. Lillard, op. cit., p. 264.

[277]Ibid., p. 270.

[278]Ibid. National Legislation Executive Almanac in Brief:

1876—$2,000.00, appropriated to employ a competent man to investigate timber conditions in the United States.

June 30, 1886—Act creating Division of Forestry in Department of Agriculture.

March 3, 1891—President authorized to establish Forest Reserves; Yellowstone Park Timberland Reserve proclaimed by President Harrison on March 30, 1891.

June 4, 1897—Present National Forest Act passed.

July 1, 1901—Division of Forestry becomes Bureau of Forestry.

February 1, 1905—Bureau of Forestry becomes Forest Service.

March 1, 1911—Weeks Law passed.

April 11, 1921—Snell Bill introduced in Congress.

May 2, 1921—Capper Bill introduced in Congress.

June 7, 1924—Clarke-McNary Bill signed by President.

April 30, 1928—McNary-Woodruff Act signed by President.

May 22, 1928—McSweeney-McNary Act signed by President.

Jan. 1, 1931—Creation of the Timber Conservation Board.

1937—The Norris-Doxey Act.

1944—The Cooperative Sustained Yield Act.

> Other Acts closely related to the Forestry program include, Civilian Conservation Corps, the Agricultural Adjustment Administration, Public Works Administration, Taylor Grazing Control Act, Farm Security Act, and Tennessee Valley Authority.

[279]"National Parks and National Forests," a statement by the National Park Service, Department of the Interior and the Forest Service, Department of Agriculture.

[280]Earl of Dunraven, op. cit., p. 34.

[281]William T. Hornaday, Our Vanishing Wild Life (New York: New York Zoological Society, 1913), p. 2.

[282]Ibid., p. 63.

[283]Earl of Dunraven, op. cit., p. 6.

[284]Ibid., p. 15.

[285]Extinct species include: great auk, Pallas's cormorant, Labrador duck, Eskimo curlew, passenger pigeon, Carolina parakeet, yellow-winged green parrot, heath hen, whooping crane, upland plover. Other effective wild life conservation advocates were Dr. Theodore S. Palmer, Edward H. Forbush, T. Gilbert Pearson, John B. Burnham, and William T. Hornaday.

[286]Earl of Dunraven, op. cit., p. 181.

[287]Ibid., pp. 182-3.

[288]Nathaniel P. Langford, "The Ascent of Mount Hayden," Scribner's Monthly, III (June, 1873), 133-40. The author does not necessarily imply that Langford reached the summit.

The author has possession of a part of Mr. Leigh's diary, numerous dictations, and items relative to "Beaver Dick."

[289]F. H. Knowlton, "The Tertiary Flowers of the Yellowstone National Park," The American Journal of Science, No. 7 (July, 1896).

[290]Chittenden says that Norris Geyser Basin was discovered from the top of Bunsen Peak in 1872. E. S. Topping and Dwight Woodruff saw a large column of steam ascending far to the south. They made an investigation and reported their find. The next day Mr. and Mrs. H. H. Stone, of Bozeman, Montana, visited the basin. Mrs. Stone was one of the first white women to enter the Park. Perhaps she was the first excepting certain members of earlier missionary parties.

[291]N. P. Langford's Diary, Second Trip To Yellowstone 1872. MS. in Yellowstone Park Library, Mammoth, Wyoming. Dr. Hayden and his co-workers returned in 1878. In this investigation they made detailed reports upon many

hot springs and geysers. The season's study, richly embellished with engravings and colored plates, was published in Hayden's Report in 1883.

[292]Lewis R. Freeman, Down the Yellowstone (New York: Dodd, Mead and Co., 1922), p. 57.

[293]P. W. Norris, Annual Report 1880, p. 7.

[294]R. Kipling, American Notes, p. 174. Also see T. A. Jagger's article, "Death Gulch, A Natural Bear Trap," Popular Science, LIV (February, 1899), 5-6.

[295]Jack Ellis Haynes states that A. F. Norris, C. M. Stephens, and J. Davis spent the winter of 1879-80 in the headquarters building at Mammoth.

[296]William Ludlow, Report to the War Department 1875, pp. 36-7. Mr. Ludlow made a reconnaissance from Carrol, Montana to Yellowstone Park and returned.

[297]Yellowstone Scrap Book, II, pp. 37, 56.

[298]Report of the Secretary of the Interior 1884, II (Washington, D. C.: Government Printing Office, 1885), p. 565.

[299]Ibid., 1889, III, p. 133.

[300]Some of these territorial officials, known in local parlance as "rabbit catchers," formed an alliance with the assistant superintendent. By this means the latter shared, as informers, the fines levied by themselves. H. M. Chittenden, op. cit., p. 113.

[301]Ibid., p. 134. See also Report for 1906, p. 522 and The Independent, Butte, Montana, Nov., 1895.

[302]H. M. Chittenden, op. cit., p. 114.

[303]Report of the Secretary of the Interior, II, 873.

[304]Report of the Secretary of the Interior, III (1889), 134.

[305]Ibid., p. 133.

[306]Henry H. Lewis, "Managing a National Park," The Outlook, LXXIV (August, 1903), 1037.

[307]Report of the Secretary of the Interior 1889, III, 129.

[308]Ibid., p. 130.

[309]Jack Ellis Haynes, Haynes Guide, p. 160.

[310]Emerson Hough, "Yellowstone Park Game Exploration," Forest and Stream, XLIII, Nos. 8-12. A series of articles covering this exploration appeared in each issue from March until August 25, 1894.

[311]T. J. Patterson, Yellowstone Park Scrap Book, I, 124.

[312]S. B. M. Young's Annual Report 1897, p. 779.

[313]Benjamin Drew, Souvenir List, Mammoth, Wyoming. One of the victims was struck over the head with the Winchester; whereas a Chicago lady was able to get a snapshot of the desperado. Rewards offered aggregated $1,100.00.

[314]Heister D. Guie and L. V. McWhorter, Adventures in Geyser Land, p. 64. Also Earl of Dunraven, op. cit., p. 206.

[315]Frederick Remington, Pony Tracks (New York: Harper and Bros., 1895), p. 192.

[316]Arnold Hague, "Soaping Geysers," Science, XIII (May 17, 1889), 384. Dr. Arnold Hague and John H. Renshawe of the Geological Survey studied the Park in 1883.

[317]John Muir, "The Yellowstone National Park," The Atlantic Monthly, LXXXI (April, 1898), 520.

[318]Land in the reserves adjacent to the Park yield 30¢ per acre from lumbering and 50¢ for grazing; whereas the water storage value alone is $12.50. Then, too, there are extensive agricultural improvements contingent upon the water supply. These would approximate $30.00 per forest acre. Statement made to the author by range supervisor, Faber Eaton, on August 9, 1943.

[319]Annual Report of the Acting Superintendent 1894, p. 661.

[320]There have been exceptions to the rule. Certain animals have been classed as predators at given times and thinned out.

[321]The average sagebrusher (camper) considers bears as an unmitigated nuisance. Because of them, he must exercise vigilance at all times or his food will be carried away.

[322]Reports of the Department of the Interior 1918, p. 827.

Strong demands were also made to open the Park for sheep grazing.

[323]Report of the Secretary of the Interior 1938, p. 6.

[324]Yellowstone Scrap Book, I, 57.

[325]Ibid.

[326]Report of the Acting Superintendent of Yellowstone National Park 1895, p. 824.

[327]These stations were located at Norris, Riverside, Fountain, Upper Geyser Basin, Thumb, Snake River, Lake Sylvan Pass, Soda Butte, Tower Falls, Fort Yellowstone, and Gardiner.

[328]There are more than thirty of these journals in the Park Library at Mammoth, Wyoming.

[329]Yellowstone Scrap Book, II, 105.

[330]R. Kipling, op. cit., p. 153.

[331]John Muir, op. cit., April, 1898, p. 510.

[332]Charles D. Warner, "Yellowstone National Park," Harper's, XCIV (January, 1897), 94.

[333]Annual Report 1894, p. 133.

[334]Eugene T. Allen and Arthur L. Day, Hot Springs of the Yellowstone National Park (Washington, D. C.: Carnegie Institution, 1935). Although Dr. Day was the director, the work was regarded as the valedictory of Dr. Allen.

[335]Theodore Roosevelt, "A National Park Service," Outlook, C (Feb. 3, 1912).

[336]S. T. Mather's "Report of The Director of The National Park Service," Report of the Department of the Interior 1918, pp. 842-3.

[337]Reports of the Secretary of the Interior 1918, pp. 842-3.

An interesting experiment, contrary to this principle, was an attempt in 1906 to raise twelve Sequoia gigantea trees near the arch at Gardiner entrance. All of the trees died.

[338]James Bryce, "National Parks the Need of the Future," The Outlook, CII (December 14, 1912), 811.

[339]Reports of the Secretary of the Interior 1918, pp. 813-4.

[340]Ibid.

[341]Ray S. Baker, "A Place of Marvels," The Century Magazine, LXVI (August, 1903), 487.

[342]F. A. Boutelle, Report of the Acting Superintendent 1889 (Washington, D. C.: Government Printing Office, 1890), p. 148.

[343]Report of the Secretary of the Interior 1937, p. 49.

[344]Short terms of service were also held by Dr. Frank E. Thone, 1923, and Alfred H. Povah, 1931.

[345]Editorial, "The Ranger Naturalist," Nature Magazine, XVII (April, 1931), 219.

[346]Exhibits were established at Rhyo-Travertine Gulch, Swan Lake Flat, Beaver Dams, Nymph Lake, Tuff Cliff, and Firehole Canyon.

[347]Report of the Secretary of the Interior 1938, p. 13.

[348]Ibid., 1918, pp. 844-5.

[349]George O. Smith, "The Nation's Playgrounds," Review of Reviews, XL (July, 1909), 44.

[350]Dwight L. Elmendorf, The Mentor, II (May 15, 1915), 13.

[351]Earl of Dunraven, The Great Divide (London, 1876), p. XI.

The Scottish Earl of Dunraven visited the Park in 1874. A peak and a pass commemorate his interest and service in informing Europeans about Yellowstone.

[352]The date of this communication was December 20, 1810.

[353]Colter's first sheet is readily identifiable, and part of another sheet may be segregated with the use of imagination and understanding.

[354]Many writers have failed to identify Gap and Sage as the same creek. They also befuddle Wind and Shoshone rivers. There is no evidence that Colter ever heard the name of Bighorn River.

[355]The figure eight results from the fact that he went to the Yep-pe camp, left it, came back, and left it again at the appropriate angles.

[356]The curious errors of the map are explained in Chapter II.

[357]Lewis evidently complained to Biddle about the variations in sheets because Clark stated in a letter to Biddle that these sheets were all of the same scale. See Stallo Vinton, John Colter, p. 47.

[358]This claim will be developed subsequently.

[359]John D. Hicks, The Federal Union (New York: Houghton Mifflin Co., 1937), p. 282.

[360]The position of Henrys River, with reference to the Snake River drainage, is almost wholly erroneous as shown on the Map of 1814. Wisers River is fictitious. The true and original Weiser River lies three hundred miles west.

[361]This hypothesis is based upon the findings of J. Neilson Barry of Portland, Oregon. Mr. Barry is a profound student of Western history and cartography. He has devoted years of intensive research in correlating journals and geography.

[362]There is a reasonable view that holds this lake to be the only real feature upon this section of the map and identifies it as Brooks Lake, but Colter never saw or knew of the main branch of the Bighorn River or its source in Brooks Lake.

[363]Clark named this mythical lake for William Eustis, who had been representative to Congress from Massachusetts. About this time he was Secretary of War in President Madison's cabinet.

Whatever Colter drew was certainly lacking Lake Eustis, Lake Biddle, and the Rio Grande, Arkansas, and Platte rivers. He was a simple frontiersman who had probably never heard of Eustis or Biddle and was not interested in mapping anything beyond his own route. Had Lewis linked Eustis and Biddle-Riddle lakes together, a possible approximation to Colter's draft might have appeared.

[364]In 1941, Paul J. Shamp, a US. forester, reported the discovery of numerous petrifications in the vicinity of Pass and Scatter creeks in the Thorofare country. This is the line of Colter's reconstructed route.

It has been the author's desire to make a search for this missing link of evidence by actually going over the route. In 1947, he made a partial exploration during a three day hike. It was enough to suggest the size of the problem.

[365]Colter may have reached Chicken Ridge by Fishhawk, Mountain, or Lynx creeks or via Falcon, Mink, or Crooked

streams. It must be remembered that this map sheet has been much mussed up. It is impossible to know what has been erased; yet, enough of Colter's map remains to provide a logical basis for the above itinerary. It is relatively unimportant which creeks he negotiated to reach Chicken Ridge. The vitally important fact is that he drew a sketch of South Arm from that angle which added to the Thumb makes an accurate map of what a trapper would have seen of Yellowstone Lake.

> [366]J. Neilson Barry has made the most intensive study of the Map of 1814. It is his opinion that Colter drew other map sheets besides the one of the Buffalo Bill country. He also has hope that these sheets may be discovered among the Lewis-Clark-Biddle papers.